LAWYERS AND THE
PURSUIT OF
LEGAL RIGHTS

LAWYERS AND THE PURSUIT OF LEGAL RIGHTS

Joel F. Handler
Ellen Jane Hollingsworth
Howard S. Erlanger

University of Wisconsin—Madison

ACADEMIC PRESS   New York   San Francisco   London

A Subsidiary of Harcourt Brace Jovanovich, Publishers

This book is one of a series sponsored by the Institute for Research on Poverty of the University of Wisconsin pursuant to the provisions of the Economic Opportunity Act of 1964.

ACADEMIC PRESS, INC.
111 Fifth Avenue, New York, New York 10003

United Kingdom Edition published by
ACADEMIC PRESS, INC. (LONDON) LTD.
24/28 Oval Road, London NW1   7DX

Library of Congress Cataloging in Publication Data

Handler, Joel F.
    Lawyers and the pursuit of legal rights.

    (Poverty policy analysis series)
    Bibliography: p.
    1. Legal aid––United States.   2. Legal
assistance to the poor––United States.
3. Public interest––United States.   4. Lawyers––
United States.   I. Hollingsworth, Ellen Jane,
joint author.   II. Erlanger, Howard S., joint
author.   III. Title.   IV. Series.
KF336.H34   347'.73'1   77–92241
ISBN 0–12–322860–3 (cloth)
ISBN 0–12–322866–2 (paper)

PRINTED IN THE UNITED STATES OF AMERICA

To Gloria, Stephen, Adam, and Frances Handler

Rogers and Lauren Hollingsworth

Pam, Lisa, and Jeffrey Erlanger

The Institute for Research on Poverty is a national center for research established at the University of Wisconsin in 1966 by a grant from the Office of Economic Opportunity. Its primary objective is to foster basic, multidisciplinary research into the nature and causes of poverty and means to combat it.

In addition to increasing the basic knowledge from which policies aimed at the elimination of poverty can be shaped, the Institute strives to carry analysis beyond the formulation and testing of fundamental generalizations to the development and assessment of relevant policy alternatives.

The Institute endeavors to bring together scholars of the highest caliber whose primary research efforts are focused on the problem of poverty, the distribution of income, and the analysis and evaluation of social policy, offering staff members wide opportunity for interchange of ideas, maximum freedom for research into basic questions about poverty and social policy, and dissemination of their findings.

Contents

List of Tables

Foreword

In the last two decades there has been increasing concern with providing more access to the legal system by groups and individuals traditionally unrepresented or underrepresented. Initially most of the focus was on ascertaining and beginning to meet the legal needs of the poverty population, especially through the Legal Services program component of the War on Poverty. Poverty law has emerged as a legal speciality, and criminal defense work for the indigent has become a much more complex one. To a large extent the new areas of the law emphasizing rights for the hitherto unrepresented have been associated with new organizations. The pace-setting activity has taken place through the federally funded Legal Services program that has involved many more clients and lawyers than the rest of the public interest law programs put together.

Lawyers and the Pursuit of Legal Rights, by Joel F. Handler, Ellen Jane Hollingsworth and Howard S. Erlanger examines the role of the Legal Services program, particularly its role in changing the law profession's inadequate provision of services to the poor. The book also examines the organizational responses of the legal profession to demands for more involvement with social change. Based largely on interviews with lawyers in a variety of practice settings over time, the monograph points to the direct and indirect mechanisms that address the legal needs of the poor and other minorities, enlarge the definitions of legal needs and rights, and, in some measure, respond to them.

The authors analyze the subtle interplay among organization characteristics and milieu, attributes of lawyers in many types of professional public interest work, and the needs and types of clients. What emerges is a picture of highly varied activity, of a profession experiencing some flexibility and socialization in unanticipated ways, of organizations able to put down roots in client and professional communities despite fairly aggressive conceptualizations of law work. Change extends beyond the Legal Rights program. Older organizations have been revived and reconstituted, or at times encouraged to broaden their spheres of interest. Within the private practice bar, several new emphases and programs have arisen to handle legal needs expressed by nontraditional client groups. Although it is unclear to what extent these professional groups and individuals can begin to handle the legal needs brought to them, much less the needs not formulated or expressed, it has been fairly well established in the last dozen years that legal rights and services can be and should be incorporated into the package of basic human services a society is expected to provide for its citizens. This is especially the case for the poor. Their rights have been elaborated as never before, and the number of professionals working on their behalf has never been larger. Legal rights for the poor may prove only an inadequate starting point for increasing social justice. The adversary professional role may prove to be too confined to incremental change and orientation and in need of a broad setting of conflict resolution devices and systemic law reform. Yet, the relatively dramatic events in the delivery of services in the last several years suggest that ferment can be quite effective in a profession.

This book is the fourth in the Institute's Poverty Policy Analysis Series. Whereas the first two entries in the series—*Progress Against Poverty: A Review of the 1964–1974 Decade*, and *A Decade of Federal Anti-Poverty Programs: Achievements, Failures, and Lessons*—constitute a comprehensive overview of the War on Poverty, *Lawyers and the Pursuit of Legal Rights*, like the third volume, *Food, Stamps, and Income Maintenance*, evaluates in depth particular antipoverty programs. As such, it makes an important contribution to our understanding of the Legal Rights movement.

IRWIN GARFINKEL
Director, Institute for Research on Poverty

Acknowledgments

It is probably impossible to convey to outsiders the full sense of what it means to work at the Institute for Research on Poverty. From the inception of the study, the Institute not only provided financial and other material support, but, even more importantly, the substantive, critical, intellectual colleagueship that is so vital to a large, multidisciplinary project. At every stage of the project, the people at the Institute made the administrative tasks less burdensome and the intellectual tasks more rewarding. Although many at the Institute lent a helping hand, we would especially like to single out the following: Bob Haveman was the director at the beginning; he immediately saw the value of the project, encouraged us to get underway, and gave valuable support during the early years. Jack Ladinsky helped immeasurably in the early stages with his great knowledge of theory and research on the legal profession and his skills in questionnaire construction. Throughout the project, we benefited greatly from discussions of common interest with the Public Interest Law project and its director, Burton Weisbrod. Jack Sorenson with Joyce Collins had the thankless task of paying our bills, managing the payrolls, and impressing on us the realities of research costs. Hal Winsborough helped solve complex statistical and methodological problems. The field work was under the direction of the Wisconsin Survey Research Laboratory, and we would like to thank the director, Harry Sharp, Tracy Lord, Charles Palit, and the rest of the staff; it was a complex, messy questionnaire. Several people provided staff support. Special thanks are due Betsy Ginsberg, Anna Wells, Irene Rodgers,

Nancy Williamson, and Pramod Suratkar. Violette Moore typed innumerable drafts with good humor and great skill.

The data on which this study rests come from more than 3000 lawyers who agreed to a very lengthy interview. We thank them for generously giving their time.

I

LEGAL RIGHTS—ISSUES AND BACKGROUND

1

The Pursuit of Legal
Rights: Issues for Research

Popular accounts of the activist lawyers of the 1960s and 1970s parallel the accounts of other young radicals of the era—a short, springlike blossom of energy followed by autumn. For the lawyers, most of the story is told in terms of the rise and apparent decline of the War on Poverty's Legal Services program. For a time, it seemed to be one of the most successful of the War on Poverty programs. Legal Services flowered during the peak of the Warren Court era. The federal judiciary, led by the Supreme Court, was fashioning new law on behalf of the poor, and poverty lawyers were instrumental in many of these cases. For several years, Legal Services seemed to attract the best young lawyers; so much so that the most prestigious corporate law firms had to meet the competition by offering their own poverty law opportunities to attract recruits (*Wall Street Journal*, 1968; 1970; Simon, Koziol, and Joslyn, 1973), a sharp contrast to the days of legal aid (Carlin and Howard, 1965; Katz, 1976). In terms of results and recruitment, the Office of Economic Opportunity's (OEO) Legal Services seemed to be a great success.

After this initial outburst of success, however, the War on Poverty gave way to the Vietnam War, and Legal Services came under repeated political attack. Various commentators, scholars, and participants in Legal Services began to write about what they saw as the decline of Legal Services. They saw the commitment of Legal Services lawyers as a fleeting one, the reform activities of the organization as vulnerable to political attack; and, by and large, they reached pessimistic conclusions about the program's long-run prospects. Of course, the quality and political approach of these accounts are quite varied, ranging from sympathy to cynicism, sadness to hostility; most are impressionistic, based on personal observation, participation, or selected interviews. Taken together, however, they present a view of an important period of social reform on the part of the legal profession, which, if correct, amounts to a critical appraisal of the lawyers who participated in these social reform programs.

In this chapter, we outline the main elements of this "popular account" of the apparent rise and decline of Legal Services and set forth questions that provide the framework for our study of lawyers and the pursuit of legal rights. Subsequent chapters detail our empirical findings, and in a concluding chapter, we discuss a theory of career paths of lawyers in legal rights activities and the policy implications of our findings.

WIDELY HELD BELIEFS REGARDING LEGAL SERVICES AND LEGAL SERVICES LAWYERS

Legal Services, as part of the War on Poverty, held a strong attraction for elite young lawyers in its initial years

The War on Poverty grew out of the civil rights struggle, and idealism and commitment to social justice ran high. Legal Services offered an important role for the legal profession in that struggle. National policy dictated that poor people were to be helped to extricate themselves from poverty, and Legal Services was part of the Community Action program designed to help poor people organize themselves in their communities for self-help. The legal system was considered to be stacked against the poor; if the poor were properly represented, the law could be changed and become an instrument for the poor instead of against them. Legal Services, particularly with its emphasis on law reform strategies, provided a means through which socially conscious young lawyers could help the poor in their professional capacity.

The law reform emphasis of Legal Services especially appealed to these elite young lawyers because the profession has long held that lawyers have unique capabilities to perform "social engineering" tasks

This argument holds that the elites of the American legal profession have always been at the center of power in society as the key advisers, manipulators, and participants in the highest circles of finance, commerce, and government (see, for example, Green, 1975, especially Chapters 1 and 2; or Goulden, 1973). This does not just refer to the "Wall Street" lawyer; the liberals had their role models, too, in the dashing young lawyers who framed the New Deal legislation and staffed some of the key regulatory agencies during that era. From both the right and the left, elite lawyers were accustomed to considering themselves as the great architects of social change. Legal education, exalted as the universal, indispensable problem-solving methodology, particularly at the prestige law schools, encouraged this self-perception. The social engineering roles portrayed the lawyer as negotiator, drafter, and problem solver. The law schools also inculcated the importance of the appellate court litigator. Because most of the curriculum was spent on analyzing appellate court cases, law students were reinforced in their view that appellate courts, and particularly the United States Supreme Court, played a crucial role in the course of human events.

In keeping with this tradition, OEO Legal Services offered an opportunity to achieve social change on behalf of the poor by winning important appellate court cases. Especially in the early years, the public emphasis of Legal Services was on law reform. The first national director of Legal Services, Clinton Bamberger, stated in 1966 the law reform goals of Legal Services in the ambitious rhetoric of the Kennedy era (quoted in Stumpf, 1968): "Lawyers must uncover the legal causes of poverty, remodel the systems which generate the cycle of poverty and design new social, legal and political tools and vehicles to move poor people from deprivation, depression, and despair to opportunity, hope and ambition [p. 711]." Practicing law for the poor, then, would not only satisfy a strongly felt social need to participate in the War on Poverty but at the same time reinforce highly regarded professional role models. It fit the traditional ideology of the appellate court lawyers in their roles as architects of society.

The commitment of the elite young lawyers to the War on Poverty was temporary and shallow

Many of these lawyers viewed their legal service jobs as brief interludes of valuable training in complex litigation. The law reform lawyers never really dealt with the poor on their terms for their problems, but used the poor for the lawyers' cases (Hegland, 1971; Agnew, 1972). They did not have to handle mundane service cases (sometimes referred to as "Band-Aid" law) in face-to-face dealings with the poor in grubby urban lower courts. Instead, they fulfilled their commitments, accomplishing real social change, by doing real lawyer's law—tough, appellate court litigation. As an additional benefit, the lawyers acquired professional skills and recognition much faster than they would have had they gone into private practice, where, in large law firms, young lawyers assist their seniors for many years.

Law reform concerns not particularly related to poverty law became faddish, and the elite young lawyers went off to do battle for the consumer and environmental movements

As the Vietnam War wound down and finally ended, the poor were all but forgotten; national attention turned to protecting the environment and the consumer. Ralph Nader had taken center stage as the lawyer–social reformer. Foundations and membership organizations subsidized lawyers to take law reform cases in new areas, and public interest law firms were created. The new groups dominated the media and gave credence to the view that they were the new wave in social reform law, attracting the reform-minded lawyer elites from Legal Services.

In the meantime, OEO Legal Services sank back into traditional legal aid, no longer disturbing to the status quo (Hiestand, 1970, pp. 175–176; 184)

Its high expectations of change through law reform were bound to fall short: Change would be long in coming, and in the meantime the press of events deflected efforts from law reform. There were three major sources for this deflection. First, the country found that it could not afford both guns and butter, so the promises to the poor were not fulfilled, and the social reform spirit became bitter and disillusioned. Second, law reformers won many court victories, but these efforts produced some negative effects. The court victories aroused a great deal of political opposition to law reform; Governor Reagan and Vice President Agnew were only the most noteworthy opponents. Housing authorities, welfare departments, city governments, and other public officials resented being sued and enjoined (Brill, 1973; Carlin and Brill, 1973). Many politicians, administrators, and legislators began exerting great pressure on OEO to curb law reform work. The Nixon-appointed people at OEO were openly hostile to law reform and even to the independence of the Legal Services program. Legislation was introduced designed to curb law reform activities and otherwise restrict the independence of Legal Services. Although this pressure was never completely successful, it did make itself felt. Static budgets forced some Legal Services offices to drop or reduce their law reform efforts in favor of handling day-to-day service cases. The program became politicized and its future uncertain. The number of law reform positions was shrinking; it was not clear that there would be the resources or the willingness to take big appellate court cases; and it was not certain how long funding for the good jobs would last (see Chapter 3).

Finally, there was growing doubt about the efficacy of the strategy of law reform. The composition of the Supreme Court had changed; important decisions began to turn against the poor, and poverty lawyers planned strategy on how to avoid the Supreme Court (Redlich, 1971). There was also increasing awareness that a court rule in itself changed little. Disillusionment with the national government led many sensitive lawyers to turn away from appellate court litigation to work with the community; they articulated the view that the route to social change on behalf of the poor and minorities comes from people in their own communities getting things together on the local level. Some of these lawyers left Legal Services or shunned it altogether and formed their own neighborhood law offices called "law communes" (Biderman, 1971a; 1971b; Wexler, 1971; *Village Voice,* 1969). Those who remained in Legal Services were service oriented in the traditional legal aid sense, not in the aggressive model that Legal Services had fostered.

When the bloom of Legal Services faded, most elite young lawyers
took traditional career paths with large law firms serving the
business community

The large corporate-oriented firms had offered opportunities to do public interest work only to meet competition from OEO Legal Services (Berman and Cahn, 1970; Ashman and Woodard, 1970; Boasberg, 1970). As the competitive pressure declined and the supply of new graduates from law schools outpaced the demand for their services, the major firms quietly abandoned their charitable gestures of offering legal services to the poor (Marks *et al.,* 1972, p. 82; Green, 1975, Chapter 11). The young lawyers did not buck this trend. A small percentage went into public interest law; and an even smaller number retained their commitments to the poor and minorities, went into the communities, or joined more radical groups, such as law communes. The remaining elite young lawyers in the environmental, consumer, and public interest law movement are treating their careers as brief interludes to pick up valuable litigation experience while doing some social good by winning a few big cases (Cahn and Cahn, 1970).

The private bar, in its last flicker of social responsibility, is
offering traditional kinds of pro bono services that are trivial in
consequence and oriented toward maintaining the status quo
(Moore, 1970, pp. 319–320; Auerbach, 1976, p. 282)

The American legal profession has always sold its services to the richest segments of society. Prior to the War on Poverty, the bar's contribution to legal aid and civil rights was negligible (Patterson, 1970; Boasberg, 1970), and basically it has remained so. There is no significant element of reform work taking place by lawyers in private practice.

THE APPROACH OF THIS STUDY

Although parts of the foregoing composite account are accurate, there are several with which we take issue. Much of the criticism implicit in popular accounts is overdrawn and based on inaccuracies or oversimplification.

Legal Services recruitment was not predominantly elite based

Popular criticism says nothing about Legal Services lawyers who were not recent graduates of the most prestigious law schools. Although it had some of the characteristics of a social movement, Legal Services was and is a government bureaucracy; hence, it drew lawyers from a variety of backgrounds who joined for a variety of reasons. Stories about the career paths and commitments of elite young lawyers may not be accurate for lawyers with different backgrounds. A major purpose of this study is to examine the recruitment, job experiences, and career paths of the full range of lawyers who participated in Legal Services and other legal rights activities.

Law reform, even for lawyers of elite background, was only part of the work and attraction of Legal Services

Even in the early days of Legal Services when specifically designated law reform units existed, many elite background lawyers, including Reginald Heber Smith fellows ("Reggies"), were not attracted to the traditional role model of the appellate court litigator. They preferred working directly with the poor and taking service cases (Cramton, 1975; also, see Chapter 3). Over the years, with the demise of special law reform units and the diffusion of reform responsibilities throughout program components, mixed workloads were the predominant pattern.

The commitment of Legal Services lawyers was neither temporary nor shallow, as shown by their period of service and their post-Legal Services professional choices

Most Legal Services lawyers remained in programs for 2 to 4 years. There are structural reasons why lawyers will leave Legal Services, not necessarily related to a change in or lack of commitment. Working conditions in Legal Services offices are poor. Lawyers are inundated with masses of cases that cause feelings of monotony and the conviction that legal skills are being wasted on routine tasks (Silver, 1968). There are bureaucratic constraints, such as continual problems of refunding and justifications and explanations to higher authorities. The prohibition on taking criminal cases is a serious constraint; nor can Legal Services lawyers help poor persons collect debts or damages; and there are pressures to avoid still other kinds of cases. These constraints make the Legal Services lawyer feel less able than the full-service lawyer to help the client. Finally, because of the press of business, Legal Services lawyers have to work hard, and there is the feeling that there should be more lifestyle amenities (particularly leisure time) to go along with foregone income.

Turnover in Legal Services is caused not only by the poor working conditions but also by professional self-images. A persistent ideal among lawyers is the model of the lawyer as the independent professional—his own boss in a small partnership with friends, engaged in a varied, personal, and interesting practice. Lawyers idealize the two principal benefits of a general, low-key practice: independence and the professional and social amenities of the small partnership. In more bucolic times, the romantic ideal was the country or small town lawyer. Even today, the ideal persists. Lawyers in large firms speak of this ideal as a desirable alternative to the rat race (Handler, 1967, p. 31; Carlin, 1962, especially Chapter 1; Smigel, 1964, pp. 293–294). Other lawyers constantly form and re-form partnerships, as if seeking a better way to practice law. Lawyers in Legal Services have these professional feelings. They want to continue to serve the "other side" of society, but they do not want to be salaried government employees. They want professional independence, the benefits of small partnerships, and the ability to serve their clients for all their problems. In other words, there are important professional reasons why lawyers leave OEO Legal Services that are not necessarily evidence of a change in commitments. Two of the important questions of this study are (a) where do these lawyers go, and (b) what, in fact, happens to their commitments.

The number of lawyers working in legal rights activities is neither static nor fixed

The popular account of the history of reform-minded young lawyers gives the impression that their numbers are relatively small and fixed, with new recruits replacing burned-out veterans, and that their attention is faddish, skipping from social controversy to social controversy. Thus, civil rights lawyers were replaced by poverty lawyers who, in turn, were replaced by environmental and consumer public interest lawyers. In part, this impression has been created by spokespersons within these various movements; for example, civil rights lawyers complained about OEO Legal Services attracting away their free legal talent (Leone, 1972), and poverty lawyers, in turn, charged public interest lawyers with abandoning the poor and minorities in favor of the middle class (Cahn and Cahn, 1970).

There are a number of inconsistencies with the notion of a cadre of relatively fixed size being constantly replaced by new members attracted to different fads. In part, there has been a substitution of social concerns: Civil rights and some poverty areas are no longer funded and supported as they were in the past, and more funds and support are going into new areas. But the reasons for these shifts are complex and represent a broadening of social concerns as much as a substitution. To give one example, a great deal of current foundation-supported public interest law is poverty-related, although it is different from OEO Legal Services in that there is less emphasis on welfare and more emphasis on health, mental health, criminal justice, and employment discrimination (Handler, 1976, pp. 100–101). Thus a change in substantive areas does not represent an abandonment of the poor and minorities. It is an empirical question whether there has been a substitution of social interests among young lawyers or a broadening of interests. There has been a great proliferation of legal rights organizations since the early days of the War on Poverty. On the surface, the growth of these organizations seems to represent an expansion of the social commitments of the legal profession beyond traditional concerns to a wider spectrum of social problems. Does this expansion dilute the talent going into traditional concerns of expand and broaden the concerns among wider segments of the profession?

Legal Services, despite political setbacks, has remained a vital program

Popular criticism of Legal Services for failing to fulfill its original mission focuses mainly on the impact of events on the recruitment and careers of reform-minded elites. It assumes that there has been a decline of law reform, that people of talent left Legal Services and new people of comparable quality were no longer attracted; but this assumption is questionable. Law reform was indeed attacked by politicians and was, for the most part, ultimately rejected by the Supreme Court. It had become less newsworthy—at least for the poor—but this did not necessarily mean that law reform did not continue in other courts or in different forms. Indeed, there is convincing evidence that law reform work continues on much the same scale, albeit often in different contexts.

Turning to other aspects of the Legal Services program, we find further evidence that the popular account of its transformation, if not its death, is exaggerated. At the field level, Legal Services offices are still being inundated with applicants for positions. The expansion of the supply of law graduates and the decline of law jobs in general does not provide the complete explanation since the volume of applicants was high before the shifts in supply and demand occurred. Reports from Legal Services offices indicate that the quality of the applicants is high; if this is true, these applicants should have other career choices. At the national level, the picture is also brighter than predicted. After a long struggle, the Legal Services Corporation Board was formed. During this intense struggle, forces sympathetic to Legal Services, including the American Bar Association (ABA) and many elite professionals, demonstrated their support. Legal Services sympathizers were able to keep obvious enemies off the board, including a former member of Congress. These kinds of victories are rare for normally low-visibility, multimember boards. In addition, the chairman of the board and the principal executive officers of the corporation are influential, highly regarded people who have demonstrated sympathetic records. Finally, the latest appropriations represent about a 25% increase in the Legal Services budget. The budget was static for many years, and in this sense the increase is a catch-up; but in these days of financial stringency, any increase for a social welfare program represents tangible evidence of political support. Legal Services, as a program, is surviving; and it has not lapsed into a moribund shadow of its former self.

Traditional career paths are not chosen by those leaving
Legal Services

Commentators on the career paths of Legal Services lawyers consider only two job categories—Legal Services or private practice. They note the vast exodus from the former, assume it is to the latter, and conclude that all of the young lawyers have returned to their true professional calling of representing the rich against the poor. Again, these assumptions are questionable. There are professional alternatives to private practice—government, teaching, and other kinds of legal rights activities jobs. In addition, all private practice is not equivalent. There is a certain amount of evidence that some young lawyers have chosen not affiliation with traditional law firms, but a practice with more of a mix of working class, poor people, and minorities. These lawyers do not view themselves as great architects of social change functioning in the milieu of appellate court litigation; rather, they have a more sober view of how social change comes about. Their path is working at the community level, helping the lower classes with their problems, and gradually building strength at the local level. Some lawyers have articulated this view; others have chosen this style of practice as a matter of taste. They are unwilling to sell their professional careers to the upper classes.

Still others, for a variety of reasons, have been foreclosed from higher-status professional jobs; large firms may not be interested in lateral entry of lawyers with Legal Services experience, or former Legal Services lawyers may not have the contacts to obtain higher status jobs. But whatever the reason, this kind of career choice results in a redistribution of legal services, in that professional services are being made available to lower social classes. Leaving Legal Services and entering private practice, then, does not necessarily mean a lack of commitment to the ideals of social justice.

The forms of private bar legal rights activity, while predominantly traditional, have become more varied in the past decade

We have already mentioned two aspects of the private bar that conflict with the popular impression. The private bar is not a monolithic group of lawyers in the service of the rich. In the political battles for the survival of OEO Legal Services, the ABA and other traditional, elitest elements of the bar were vigorous in defense of the program. The leadership of the ABA, as well as a few important state and local bar associations, have also come out in strong support of public interest law (Fellers, 1975, p. 1053; Handler, 1976, p. 105; Klaus, 1976, pp. 136, 139). In addition, lawyers on their own have a history of charitable work— called *pro bono* (Green, 1975, p. 243). Finally, in discussing some of the impressionistic evidence about subsequent careers of former poverty lawyers, we mentioned that some of private practice is serving lower social classes. In other words, there are legal rights activities going on among private practitioners; we will examine later how much and what kind.

It is obvious that any study of the social commitments and activities of the legal profession must include lawyers in a wide variety of professional settings. What has happened to Legal Services is a critical part of the story, but it is only one part. There are many ways in which reform-minded lawyers can meet their commitments in professional work. In addition to Legal Services, one must also examine civil rights, public interest law firms, and the whole range of activities of private practitioners. These include not only pro bono activities but also lawyers who, by choice, are serving lower social classes; there are private practice legal services as well as public and charity-supported legal services.

SUMMARY

All of the legal activities to be discussed have one characteristic in common: They are oriented toward the delivery of legal services to individuals or groups who have not had their share of representation. In a democratic legal order, one of the basic rights of citizens is that of legal representation; in broadening the base of representation, lawyers are involved in the pursuit of legal rights for their clients. People may be lacking in legal rights for a variety of reasons: They may lack the resources with which to purchase legal representation; they may be denied information about their rights or about how to obtain representation; or they may be aware of their rights but lack the ability to organize themselves to obtain representation. Thus the pursuit of legal rights includes representation of the poor, minorities, civil libertarians, political causes, traditional charities, consumers, environmentalists, and other social reform groups interested in a variety of causes. We write of the pursuit rather than the attainment of legal rights because we are quite aware that simply having a lawyer to represent one's interest may not be enough to achieve substantive justice, which is the ultimate legal right. However, it is our position that in order to achieve substantive justice, there must first be procedural justice, and that this procedural justice in turn depends on equality of representation. In this monograph, we are dealing with only one part, but a crucial part, of a large enterprise.

For ease of presentation, we refer to efforts to expand legal representation to individuals and groups who have been underrepresented in the past as *legal rights activities*. As we discuss in Chapter 2, legal rights activities have a long history in the bar, beginning with legal aid work and the pro bono work of private practitioners. These efforts were, and to a certain extent continue to be, niggardly and paternalistic. Free legal representation was only guaranteed to those charged with the most serious criminal offenses. Civil legal aid programs were very small and restricted to "worthy" cases; representation was not generally available for divorce or bankruptcy. There was little litigation; most client problems were handled by referrals or office advice consisting of a single appointment. Legal rights activity was conceived of as charity in a traditional sense—moralistic, paternalistic, and supportive of the status quo. In this study, "traditional" legal rights activities are contrasted with "aggressive" legal rights activities. In both behavior and ideology, aggressive legal rights activities are the opposite of the traditional. Aggressive legal rights activities include a willingness to litigate and take on law reform cases, to take a client's perspective, and to view clients as underdogs challenging society. Aggressive legal rights activities encompass both test-case law reform litigation and service work. It is the attitude and perspectives of the lawyers, as well as their behavior, that make the difference.

Traditional and aggressive legal rights activities are presented as opposite ends of a continuum. Although distinctions among the various lawyers and organizations will often not be clear-cut, locating them along a traditional–aggressive continuum will provide a useful way of analyzing the changing developments in legal rights activities.

The basic policy question is this: Even if we do find a variety of legal rights activities, what does this mean for society? Why should society be concerned about the careers of lawyers in legal rights activities? The answer, as we hope to show, is that legal rights activities play an important role in calling attention to problems of the poor and the unrepresented and in sensitizing society to their legal needs. In Chapter 2, we show how aggressive legal rights organizations uncovered problems of the poor and minorities; brought them to the attention of the country; and persuaded courts, agencies, and legislatures that these problems were legal needs that should be remedied through the legal system. These organizations created a revolution in legal thought on behalf of the poor and the unrepresented and changed the legal consciousness of our society.

In the course of uncovering legal needs and sensitizing the country, legal rights organizations played other crucial roles: They provided the structures that recruited and trained lawyers who wanted to work in these areas. Without these structured opportunities, a great many of the legal rights careers of young lawyers would have aborted. The organizations performed a cycling effect through turnover; lawyers left the organizations after a tour of duty but continued their commitments in other jobs. In performing all of these roles, the organizations delivered legal services to the poor and the unrepresented.

In the following chapters we do two things: describe the range of legal rights activities and organizations and locate them along the traditional–aggressive continuum, and examine the careers of lawyers who engage in various legal rights activities in terms of recruitment, job experience, and subsequent careers. Chapters 3 through 6 deal with the first type of question: What were the nature and extent of legal rights activities? What clients were served, and for what types of matters? Where was the work being done, and what implications did such work carry for client groups? What were the working conditions? How have any of these characteristics changed over time? The chapters addressing these matters are chiefly descriptive. They describe legal rights activities in Legal Services, public interest law, and the private bar.

Chapters 7 and 8, which deal with career paths, are both descriptive and analytic. The lion's share of the study deals with OEO Legal Services because it is by far the largest of the original legal rights organizations and, as we shall see, the most important recruiter and trainer of lawyers engaged in legal rights activities. But other professional settings, including the private bar, are examined as well. The concluding chapter summarizes the findings and discusses policy implications, particularly the importance of organizations for career paths and for meeting the legal needs of the poor.

The major omission from this study is the government lawyers. There is a long tradition of socially committed lawyers working for the government, either on a short-term basis or in permanent careers. During the period we are concerned with, young lawyers joined the Civil Rights Division of the Justice Department during the Kennedy years or the Federal Trade Commission and other consumer and environmental protection agencies at both the federal and state levels. In theory and, we think, in practice, these government lawyers are indistinguishable from the lawyers with whom we are concerned. They are excluded from this study only because of budgetary considerations and sampling problems.

2

Organizations and Legal Rights Activities

This chapter emphasizes the history and scope of organizations involved in legal rights activities in order to show the expansion of legal rights efforts, the relationship of this expansion to other political events, and the resulting range of alternatives open to the lawyer interested in pursuing legal rights activities in the 1970s.

In the process of formation and through their continual efforts to mobilize resources, organizations develop ideologies and define legal needs that attract lawyers and provide the focus for their work. Organizations have been, and continue to be, the principal mechanism for defining the legal needs of the poor and unrepresented, changing the legal consciousness of society, and recruiting and training most of the lawyers in legal rights activities. The structured job opportunities that organizations provide are most important in directing young lawyers toward continued careers in these activities. The success of organizations in winning cases, obtaining publicity, and attracting public support generates new organizations and other efforts to offer similar kinds of opportunities in the two major sectors of the legal profession—private practice and government.

ANTECEDENTS

Traditional Legal Rights Activities

In the legal profession in the United States, reduced-fee work for the poor historically depended on the willingness of individual lawyers in private practice. In part, this was charity by lawyers; in part, it was an effort to justify the public service image of the profession. The reigning belief was that although the legal system essentially worked well some people needed better access to it. If these people could not afford fees of lawyers, it was the obligation of the profession to assist them without charge. Individual practitioners had the responsibility to make some of their time available to satisfy this professional obligation. No- or low-fee work for the indigent was called pro bono (from *pro bono publico*, for the public good).

With the organization of the American Bar Association and similar groups at the state level in the late nineteenth century, canons of ethical conduct were defined (1908); but these canons were limited in that they only mandated defense of indigent prisoners and did not deal with obligations toward the indigent in civil disputes. Moreover, even the obligation to prisoners was narrowly construed and often ignored.

During the latter part of the nineteenth century, some lawyers and bar associations turned their attention to creating a more organized method of handling the legal problems of the poor as an alternative or supplement to the obligations of individual lawyers. The first legal aid society was established in 1876 in New York City as part of an organization that attempted to ease the transition for German immigrants in the United States. Within a few years, legal aid organizations were extended to other immigrants and indigents, although on a modest scale. The resources of the legal aid offices were slender: Only a few lawyers associated with them; they did legal aid work on a part-time basis and often handled the cases at their own private offices. The legal aid service was supported mostly by private subscriptions, although some offices had modest municipal subsidies, and some also took cases on a contingency basis (Pipkin, 1919).

In 1919, Reginald Heber Smith, in a survey of legal aid needs in the United States, found that approximately 40 organizations existed in 37 cities. Some were freestanding; others were housed within private charitable agencies, parts of public bureaus, or affiliated with law schools (Brownell, 1951, pp. 10–11). Some programs undertook criminal work for the indigent, although this was not common. Shortly after the publication of Smith's *Justice and the Poor* (1919), and largely in response to its admonishing tone, the ABA established a standing committee on legal aid, headed by Smith, in an effort to strengthen the service.

During the first half of the twentieth century, the legal aid model spread, though slowly. Legal aid offices, however, were not intended to replace the activities of private lawyers on behalf of the poor as part of their professional obligations. In smaller cities, two different types of organizations with roughly the same consequences emerged. One was a lawyer referral program, with a part-time secretary who put needy clients in touch with lawyers who were willing to be listed. The other was a lawyer who undertook the work himself or was responsible for a younger member of his firm who did the work. Either way, the lawyer in charge of a legal aid committee or a lawyer referral committee often held his position at the behest of the city or county bar association. Costs were low for both arrangements and usually borne by bar organizations.

In both the large and small cities, most programs were small in terms of professional staff and available time. When Emery Brownell surveyed legal aid for the ABA in 1947, he found only 70 facilities operating. Thereafter, with more vigorous bar support, proliferation became more rapid. By 1963, there were 249 legal aid offices. However, despite the large number of offices, legal aid was severely constrained by lack of funds; in 1964, the entire bill for legal aid was only a little more than $4 million, an average of approximately $16,666 per program. Community funds provided more than half of the total funding, lawyers and bar organizations another 17% (Voorhees, 1970).

Partly to limit work load, but also for moralistic reasons, legal aid offices established guidelines concerning the types of cases they would accept. Family cases usually made up a large percentage of the service load, though divorces were handled only very reluctantly (Mayer, 1967, p. 97). Adoption, bankruptcy, civil mental commitment hearings, juvenile proceedings, and administrative hearings were also often refused (National Legal Aid and Defender Association, 1964). The second most common category of cases was landlord–tenant, especially in major metropolitan areas. Consumer problem cases were numerous; they included installment purchases, repossession of merchandise, and fraudulent sales.

Legal aid emphasized service to individuals exclusively. There was no law reform or class action litigation; only a minimal effort was made to uncover problems of the poor and sensitize society to legal needs. Emphasis on individual services stemmed from the assumption that the law was just—that for poor people the problem lay not in the nature of the law but in obtaining access to the law. Logically, the more lawyers who made time available to the poor (on an individual, one-to-one basis), the more likely it was that the legal system would operate fairly. However, offices were usually so poorly funded that they had to set very strict eligibility standards in order to keep down the caseload limit. They avoided community education or publicity so that their work schedules would remain tolerable. Studies have shown that, for most

legal aid clients, access to the legal system consisted of only one interview with a legal aid lawyer (Mayer, 1967, p. 101).

In large metropolitan offices, the low pay, type of legal work, and
crushing caseload discouraged ambitious lawyers from entering legal
aid. Legal aid positions were often accepted only until something better
became available. For lawyers unwilling to try their fortunes in private
practice, legal aid positions had the advantage of steady employment,
however modest the pay and professional status (see Katz, 1976).

Despite the obvious shortcomings of legal aid, it served an important
public relations function for the organized bar. Quite often, prestigious
members of the bar lent their names and some of their time to legal aid
or to high-level bar association panels concerned with it. Even if most
lawyers had no time for legal aid, it won a definite niche for itself in the
legal profession.

For the criminally accused, representation has most often been
through the assigned counsel system, the dominant mode of providing
such aid for over a century (Nagel, 1973; Hornstein, 1973; Silverstein,
1965). In this system, a practicing attorney is assigned to the defense by
the judge, usually without compensation. Assigned counsel systems
have varied in the crimes included, the point in the proceedings where
the assignment is made, and the method of selecting the lawyers.
Generally speaking, young lawyers have welcomed assignments. If they
were in small firms or on their own, it gave them experience and
visibility. If they were in large firms, it provided variation from a
business practice. More experienced lawyers, on the other hand, have
usually tried to avoid assignments and, it was claimed, tended to give
assigned clients a minimum amount of service. Needless to say, the
quality of the assigned counsel system varied enormously.

Despite the shortcomings of this system, widespread viable alternatives have been slow to emerge. Although the first public defender
office for the criminally accused was established in Los Angeles County
in 1910, until 1960 the growth of defender programs with salaried
lawyers working exclusively in defense of criminally accused indigents
was very slow, even in comparison with the growth of legal aid
societies. In 1917, there were 5 defender programs; in 1947 there were
only 29 (including 4 legal aid societies doing substantial criminal work);
and of these 29, 13 were in two states. By 1960, 90 such programs existed,
and three basic organizational patterns had emerged: public defenders
defined by statute and paid by public funds, public–private programs
with some funds from the private sector, and programs with all financing from private sources (usually bar associations). The dominant pat-

tern, however, was public—more than 75% of defender funding came from tax sources, as opposed to the 7% that legal aid organizations received from public sources (Brownell, 1951, p. 35).

Why did defender programs languish behind legal aid? Legal aid was handled privately by local bar associations with the support and encouragement of the ABA. The administration of criminal justice, on the other hand, is not a private affair; and until recently, it was not even a national concern. Criminal justice administration is primarily in the jurisdiction of state and county governments. The cooperation of local public officials would be needed before any defender program could be established. Defender programs may also have languished because of different perceptions about the worthiness of the criminally accused as compared to the legal assistance client, especially since the latter was screened. At any rate, no prestigious nationwide organization of professionals advocated defender programs, nor was there a specialized organization for promoting defender programs until 1960 when the National Legal Aid Association broadened its concerns to become the National Legal Aid and Defenders Association (NLADA). Concerns with protecting the indigent criminally accused were instead expressed in the elaboration and extension of the assigned counsel system. Although under serious attack during the 1960s, the system showed no signs of withering away.

In sum, although there had developed a long tradition of charitable legal work for the poor, and although this tradition was supported by the elites of the profession, it remained in fact in the backwaters of the profession. Legal aid offices and defender programs were for decades few in number, and even when they became more numerous, they were poorly financed; they were staffed either by lawyers looking for something else or by those seeking security from a competitive society. With few exceptions, young, activist, social-minded lawyers would not join legal aid or defender programs.

Nevertheless, at the time they were first formed, legal aid and public defender programs were a meaningful reform because they at least began the broadening of the delivery of legal services. They provided an organizational setting for traditional legal rights activities which supplemented the pro bono efforts of private practitioners. These legal rights efforts were paternalistic, moralistic, and limited in the services they delivered. They conceived of their role as that of handling problems thrust upon them rather than seeking out the problems of the poor. In part, it was because of dissatisfaction with traditional legal rights activities that Legal Services programs and a major expansion of the defender efforts were initiated in the mid-1960s. On the other hand, as we discuss shortly, traditional legal rights activities were not replaced in the 1960s; they continued to grow.

Early Aggressive Legal Rights Activities

About the same time that these first steps were being made to expand traditional legal representation for the indigent, major efforts were being made in the use of litigation to achieve broad social reforms. The most influential early organizations pursuing this strategy were civil rights organizations, particularly the National Association for the Advancement of Colored People. The NAACP, founded in 1909, relied heavily from the very beginning on the use of test-case litigation, with great courtroom success. Through a series of cases, the NAACP brought to the attention of the courts, and through the courts to the larger society, the existence, nature, and legal implications of racial discrimination. As a result of NAACP cases, the United States Supreme Court invalidated anti-black voting restrictions (1915), housing segregation ordinances (1917), and the exclusion of blacks from juries in criminal cases (1923). These cases attracted a great deal of support, both white and black, to the organization. The membership of the NAACP expanded rapidly (there were 30,000 members in the 1920s). However, in spite of this growth and the continuing stream of legal activity, the legal staff remained small (Meier and Rudwick, 1970, pp. 3–4; Kellogg, 1967, pp. 9–42).

In 1939, the NAACP established the Legal Defense and Educational Fund, Inc. (popularly known as the "Inc. Fund") not only to handle its own legal work but also to work with other civil rights groups on civil rights cases. The Inc. Fund, with its small staff (three lawyers in the middle 1940s and only nine in 1963), fought numerous test cases in a wide range of areas (education, voting rights, housing and restrictive covenants, transportation, and public accommodations) and continued to win. By 1952, the Inc. Fund had won 34 of 38 cases argued before the Supreme Court. The regular staff was assisted by volunteer attorneys throughout the country, though it bore most of the load itself, especially prior to 1960 (NAACP Inc. Fund, 1969, p. 6; Washington, 1971, p. 173).

Inc. Fund achieved its greatest fame in *Brown* v. *Board of Education* (1954)[1], which was followed by successes in cases involving segregation in buses, golf courses, bathhouses, courtrooms, voting, marriage, public accommodations, housing, and other state activities. In the era of the

[1] *Brown* v. *Board of Education*. 1954.

Warren Court, it seemed as though every year following the *Brown* decision, reformers could count on not one, but several Supreme Court decisions on behalf of the disenfranchised of American society. A great many of these cases were class actions, a model of social reform that was openly encouraged by the Court itself. As the Court saw it (*NAACP* v. *Button* 1963), "[U]nder the conditions of modern government, litigation may be the sole practicable avenue open to a minority to petition for redress of grievances."[2]

It would be difficult to overestimate the influence of the Inc. Fund class action litigation strategy on the subsequent development of legal consciousness and legal rights activities. Supreme Court victories had enormous appeal: At the stroke of the judicial pen, so it seemed, legal rights and legitimacy were given to disadvantaged groups. The executive and legislative branches of government, thought to be hostile and indifferent to the claims of blacks and other minorities, appeared to be circumvented. The style and location of the litigation were important in influencing lawyer recruits. Young, elite, motivated lawyers would work with the leaders of the organization, and their legal work would be aired in the prestigious federal courts, often at the appellate level. The legal training of young lawyers and the law school conception of the role of law and lawyers in social reform concentrated on appellate court litigation. The Warren Court and the NAACP litigation seemed to be the perfect examples of what law, lawyers, and legal education were all about.

As we shall see, this model of class action law reform strategy became the single most important influence in the development of OEO Legal Services, consumer and environmental law, and public interest law: It became the popular standard for measuring the quality and effectiveness of other legal rights activities. In time, it also became the focus of political attacks on legal rights activities.

The other principal civil rights and civil liberties organization was the American Civil Liberties Union. The ACLU emerged in 1920 as the successor organization to the American Union Against Militarism, the Bureau for Conscientious Objectors, and the National Civil Liberties Board. These organizations had been concerned with United States involvement in a European war, fair treatment of conscientious objectors, and prosecutions under the Espionage and Sedition Acts. During the 1920s, the ACLU was concerned with censorship, deportation, and harassment of the IWW and other labor groups. Gradually, branches of the ACLU were created in the nation's largest cities, loosely coordinated

---

[2] *NAACP* v. *Button*. 1963. 371 U.S. 415.

through a national office that had slender resources (Johnson, 1963, p. 53). Few branches retained attorneys; most of the work was done by volunteer attorneys (both members and outsiders).

During this period, the ACLU was weakened by an internal controversy over the desirability of identifying with radical labor activities. Nevertheless, the ACLU continued to grow, only to be confronted by a much more intense controversy in the 1940s over the question of allowing admitted Communists to hold positions of leadership. Internal dissension plagued the organization for the next two decades (James, 1973, pp. 26–27).

Because of a lack of funds and a strong organizational base, the work of the ACLU prior to 1960 consisted mainly of filing amicus briefs rather than direct litigation. Nevertheless, the ACLU did considerable civil liberties work in times that were generally not sympathetic. Important ACLU cases were well known to law students and young lawyers interested in civil liberties. While the ACLU's work never achieved the great fame of the NAACP's, it did represent a steady tradition of appellate court law reform work. The ACLU also worked closely with several other organizations with civil liberties interests, serving as a resource and kind of sponsor for them.

For a brief period, the National Lawyers Guild also influenced reform work done by lawyers. Organized in 1937 as a nationwide professional organization counter to the ABA, the guild enjoyed a period of success and then fell on hard times in the 1940s and 1950s during its long fight to avoid being placed on the attorney general's list of subversive organizations. Although it was ultimately successful in remaining off the list, membership declined steadily, and the guild's influence virtually disappeared until the late 1960s. Whatever its organizational problems, the guild's activities in protection of dissidents and in other civil liberties problem areas were an important factor in the emergence of a reformist, socially activist community in the legal profession.

LEGAL RIGHTS ACTIVITIES IN THE 1960s: THE EMERGENCE OF AGGRESSIVE LEGAL RIGHTS AS A MAJOR THEME

The activity, spirit, beliefs, and symbols of the New Frontier of the Kennedy administration encouraged the idea that law could be used on behalf of the unrepresented. Much of the activity of the administration was based on the assumption that the institutions of American society could be activated and reordered to achieve social justice; government agencies could and should serve as protectors and advocates of the downtrodden (the Civil Rights Division of the Justice Department and VISTA [Volunteers in Service to America], for example); private groups of various types could save the cities, change the power structure of the South, and end nuclear testing, to mention only a few objectives. The individual citizen working in social reform organizations was seen as capable of affecting the machinery of government and the future of society. The thrust of these beliefs was twofold: that government agencies could spearhead reform and that citizen action should be taken against parts of government reluctant to change society.

The spirit of activism, despite many defeats, disappointments, and delays, continued during the 1960s, though in an appreciably different form after the assassination of President Kennedy and the continuation and escalation of the Vietnam War. Much of the literature concerned with the ideological shifts of the 1960s has focused on events on university campuses. Although campus events were only a partial reflection of the times, they serve quite well to illustrate the optimistic belief that the legal system, when pressured, could assure equality for all, the hopefulness of ending poverty at home and abroad, and finally, the disillusion with government and the creation of new antigovernment and antiestablishment organizations. The first large-scale activist involvement of students and liberals was triggered by the southern black student sit-ins in the beginning of 1960. The sit-ins spread rapidly throughout black colleges in the South, while northern students supported these efforts by picketing and boycotting northern branches of the chain stores where the sit-ins took place. The student movements in the early 1960s envisaged reform rather than radical change of society. The protest and dissent of this period were, on the whole, committed to the nonviolent tactics developed by Martin Luther King, Jr., and were optimistic about the responsiveness of universities and government. Students were mobilized to organize the poor, engage in civil rights work, work on voter registration, and work in the South, Appalachia, and the northern urban ghettos. When President Johnson announced the War on Poverty, nearly 1000 volunteers went to Mississippi to work for the Mississippi Freedom Democratic party.

Although the ferment of the early 1960s was supportive of more social activism in the legal profession, the events of the rest of the decade carried different implications for the responses of the legal profession to issues about social reform and the unrepresented. Disillusionment and new pressures—the murders of three students working for civil rights in Mississippi, the rebuff of the Mississippi Freedom Democratic party at the 1964 Democratic national convention, events in Vietnam, the failure of the War on Poverty, the credibility gap with the administration, and the university response to student protests—put an end on campus to the faith in social reform. The events of the second half of the 1960s included bloody urban riots; mounting protest against the war in Vietnam, often involving massive arrests; police encounters; a national administration perceived by many as hostile and guilty of endless duplicity; and the defeat of the McCarthy forces at the 1968 Chicago national Democratic convention. For many, both students and others, these events and others led to the conclusion that existing social reform rhetoric was useless. After 1968, the liberalism of the early 1960s was found first ineffective and then inapplicable. For some, more radical lifestyles and objectives, openly challenging government, seemed to offer the only acceptable way of changing the status quo.

A radical choice was possible only for a limited number of the people who had been caught up with the social reform hopes of the early 1960s. Some withdrew; a small number became actively hostile to the forces with which they had once identified; and for most, a different kind of commitment to social reform work probably resulted, more circumscribed and less ambitious. Rather than talking of the abolition of poverty or the other grandiose goals of the Great Society, latter-day liberals turned to reform of local politics, to consumer leagues, environmental preservation, and local organizations concerned with equal opportunities and delivery of better educational and medical services in communities. The incremental view of social change, though not well articulated, prevailed.

These changes in ideology were reflected in changing efforts to use the law for the unrepresented. During the 1960s, there was an initial period of optimism about change through law reform, then a period of radicalism and disillusion, and finally, at the end of the decade, the acceptance of goals of middle-range change through incrementalism. These emphases worked themselves out in the tenor of organizations in the legal profession and in the professional opportunities for either full- or part-time participation in legal rights activities.

Civil Rights and Law Reform

As the legal profession, especially young lawyers, came to grips with the spirit of the early 1960s, there was really only one applicable historical model. Traditional legal aid was never seriously considered as a viable method by which society could be restructured. Government service had also fallen into disfavor as a result of the Eisenhower years and the reluctance of government to respond to the most burning social issue of the day—civil rights for blacks.[3] Test-case litigation of the ACLU type continued to attract its small group of adherents, but this kind of social reform work was either too traditional or too professionally antiseptic to capture the spirit of the decade. The ACLU functioned largely within the established legal profession, as a conscience rather than as a counter or outside challenge group. Appellate civil liberties and criminal litigation often attracted lawyers interested only in the chance to win an appeal, irrespective of the nature of the case. This type of disinterested, highly professional appellate work is not the stuff of which social movements are made.[4]

The early part of the 1960s belonged to civil rights for blacks. The model was the NAACP and the Inc. Fund. Eventually, a number of strands were bound together in the 1960s—civil rights, civil liberties, poverty law, environmental protection, and consumerism; but clearly, for at least the first half of the decade, the civil rights movement was the most conspicuous area of activity for reform-oriented lawyers. Moreover, civil rights activity set a tone for other legal rights organizations and established the most influential pattern.

During the years of desegregation campaigns, voter registration drives, and sit-ins, civil rights groups faced an acute shortage of legal help. Few lawyers in the South would represent blacks in these kinds of matters; and those who did so suffered severe reprisals (Carter, 1963; Pollitt, 1964; Honnold, 1966).[5] The NAACP had only limited funds and personnel. This shortage of legal manpower meant that a movement or campaign could be effectively controlled or slowed if its leaders could

[3] A conspicuous exception to the low regard in which social reform-oriented lawyers held government work was the Civil Rights Division of the Justice Department, created in 1957. The attorneys general of the 1960s (Robert Kennedy, Nicholas Katzenbach, and Ramsey Clark) and the heads of the Civil Rights Division (Burke Marshall, John Doar, and Stephan Pollak) attracted many dedicated young lawyers interested in civil rights. In 1965, there were 86 lawyers in the division; by 1970, there were 136. Most of the litigation brought by the Civil Rights Division was in education, but large numbers of cases were also filed in the areas of public accommodations, interference with civil rights, employment, and housing.

[4] Jonathan D. Casper (1972), points out that although lawyers who were either group advocates or civil libertarians were sensitive to broad issues in the areas of reapportionment, loyalty–security, and civil rights; lawyers presenting criminal justice litigation were interested in winning, not in broad issues.

[5] The Congress for Racial Equality (CORE) had most of its legal work done free by the New Orleans black firm of Robert Collins, Nils Douglas, and Lolis Elie, although the amount of work was far greater than the firm could handle (Meier and Rudwick, 1973, pp. 115, 151).

be jailed or otherwise halted through the legal system. The fact that a civil rights leader could ultimately win in the courts was irrelevant if legal help was unavailable. In response to this urgent need for legal help, three organizations of lawyers and law students were created between 1963 and 1965: the Law Students Civil Rights Research Council (LSCRRC), the Lawyers Committee for Civil Rights under Law (LCCRUL), and the Lawyers Constitutional Defense Committee (LCDC).

After a 1963 summer experience in the South assisting civil rights lawyers, 10 northern law students established the Law Students Civil Rights Research Council. The purpose of the organization was to make large numbers of law students available for civil rights work. During 1964, chapters were founded at many law schools; members worked both in the South and in their school communities in a variety of capacities. It is difficult to estimate how many law students were "interns," as they were often called, during the early and middle 1960s, but they helped popularize student activism in the law schools they attended (LSCRRC, 1972).

The Lawyers Committee for Civil Rights under Law was formed in response to a plea in June 1963 by President John Kennedy and Attorney General Robert Kennedy, who urged the legal profession to create an organ to address itself to social upheaval and other problems connected with the enforcement of civil rights. There was no difficulty in recruiting more than 200 prestigious lawyers for committee membership. The first act of the program was to send volunteer lawyers into the South for 2- to 3-week periods, but later LCCRUL staffed a permanent office in Jackson, Mississippi and worked with other civil rights attorneys already on the scene (Countryman and Finman, 1966, pp. 556–557). Sizable chapters were created throughout the country, emphasizing test-case litigation. In later years, the organization broadened its concerns, although it continued to recruit and train young lawyers interested in civil rights work (Marks et al., 1972, pp. 126–137). In part because of the visibility of the auspices of its creation and in part because of the professional prominence of early participants, LCCRUL attracted considerable attention and was recognized as a vehicle for bringing high-powered talent to focus on social impact litigation.

Less prestigious and less enduring was the Lawyers Constitutional Defense Committee, created in 1964 by Carl Rachlin of the Congress of Racial Equality (CORE), with the aid of the ACLU, the NAACP, the Inc. Fund, the American Jewish Committee, the American Jewish Congress, and the National Council of Churches. Staffed with volunteer lawyers,

LCDC operated offices in six southern cities in 1964 and 1965, sending 125 lawyers to the South in 1964 and 70 in 1965.[6] Thus the early 1960s witnessed the emergence of aggressive legal rights activities pressing into the trouble spots of discrimination. The effort was primarily through voluntary organizations; the subject matter was civil rights for blacks; and the basic strategy was law reform litigation, following the lead of the NAACP and the Inc. Fund.

The Struggle between Traditional and Aggressive Legal Rights

Just as many began to feel that adequate legal assistance might be available for civil rights organizations, a displacement of enthusiasm occurred as the War on Poverty drew the nation's attention away from the civil rights movement. By 1965, a program for lawyers had been added to the War on Poverty, and for many lawyers the focus of attention became not the quality of legal defense of southern blacks but representation of the poor. Although for a few years in the mid-1960s the two movements of civil rights and the poor seemed to dovetail, by 1967 it was clear that whereas civil rights law had previously been "in," poverty law seemed to some extent to have replaced it (Leone, 1972).

Poverty law, as expressed in OEO Legal Services, had its structural roots in the Ford Foundation's Grey Areas programs, in the President's Committee on Juvenile Delinquency, and most important, in Mobilization for Youth (MFY) in New York City. All of these programs were efforts to reach the poor and other disenfranchised. groups and, by offering them new or different resources or tools, make more likely their participation in the mainstream of American life.

The Ford Foundation's Grey Areas program was broadly gauged to confront and change the whole texture of life in decaying or blighted urban areas. The Foundation made grants for broadly designed demonstration projects. According to Paul Ylvisaker (quoted in Moynihan, 1969), the point was "to experiment with new ways of improving the social conditions of the central city and of opening new opportunities to those now living in these urban 'grey areas' [p. 36]." Of the six Grey Areas grants, that in New Haven provided the most appropriate model for the future Legal Services program. From the outset, New Haven's antipoverty program, Community Progress Incorporated (CPI), in-

---

[6] This organization is discussed in more detail in Meier and Rudwick (1973 pp. 271–273).

cluded a legal assistance program (Murphy, 1971, pp. 71–74). Conflicts immediately developed between the lawyers, who maintained that litigation was an essential part of their professional role in helping the clients of the program, and the executive director, who thought that the organization could function best by not suing other governmental institutions.[7] What survived the early tense days was a modified legal program independent of CPI, the New Haven Legal Assistance Association. The lessons of the New Haven experience were twofold: Legal services should be supported as part of any antipoverty efforts, but housing them in community action programs might prove untenable if there was to be aggressive client representation (Cahn and Cahn, 1964).

Roughly contemporaneous with the Grey Areas program was the President's Committee on Juvenile Deliquency and Youth Crime, which also worked through demonstration projects emphasizing vocational training, employment services for young people, and community service centers. To a considerable extent, the programs funded by the committee overlapped the Grey Areas list.

The most famous program, funded by both the Ford Foundation and the president's committee, was Mobilization for Youth in New York City. Conceived as an experimental application of a theoretical analysis of the roots of delinquency, it was known and attacked for its militant self-assertion of the poor. The program was concerned primarily with youth employment and training programs for the area of New York City below Fourteenth Street on the East River. Service projects began in four major divisions: Educational Services, Employment Services, Services to Individuals and Families, and Community Development (including Services to Groups) (Heifetz, 1969, p. 23). Legal Services was added as a fifth division in 1964, with the following aims: direct service to and referral of clients; legal orientation for MFY staff, clients, and community leaders; and use of law as an instrument of social change (Appleby, 1969, p. 36). The third goal was the most important for MFY.

To implement its commitment toward social change, MFY's legal component considered the test case as the primary vehicle for creating new law as well as establishing the rule of law in the administrative processes of welfare programs. The most important legal needs of the poor were thought to be those that concerned their relations with public service programs such as welfare and housing. Also of concern were certain aspects of criminal law (pretrial representation of youth, espe-

---

[7] Murphy (1971) writes: "This tension between the professional dictates of the lawyers and the strategic concern of the agency's executive director was never fully resolved to the complete satisfaction of either [p. 116]."

cially), consumer problems, and developing coordination between social workers and lawyers (Grosser, 1964, p. 74). Although MFY's legal
program initially had only four attorneys and a downtown location, it
rapidly increased its staff, established ties in neighborhoods, and built
a very large caseload. Almost from its inception, the MFY program was
involved in bitter controversy as to what extent community organization was appropriate.

Edward Sparer's energetic direction of MFY's legal unit, Jean and
Edgar Cahn's 1964 article suggesting the ways in which neighborhood
law firms might be structured to respond to the needs of the poor, and
the 1964 Conference on Law and Poverty all contributed to the development of a general consensus by late 1964 that the federal government should make a sizable investment in adding a legal services
component to the War on Poverty programs (Grosser, 1964). Moreover,
it was argued that to be consistent with the goals of the War on Poverty,
federally funded legal services were to be aggressive rather than traditional. Legal services would be client oriented and would stress social
change through litigation.

The issue was immediately joined between the traditionalists and
those who argued for aggressive legal rights. Initially, the controversy
over the goals and style of Legal Services focused on what role existing
legal aid societies and local bar associations would have in the new
program. Both the ABA and the NLADA were hostile to the massive
funding of new legal organizations if carefully shepherded legal aid
societies were to be passed over. Their argument was a simple one:
More than 200 legal aid societies (or committees of similar organizations) already existed, and there was no reason not to build on their
strength by allowing them to apply for new funding as Legal Services
programs. Critics of legal aid pointed out the faults of legal aid societies
and warned that no program associated with them could accomplish the
general law reform objectives stated for Legal Services (Carlin *et al.*,
1966). Legal aid societies, they claimed, were too cautious, too service
oriented, too supportive of the establishment and the status quo, too
inexperienced in dealing with the kinds of cases that really mattered, too
accepting of the structure of the law and its injustices, and too tied to local
influentials—in short, too traditional (Pye, 1966). The compromise was
that legal aid societies could apply to be Legal Services units but would
not be considered to be entitled automatically to Legal Services grants. At
the same time, lawyers not affiliated with a legal aid society could apply
for funding in the same local areas. Their applications would be considered alongside those of the legal aid societies; one might be funded, or
both. NLADA immediately undertook a campaign to instruct legal aid

societies in how they might obtain the federal money, and applications began to flow (Pye, 1966, pp. 224–226).

The other compromise related to the role of the bar and the extent to which a local bar association had to approve a program before it would be funded. Understanding on this point differed, but many lawyers and commentators clearly believed that a veto power existed. Early critics of Legal Services and of the legal aid model doubted that the goals of the War on Poverty could ever be realized if the bar retained this degree of control in the area of Legal Services (Wright, 1967). Although the ultimate question of whether a local bar association had a veto was never fully resolved, it was generally agreed that some kind of bar endorsement was necessary for federal support. Another manifestation of bar influence was the requirement that roughly half the governing board of a Legal Services program had to be lawyers.

Partially in return for these concessions, and as the culmination of a half-century of support for the general idea of aid for the indigent, the ABA in February 1965 passed a statement of approval and support for the new Legal Services program. The sanction and continuing support of the ABA were invaluable to Legal Services, particularly as they acted to influence otherwise doubtful bar associations. It was generally acknowledged that most local bar associations were at least somewhat hostile to the idea of Legal Services. And the more the Legal Services unit departed from the legal aid model, the greater the likelihood of hostility. The ABA's role in defending Legal Services, both from local bar association attacks and political attacks, became very important (Pye and Garraty, 1965–66). No doubt, part of the reason for ABA support of Legal Services stemmed from the desire of the profession to protect itself from interference from outsiders; but as the years passed, the ABA became more generally supportive of the content and achievement of Legal Services (ABA 1970; 1971a; 1971b). The issue of the responsibility of the lawyer to a client, removed insofar as possible from the pressure of outsiders, motivated the ABA toward support of Legal Services, so long as the program put no obstacles between professional and client and local lawyers could be community resources to ensure reliability in program activity.

In the early days of Legal Services, the stress was understandably more on getting programs funded and under way than on agreement as to purposes. For that matter, there were many different views of the function of Legal Services and many different interpretations of the language in which the program was initially clothed. With a new program, terms like social change and social reform meant different things to different people. The real tests lay in what happened in field-level offices and how strong a role the national office played.

According to Philip J. Hannon (1969, p. 242), in the early days of OEO about half the grants went to existing legal aid societies; and most of the first Legal Services budget was allotted to local bar associations or bar-sponsored groups of lawyers (Bamberger, 1965–66). By the end of 1965, about 27 projects were in operation (Pye, 1966, p. 230), and seven regional offices had been established. In 1967, nearly 1200 lawyers were working in approximately 250 different projects, with 850 offices.[8] The number of attorneys employed by Legal Services grew steadily until 1972, with peak size somewhat over 2000. Similarly, the number of projects increased until 1972, when there were about 280. Funding, which had begun at a level of $27 million in fiscal 1966, was $71.5 million by fiscal 1972; it was held at this level until 1976, when the program was reorganized at the national level and funding increased.

Many organizational changes occurred in the early Legal Services years. As the number of programs increased, 10 regional offices replaced the 7 of the first years. Back-up centers were established that engaged in research and appellate litigation in specific problem areas such as health, housing, and juvenile delinquency, although in a few instances they were created to support programs in a given geographical area or state rather than a specified policy area. There were continual efforts to rationalize the operation of field offices. In the early days of Legal Services, when there had been great urgency to establish programs, some very small programs—one-attorney offices in many cases—were funded. In subsequent years, many smaller offices and branch offices were curtailed or merged. As much as possible in metropolitan and highly urbanized areas, programs were encouraged to combine so as to meet more effectively the range of urban problems. The amount of program turnover, unfortunately, cannot be measured—some programs that were terminated had never, in fact, opened; others were merged or restructured under new names. At the top of the Legal Services bureaucracy, there was also considerable personnel turnover. Between 1965 and 1972, there were seven directors whose average stay was only a bit more than a year, and the pattern for other top administrators was similar.

In most cases, Legal Services offices had the benefit not only of the lawyers directly employed by them but also of the assignment of lawyers who were holders of Reginald Heber Smith ("Reggie") fellowships and of VISTA lawyers. The Reggie program, begun in 1967, grew from an entering class of 50 to 250 a year. Almost all Reggies were

---

[8] There are no precise data on either the number of attorneys employed or projects funded for the early years of Legal Services. Programs that were funded did not always open, much less continue. And while program grants were partially determined on the basis of the number of attorneys to be employed, slots were often unfilled.

assigned to neighborhood Legal Services offices, usually for 1-year periods, but later for second or third years if the Reggie so wished. It is not surprising that many Reggies remained in programs as staff attorneys when their fellowships ended. Since Reggie fellowships were prestigious and paid a salary higher than most regular Legal Services jobs, they were usually a source of recruitment of special talent. After 1970, the Reggie program increasingly recruited minorities, which carried implications for minority representation in neighborhood programs as well. In much smaller numbers and with much less pay and shorter assignments, VISTA lawyers also supplemented the staffs of Legal Services programs. VISTA, often called the domestic Peace Corps, recruited people of all ages and skills to work in different human service delivery systems. Lawyers in VISTA had assignments to many types of organizations other than Legal Services, but local Legal Services offices often had VISTA volunteers who were not lawyers.

Although the conflict over whether Legal Services was to be traditional or aggressive was compromised initially by the decision to receive and fund applications from existing legal aid societies and programs with a heavy bar influence, the early leadership of Legal Services pushed hard for an aggressive program. The first director, E. Clinton Bamberger (quoted in Stumpf 1968), stressed the law reform mission of Legal Services and downplayed services.

> We cannot be content with the creation of systems of rendering free assistance to all the people who need but cannot afford a lawyer's advice. This program must contribute to the success of the War on Poverty. Our responsibility is to marshall the forces of law and the strength of lawyers to combat the causes and effects of poverty. Lawyers must uncover the legal causes of poverty, remodel the systems which generate the cycle of poverty and design new social, legal and political tools and vehicles to move poor people from deprivation, depression, and despair to opportunity, hope and ambition [p. 711].

Along similar lines, in 1967, Earl Johnson, Jr., director from 1966 to 1968, said

> [T]he primary goal of the Legal Services Program in the near future should be law reform: bringing about changes in the structures of the world in which poor people live in order to provide, on the largest scale possible consistent with our limited resources—a legal system in which the poor enjoy the same legal opportunities as the rich [1967, p. 4].

The extent to which law reform should be emphasized, as stated by Bamberger and Johnson, quickly became the single most important question in the development of Legal Services. Divisions over the wisdom of a law reform strategy were not necessarily along liberal versus conservative lines; there was also the question of practicality.

Vigorous law reform might be too much for local bar associations and the local establishment to swallow, jeopardizing support at the local level. There was the problem of allocation of scarce resources—the more law reform work an office did, the more it might have to turn away service cases. There were disagreements about which approach would serve the needs of the poor best and about the types of problems each approach was best suited for. After some early hesitation, by the spring of 1967 law reform emerged as the dominant official ideology of OEO Legal Services and became a specific aspect of program evaluation. The national office of Legal Services and the regional offices lent their efforts toward increasing the amount of law reform work.

By 1969, community education, economic development, and group representation were also areas of stress. Earl Johnson's 1967 address to the University of Kentucky Law-Alumni Day Program indicated willingness on his part to pursue these areas (Johnson 1968). Burt Griffin (cited in Hannon, 1969), director in 1968, showed similar leanings:

> We must leave our offices and go out among the least fortunate of our citizens. . . . We must help them form unions, co-operatives, condominiums, neighborhood associations, and community development corporations for their own betterment [p. 249].

All these areas of activity proved extremely difficult to foster. It was one thing to tell programs that they would be evaluated in terms of their efforts to achieve particular goals; it was quite another to implement the findings of the evaluations.

Ironically, while the political fight was going on over the future of law reform in Legal Services, doubts were being raised by Legal Services lawyers and others concerning the efficacy of law reform. The argument was advanced that law reform, almost by definition, was inappropriate and unattainable within the Legal Services program framework; that no matter how aspiring and energetic the lawyers, they usually failed in their law reform work. What did it really matter if agency or state rules about welfare dependency were overturned by a test case? The state or agency had enormous administrative discretionary authority and could eventually outmaneuver the Legal Services clients and attorneys so that overall practices remained the same (Handler, 1966; Stumpf, 1973, p. 4; Krislov, 1973; for a different view, see Sullivan, 1971). When law reform work was visible and successful, the political repercussions were enormous. The Reagan–Murphy attacks on Legal Services in 1967 and 1969 were prompted by the suits against various state agencies and programs filed by the California Rural Legal Assistance Program (Hiestand, 1970).

In many other states and communities, politicians and bar groups treated Legal Services programs with thinly disguised hostility.

Though the immediate threats to Legal Services posed by Reagan and Murphy were blunted, there were other political attempts to curb the law reform activities of Legal Services. There were efforts to regionalize and weaken the program by putting Legal Services under the authority of Community Action program (CAP) regional directors or state governors. Initially, Legal Services had been created as a semiautonomous program within the Community Action program of OEO. The arrangement was imperfect and, on occasion unworkable, when CAP promoted decentralization of the Legal Services programs and administration by the laity with Legal Services personnel only advisory in role. Various state governors and agency heads thought that more state or local control of programs would effectively control law reform suits against public authorities. Although CAP leaders and state governors had little in common, they did agree on the desirability of regionalization of Legal Services and won the backing of OEO leaders. The political troubles intensified when Donald Rumsfeld, as head of OEO, pushed hard for regionalization. This move was thwarted, but one of the casualties was Terry Lenzner, the national director of Legal Services, who was very popular with the law reform elements in the program. Morale in Legal Services reportedly sank, and the political warfare continued. Legal Services had to fight vigorously every year for budget increases, and the amounts requested by the program were severely reduced (Pious, 1972). Eventually, the shape and composition of a national corporation to run Legal Services and the sorts of restrictions that should be put on the law reform and other political activities of Legal Services offices emerged as the main political issues (Pious, 1972; Karabian, 1972).

Another criticism was that law reform had jaundiced the prospects of Legal Services by affecting recruitment patterns. Law reform, as an ideology, appeared to be very important in recruitment in Legal Services. The possibility of doing law reform and appeals work added to the glamour of a Legal Services position, and it has been argued that this attracted graduates of elite schools who were solely interested in doing law reform and appellate work. Critics held that participation by these elites had a number of drawbacks: Law reform became too much a subject of emphasis; lawyers from nonelite law schools were discouraged from doing law reform work; and graduates from elite schools left after short periods, posing serious problems for programs that hoped to carry on some continuity of law reform work. The argument here is much like that applied to participation of law elites in civil rights work:

They left very large gaps when they returned to their normal settings, and organizations suffered greatly. According to this argument, a more realistic and more satisfying work plan should deemphasize law reform work and seek better kinds of service work or, alternatively, recruit different personnel (Griffin, 1967).

In July 1974, after several years of bargaining, the various conflicting forces at the national level were able to compromise and produce a new governing statute called the Legal Services Corporation Act. Under this act, Legal Services is run by an 11-person board of directors appointed by the president with the advice and consent of the Senate. A majority of the board must be lawyers admitted to practice. The statute contains a number of attempts at restricting the more controversial aspects of Legal Services. There is an attempt to cut down on law-reform litigation. The back-up centers are to be restructured. The corporation itself can undertake research, training, and clearinghouse activities but cannot contract out any of these functions or engage in litigation on behalf of clients. The intent is thus to keep research under the direct control of the board and prevent any activism. Another restriction on the corporation (from the Legal Services Corporation Act of 1974) forbids contracting with "any private law firms which expend 50 percent or more of their resources and time litigating issues in the broad interests of a majority of the public [Section 1007],"[9] that is, public interest law firms.

The Legal Services Corporation is directed to issue rules and regulations governing the activities of lawyers in its employ. Some of these restrictions include prohibitions against participation in public demonstrations, picketing, or civil disturbances; violations of court injunctions; any political activity; any voter registration activity; transportation of voters or prospective voters; the incitement of litigation; training programs "for the purpose of advocating particular public policies or encouraging political activities"; and legal assistance for desegregation of schools, to procure nontherapeutic abortions, or to challenge violations of the selective services or armed forces laws. In addition, local offices are required to solicit the local bar associations for staff positions and to give preference in hiring to qualified local persons.

It is uncertain how this new statute will be administered and what effects it will have on the future of Legal Services. The membership of the board and the leadership of the corporation indicate that integrity, quality, and independence of Legal Services were strongly and effectively supported by the organized profession and other influential political actors. Leading critics of Legal Services, including a

[9] Legal Services Corporation Act. 1974. 42 USC 2996.

former member of Congress, were kept off of the board. The chairman of the board is Roger Cramton, dean of Cornell Law School and former head of the Administrative Conference. The president of the corporation is Thomas Ehrlich, former dean of Stanford Law School; the executive vice-president is Clinton Bamberger, the first head of OEO Legal Services and former dean of Catholic Law School. These three influential people should be able to lead Legal Services out of the political wilderness of the Nixon years. They are sympathetic, energetic supporters of Legal Services. One of their first acts was to find a way to save the back-up centers, one of the more prominent symbols of law reform. The corporation leadership has taken a strong stand in expanding services with new programs and much larger numbers of lawyers.

Although future directions of Legal Services are not clear at this point, a few general points can be made. The organization of Legal Services at the national level, with its strong bar association support, indicates that the program will be most likely to continue in the future; it seems to have won its battle for survival; and barring a dramatic change in political climate, it is unlikely that future elected politicians will try to kill or seriously damage the program. At the minimum, the program will have increases in financial support. How high these levels will rise, and how fast is unknown.

Although the national office is now vital, knowledgeable, and energetic, we would expect a minimum amount of control and direction of field-level operations. As we point out in the next chapter, Legal Services at the field level was rather impervious to the political fortunes and misfortunes of the program at the national level. The field offices remained the most important recruiters and trainers of legal rights activities lawyers; we would expect this importance to continue.

The development of Legal Services can be summarized as follows. The idea of Legal Services as part of the War on Poverty grew out of aggressive legal rights activities of the early 1960s; this ideology was pushed hard by the early national leadership, seems to have a good deal of sympathy with the present national leadership, and, as we shall see, survives in Legal Services today. At the same time, some Legal Services programs—often those that were re-funded and renamed legal aid societies—take a very traditional approach to legal rights. Just as many field offices were able to resist the conservatism of the Nixon years, some resisted the aggressiveness of the Johnson years. Finally, although a large part of Legal Services is service work, it does not have a traditional orientation. As is pointed out in the next chapter, the service work done by most Legal Services offices is different from traditional legal aid; there is much more litigation; and the lawyers for the most part appear to take a client perspective. On our continuum, this service component of Legal Services (which constitutes the bulk of legal services work) is in the middle area because it is not as aggressive as the law reform component of this or other organizations, but its approach is still fundamentally different from the nonlitigation, paternalistic, moralistic approach of traditional legal rights activities.

Public Defenders: A Traditional Program Marked by Little Change

At the time that the federal government was undertaking a sizable investment in lawyers for the civil problems of the indigent through Legal Services, defender programs were beginning to grow rapidly, both in number and size. By and large, defender programs were built on the base established prior to 1960. Although there has been more concern with appellate work in the past decade, there was no centralized administration for defender programs advocating reform activity. The problem of service versus reform among defenders was never very significant.

Defender programs began to improve after the 1963 Ford Foundation grant for the National Defender Project (NDP). The project was an effort to increase the number of programs, to improve operations, and to win greater acceptance of defender programs as the best method for defending the criminally accused indigent. The National Defender Project included the funding of 73 projects in a variety of circumstances—small counties, large metropolitan centers, statewide, and some federal—as well as different working arrangements with law schools and through legal aid societies and private defender organizations (*Legal Aid Briefcase*, 1968).

In 1961, defender programs existed in only 3% of the counties of the nation and served only about one-quarter of the population; by 1973, 650 defender programs were providing services in 28% of all United States counties, reaching two-thirds of the population. In addition, 16 states have organized and funded defender services at the state level (NLADA, 1973, p. 13). The National Defender Project, plus the Supreme Court decisions mandating the provision of lawyers for indigents in the criminal justice system, served to focus attention on defender programs. In large urban programs, in particular, changes have included increased staff; more use of volunteers, students, paralegals, and investigators; better funding; more appeals work; more office specialization; more training; and improved procedures for working with clients. Although the number of programs and the size of some have increased, a NLADA defender survey (1973, pp. 14–15) revealed that only one-half of the existing 650 systems are really offices with staff attorneys or other staff. The other systems have only one lawyer, unassisted. Approximately 5000 lawyers are providing defender services in state courts throughout the United States; of these lawyers, half are part-time.

The traditional image of defender work suggests that it offers low pay, little prestige, and poor working conditions. Lawyers have been thought to move out of it rather quickly. Career defender work, unless federal, was unlikely and atypical. The 1973 Defender Survey reported that 39.2% view their defender employment as a career position.[10] (Metropolitan defenders are more likely to look upon their jobs as career positions than are rural defenders.) On the other hand, nearly half the chief defenders have held their positions 2 years or less. Of the defenders, 57% were under 30 years of age, and 63% of the staff attorneys reported salaries lower than those paid the prosecutors' staff attorneys (NLADA, 1973, p. 17). Anthony Platt has stressed the burned-out effect that defenders feel, comparable to what many Legal Services lawyers have reported (Platt and Pollick, 1974).

Developments in the defender programs in some ways parallel the development of Legal Services and in others are a reaction to Legal Services. A small number of defender offices in the country became high prestige law reform offices, attracted a great deal of publicity, and recruited from social-reform-oriented elite young lawyers. For a time, positions in these offices were considered to be as desirable as positions in the best Legal Services offices. The other attraction of defender positions sprang from the growing disenchantment and radicalization of some young lawyers that occurred in the late 1960s. As the Vietnam War and the counterculture increased, some young lawyers began to work more and more in draft, drug, and political cases. For increasing numbers of lawyers, criminal law practice became more attractive; but it was not the traditional criminal law practice for which a prosecutor's office had been the usual training ground but criminal practice with political and social reform overtones for which the public defender's office became the training ground. On the whole, the defender program grew in size but retained its traditional orientation.

A Panorama of Other Efforts

As Legal Services grew, organizations engaged in legal rights activities in the voluntary sector and in the profession also continued to

---

[10] Of the 233 public defenders who participated in the survey, 115 were full-time, 108 part-time.

grow, taking different positions along the traditional–aggressive continuum. The dominant position, however, was aggressive legal rights activities.

Aggressive Independent Organizations

Just as the voluntary organizations, particularly the NAACP, the Inc. Fund, and (to a lesser extent) the ACLU, set the pace in the early 1960s, voluntary organizations, and some types of private organizations, provided the cutting edge of aggressive legal rights activities in the second part of that decade. The most prominent were organizations developed by Ralph Nader, foundation-supported public interest law firms, and law communes.

The premise of Nader was that unrepresented consumers could defend themselves if more information were made available to them and if they organized to determine and implement their collective will. Investigation and exposé were the key ingredients for the dissemination of information. Goals were enforcement of neglected legislation, passage of new legislation, or alteration of practices by public or private authorities. Nader had great appeal for young lawyers. He was a lawyer himself; and although he called on other professionals for particular kinds of expertise, he felt that the aggressive lawyer as a problem-solving generalist was best suited for his crusade.

The civil rights movement was waning, at least for whites. Some young lawyers were also seeking alternatives to OEO Legal Services or were antigovernment. There was a substantive attraction to the Nader movement. Nader was anti–big business. He was for the little person, the consumer, the victim of giant public and private bureaucracies. Nader's movement represented a facet of participatory democracy: Little people could get together and with a skilled, sympathetic lawyer make their voices heard. Working for Ralph Nader combined missionary zeal with camaraderie; self-sacrifice; independence from government, business, or private law practice; a vision of a new democratic society; and, for most, an exciting professional life in Washington, D.C. By the late 1960s, the appeal of the Nader organizations to law graduates rivaled the drawing power of Legal Services. To many, the Nader organizations seemed much more reform oriented than Legal Services, and they required no case-by-case service activity. They offered the attractions of working exclusively with like-minded people, a great deal of organizational autonomy, and no outside political interference. Another attraction was that since organizations were small, the workers were also the principals. Extremely low salaries did not seem to hinder recruitment.

The Nader organizations have been well known for their use of research teams whose findings have been published in numerous volumes. They focus, for the most part though not exclusively, on the failings of federal regulatory agencies. In addition to organizations more or less directly under his control, Nader has a strong interest in some organizations which are financially independent; and several former Nader lawyers have started their own organizations, which function with varying degrees of autonomy. Most of Nader's organizations have operated on very modest amounts of money from the General Motors settlement, from Nader's fees for appearances and speeches, from small foundation grants—the Stern, Field, Midas, Norman, and Wallace-Eljabar foundations, among others—and from donations to Public Citizen, Inc. By 1974, Nader or Nader-type organizations had emerged in the areas of auto safety, aviation, health research, corporate responsibility, land use, water cleanliness, food safety and standards, women's policy, science, and citizen action, among others. Public interest research groups had been founded in a number of states, often through university student support.

There is a large amount of transition in Nader organizations. The staffs are small and often supported by only small amounts of money.[11] Despite this, most groups involve at least one lawyer, with volunteers, students, and other professionals playing important roles in the larger projects. The focus of each group may change somewhat with the preferences of staff members; in several instances, parent groups have spawned satellite organizations as departing personnel have created new groups. With the formation of independent public interest groups in many states, often relying on student workers, the Nader thrust is quite decentralized. The formal appurtenances of organization have never been of great interest to Nader and his co-workers. What they have been concerned about is the institutionalization of advocacy for consumers—whether that advocacy is expressed in private study–research groups or by subunits in bureaucracies charged with consumer responsibilities in response to an aroused public.

In the late 1960s, groups of social reformers began to feel that the lack of representation that had been demonstrated to apply to blacks and to consumers applied more generally throughout American society. In particular, it was felt that the government regulatory agencies supposed to represent the public interest often failed to do so and that they were captives of the special interests that they were supposed to regulate. The idea that there was a need to represent the unrepresented—the public interest—before government agencies received its initial strong

[11] For perspectives on organizational structure and function, see Gerlach (1971).

sanction in a 1966 court of appeals decision involving a Federal Communications Commission license renewal proceeding.[12]

In this proceeding, the United Church of Christ sought to represent groups of blacks as listeners. The court granted the group the right to present their case on the grounds that the commission no longer effectively represented listener interests. This ruling was applicable to many kinds of groups before many different government agencies. The term *public interest* began to be used to express the idea that the problem of inadequate representation applied through all sectors of society. In the late 1960s, public interest law firms emerged in which salaried lawyers worked to secure more citizen rights vis-à-vis government, mainly in consumer and environmental problem areas and later with poverty and minority-related problems. Public interest law firm work was almost entirely test-case law reform.

The proliferation of foundation-supported public interest law firms began in 1970 with the Ford Foundation's decision to become a principal source of support for public interest law organizations (Harrison and Jaffe, 1972). The number of foundations that support such firms is not large. Ford is clearly the leader in terms of both amount of support and number of organizations supported, but other foundations—the Carnegie Corporation, the Field Foundation, the Stern Family Fund, the Edna McConnell Clark Foundation, and the Rockefeller Brothers Fund, to name a few—also contribute varying amounts of money to public interest law.

In Chapter 4, we describe in detail the organization and work of public interest law. The importance of public interest law is that it represented another distinct phase in the growth and development of aggressive legal rights activities. It presented young, socially minded lawyers with new areas of interest and new organizational settings. Just as OEO Legal Services appeared to present an alternative to civil rights work, public interest law appeared to replace Legal Services as the cutting edge of social reform.

In addition to foundation-supported firms, some private law firms identified themselves as public interest law firms. Very few of these private public interest law firms support themselves solely from public interest law work; that is, either they have sufficient public interest clients (like the Sierra Club) that pay fees, or they obtain grants for specific projects. Most private public interest law firms have a mixture of regular clients and public interest clients. Lawyers in such firms

[12] *United Church of Christ* v. *Federal Communications Commission.* 1966. 359 F.2d 994, D.C. Cir.

tailor their caseloads so as to do a considerable amount of free or low-fee work for cases or clients that they define to be in the public interest. Most often these firms are wholly dependent on regular client fees for income. The total number of lawyers involved in these firms is small, perhaps only about 100 (Halpern and Cunningham, 1971).

In a sense, the law commune is a radical version of the private public interest firm. Communes attempt to limit their work to kinds of cases or clients along radical, political, ideological lines, charging only if clients have funds. The overriding aim of the communes is political activism rather than the traditional practice of law. The usual, and preferred, clients are criminal defendants, political activists, radicals, students, and other youth in varying forms of alternative culture (Braudy, 1971; *New York Times*, 1971; *Washington Post*, 1970). Law communes are discussed in more detail in Chapter 6.

A variety of other organizations also deserve mention here, although several will be discussed in more detail in subsequent chapters. Several "counter" or alternative bar associations have been formed. Perhaps the best known of these is the revived National Lawyers Guild, which was transformed into a radical political organization by student activists and young lawyers in 1967. A parallel organization, the National Conference of Black Lawyers (NCBL), was organized in 1968–1969, to "use the skills of the black bar in struggles against racism and for the liberation of black people." NCBL activities have included, among others, the defense of politically unpopular people, affirmative suits on community issues, and monitoring of government activity affecting the black community.

The organized bar has also engaged in efforts which although not as aggressive as those of nonbar groups have had a law reform orientation. Best known is the public interest law firm funded by the Beverly Hills Bar Association. Several other bar associations are considering or have started similar projects, although how aggressive or traditional is uncertain. In addition, the American Bar Association has approved a special committee report strongly supporting public interest law, and the Lawyers Committee for Civil Rights under Law has continued its earlier concentration on law reform.

Service-Oriented Independent Organizations

Another type of organization, generally more traditional than the bar-sponsored groups, has emerged in several cities. Lawyers have been organized by ghetto or foundation organizers to provide volunteer legal services; supported by the lawyers themselves, large private law firms, or occasionally by small subsidies from local bar associations.

Community Legal Organizations (CLO) of New York City, founded in 1968, uses volunteers and employs several staff lawyers on a full-time basis (Rosenthal *et al.*, 1971). Chicago Volunteer Legal Services, founded in 1964, grew to 250 attorneys by 1973. The more aggressive Chicago Council of Lawyers was founded in October 1969 and grew to more than 1200 members. The Council of New York Law Associates, founded in 1970, acts primarily to disseminate information about pro bono activity and only secondarily as a service organization or in an investigative capacity. With about 1600 members, the New York council has become somewhat more action oriented in the past 2 years, but it remains more of a clearinghouse than anything else. Councils were also formed in Washington and San Francisco. Several other communities have or had rather similar programs, varying in size, in type of preferred clientele, and in kinds of cases handled, but overall, their emphasis is on one-to-one case service and not on law reform work. However, we suspect that at least some of these lawyers have been influenced by aggressive legal rights ideology. Certainly, large numbers of professionals have become involved in these service organizations which provide a structured setting for the delivery of traditional services.

Regularized pro Bono Activities by Large Private Firms

Chapter 5 discusses the pro bono activities of private lawyers. Most of this work, carried on by individual practitioners, is of a traditional sort. In some large firms, however, pro bono activity is organized. Around 1968, it was widely believed by many hiring law firms that the best law graduates were not interested in traditional jobs and would seek jobs in Legal Services (or similar activities) unless traditional firms had attractive pro bono programs in which they might participate.[13]

Although the actual deflection of talent away from private law firms was probably small, it is clear that some Legal Services programs were successful in attracting very able people. Law firms concerned with

---

[13] *Wall Street Journal* (1968): "While most law students still do strive to get a lucrative job with a corporation or a firm or a traditional Government post, an increasing number are opting for low paying jobs that they consider more challenging and . . . socially rewarding . . . those that are choosing to stay away from Wall Street are often the brightest students [p. 1]."

In the same tone, a more recent *Wall Street Journal* article (1970) reported: "The hiring partners in most firms agree that they get many more questions about opportunities for public service work from law school seniors interviewed today than in the past. Young lawyers themselves say such opportunities play an important role in their decisions to join a given firm [p. 1]."

hiring the best thus had an incentive to create in-house programs for pro bono work. These programs are discussed in Chapter 6.

Impressionistic evidence suggests that the pro bono interest of traditional firms is on the wane. Perhaps, as suggested by some critics, there was no real commitment on the part of traditional law firms; and once the competition from OEO Legal Services declined, their interest in offering nontraditional alternatives to new associates slackened. It is also reported, again on an impressionistic basis, that applicants for jobs in traditional firms no longer inquire about pro bono opportunities. If true, this change in professional orientation may be the result of a softening job market for lawyers or may reflect a more general decline in interest in social reform. The pro bono programs of law firms have varied in the extent to which they depart from traditional service patterns, but their very existence has meant more professional opportunities to be introduced to the problems of the underrepresented.

SUMMARY AND CONCLUSIONS

Our concern in this chapter has been to indicate the wide variety of activities that are a part of efforts in the legal profession to broaden legal representation. In describing these legal rights activities and how they have emerged from the traditions of the profession, we have emphasized the roles of organizations, especially Legal Services. We have also indicated how these organizations have been related to broader social reform activities of the 1960s.

By the later 1960s and early 1970s, legal rights activities had expanded into a wide variety of organizations. Both traditional and aggressive organizations served the legal needs of the poor and the unrepresented, but aggressive organizations played a much different role in the development of legal needs. The essence of the aggressive organizations was to chart out new areas, uncover problems, define them in terms of legal needs, and sensitize the country to the issues. They were a creative force in the development of legal consciousness on behalf of the poor and the unrepresented; and in this respect they functioned very differently from traditional legal rights organizations which were more or less content to respond to the demands thrust upon them.

Organizations also performed another crucial role: the recruitment, training, and cycling of lawyers interested in pursuing careers in legal rights activities. Young lawyers interested in pursuing legal rights careers had a choice of working in government, the voluntary sector, private practice, or bar association organizations; moreover, within each of these settings, they could select organizations that were aggressive, traditional, or a mixture. In short, there has been growth in a number of different directions. Although organizations engaged in aggressive legal rights work have been the most prominent—at least in terms of publicity and controversy, if not of results—there has also been a steady growth in mixed and traditional organizations. Legal rights activities developed into a rich and variegated enterprise, with a wide array of full- and part-time opportunities for participation.

In terms of the number of full-time lawyers it has involved, Legal Services is clearly the largest organization by far, employing more lawyers than most of the other legal rights organizations put together. For this reason, it is Legal Services that will be highlighted in the remainder of this study. To what extent are popular beliefs about recruitment in Legal Services borne out? What are the main activities in Legal Services, and what strains are evident? What impact has the organizational experience had on career choices for lawyers who have left Legal Services? How are different types of Legal Services work and attitudes related?

At the same time, we will report on other organizations, including public interest law firms and organizations within the private bar. What types of activities do they engage in? How are they organized? What are their chances for survival? What are the attitudes and experiences of participating lawyers?

Finally, outside of organizations, what types of legal rights activities are being carried on by individual practitioners? Some practitioners are involved with voluntary or professional organizations described in this chapter; most are not. To what extent are private practitioners involved, and what implications do their activities carry for the future of legal rights work?

The conclusion that we draw is that legal rights work is a growing, dynamic field in which, over time, structures will emerge—some to disappear, some to survive. What others have described as waning and waxing of interest in legal rights activities is, in our eyes, a more subtle process: a substitution and broadening of interest in such work, with different organizations highlighted at different times.

II

LEGAL RIGHTS
ACTIVITIES TODAY

3

Legal Services

Since the Legal Services Corporation is the largest legal rights organization, its work and personnel are central to any discussion of legal rights. In its early days, the War on Poverty's Legal Services program achieved great success: It received good publicity, grew, attracted young recruits, built caseloads, and developed law reform cases. It also survived the demise of OEO. Some have interpreted the fact that Legal Services budgets were not cut during the early 1970s, when OEO was being weakened and ultimately dismembered, as a sign of strength. Despite the strenuous efforts of its enemies to kill or emasculate the program, its supporters continued to rally to its defense. The program lives—but how well? The great political controversies have taken place at the national level. It is claimed that at the field level the battle for the preservation of the program has been lost; that it has been converted from a powerful engine of social reform on behalf of the poor to traditional legal aid; and that, because of this change, it no longer attracts the cream of the young legal talent. Morale is said to be low, working conditions poor, work shoddy, and turnover high.

In this chapter, we are concerned with some of these questions. First, we want to know what kind of activity Legal Services lawyers are doing—the kinds of clients they serve, the types of problems they deal with, the legal services they perform, the mix of law reform and service cases—and the extent to which these activities have changed over time. Is it true, for example, that Legal Services has been converted to traditional legal aid? Second, we shall be concerned with the lawyers. How do the lawyers themselves view their working conditions; why did they join Legal Services and why do they leave? Have job satisfaction and morale changed over time? To what extent does Legal Services continue

51

to provide an attractive structural alternative to private practice? These questions are discussed on the basis of interviews with large numbers of past and present Legal Services lawyers. (See Appendix A for sample construction and other methodological aspects of the study; and Appendix B for the questionnaire used.)

THE WORK OF THE OFFICES

From the earliest days of the program, the principal areas of activity for Legal Services lawyers have been family, consumer, housing, and welfare law. Table 3.1 shows that in 1972, as in 1967, these four areas

Table 3.1

Work Done by Legal Services Lawyers

	Percentage of total workload	
Type of work	1967	1972
Family	30.4	21.7
Consumer	24.1	21.6
Housing, landlord–tenant	18.2	23.3
Welfare	6.2	12.2
Employment	2.9	5.3
Juvenile	2.0	4.6
Criminal	4.4	.5
Others mentioned (each less than 2%)	11.8	10.8
Total	100.0	100.0

accounted for almost 80% of the activity of the lawyers, although in 1972 a few other areas claimed some attention (employment, juveniles). There were, however, shifts within these areas: In 1967, family matters accounted for 30.4% of the lawyers' work; by 1972, the family category dropped to about 21.7%. Many Legal Services offices developed highly specialized or routinized methods for dealing with uncontested divorce actions, the most common subcategory in the family area. Use of paraprofessional and automatic programed machinery have enabled some programs to handle a very large volume of divorces. Other programs try to minimize their personnel investment in divorce work by office specialization, assigning attorneys exclusively to family matters.

At the same time, welfare and housing activity rose.[1] Legal Services programs have also pioneered in specialized speedy techniques in these areas. Standard forms have been developed for several kinds of landlord–tenant cases; and in the welfare area, Legal Services programs have trained lay advocates to assist clients in welfare department administrative hearings.

As Legal Services programs have matured, they have taken more advantage of the benefits of specialization, using models similar to those employed in large private firms and bureaucracies. About 70% of lawyers who mentioned a specialty (in 1972) mentioned one of the four service areas— family, consumer, housing, or welfare. Presumably such specialization has promoted greater efficiency and expertise. Although smaller programs have much less specialization, they have also tried to benefit from routinization in order to handle more cases. Some attorneys in specialized units spend all their time in particular areas, but most attorneys do not; overall, Legal Services lawyers work as generalists.

What accounts for the seemingly decreasing emphasis on family law cases over time? There are a number of possible explanations. Legal problems dealing with the family are not susceptible to solution merely by the passage of time; a separated couple must get a divorce if either spouse is to remarry. Consequently, one would expect a backlog of families with marital problems waiting for legal services. However, with consumer, housing, and welfare problems, those involved can use nonlegal, self-help solutions or make other adjustments. Goods are repossessed, tenants are evicted, applicants are denied relief; although there may be suffering and injustice, problems get solved without lawyers and tend to disappear over time. This difference, then, between family law problems and other problems could explain the gradual decline of family law matters—as Legal Services continued, the backlog would gradually get unjammed.

Another reason could be the adverse publicity that Legal Services received as a result of handling a large number of divorces. Part of the

---

[1] The sample is described in Appendix A. The percentages in this section are based on response to the question "What are the major areas in which you handled services cases?" and thus are only a rough indicator of the total effort of Legal Services offices in these areas. It is reasonable to infer, however, that some change did take place.

In addition, lawyers reported these areas for the most recent year that they were in Legal Services, not specifically for 1967 or 1972. Some of the 1967 sample, and most of the 1972 sample, were still in the program when interviewed in 1973. Thus, the 1967 and 1972 figures are at best only approximations of early and recent activities. Throughout this chapter, Reggies are excluded from means and distributions.

controversy about Legal Services centered on its identification as a publicly supported divorce mill. Traditional legal aid, prior to the advent of OEO Legal Services, also suffered from this kind of attack. Charitable legal services were supposed to be for the deserving poor for worthy ends; divorce was never considered a proper object of charity, and few legal aid offices handled divorces except under exceptional circumstances. To a considerable degree, these attitudes carried over to OEO Legal Services. The national office and many neighborhood offices were sensitive to the divorce-mill charge, and pressure was exerted to hold down the number of divorces. This also may have accounted for the proportionate decline of family law matters as an area of activity.[2]

Type of work did not vary much from one region of the country to another. Programs in larger cities reported more work with housing problems, but other types of work did not vary with city size. Both housing and welfare work were more commonly reported in the Northeast than in any other area; but there were no relationships between geographical area and consumer, marital, or other major types of work. Programs have varied in the extent to which they have institutionalized advocacy for migrants, consumer problems involving major financial institutions, etc.; but for the most part program workload similarities stem from the common problems of the poor, which appear to vary only marginally according to geography and extent of urbanism.

As Chapter 2 indicated, one of the great controversies in Legal Services had to do with service work versus law reform work. The early national directors, Clinton Bamberger and Earl Johnson, stressed the law reform role of Legal Services; this would distinguish Legal Services from old-style legal aid. Law reform was also the main reason for the rise in the political difficulties of Legal Services. More recently, it has been said that law reform has been drastically reduced in Legal Services and that this is one of the major reasons for the supposed decline in the program.[3]

According to the reports of Legal Services lawyers, there was not a great deal of change in the distribution of time between service and law reform work between 1967 and 1972; in fact, there was even a slight increase in reform work. The lawyers were asked how they and their offices divided their time between these two activities. In 1967, the average law reform time reported for offices was 21%; in 1972, the

---

[2] Alternatively, it could be that although fewer lawyers reported doing family work, the overall amount of time and number of family law cases remained the same.

[3] For controversy about the role and amount of law reform in Legal Services programs, see Rothstein (1974); Champagne (1974); Feuillan (1973); Brill (1973); Carlin and Brill (1975); Stumpf et al. (1975).

percentage was 24.6. As to the lawyers' distribution of time, we note the same trend. In 1967, the average proportion of time the lawyers report having spent in law reform work was 25%; in 1972, it was 31.2%. Thus, using either indicator, common knowledge proved wrong; if there was any change, it was in favor of more law reform, rather than less. In addition, in 1972, more Reggies were available to Legal Services programs. Reginald Heber Smith fellowship recipients spent more time in law reform work than did other Legal Services lawyers (39.5% of their time).

The line between law reform and service work is not distinct; moreover, our data rely on classification by the respondents themselves. In this connection, it is interesting to note that overall the respondents said they were doing more law reform work than were their offices. In fact, we cannot say how much law reform is going on in Legal Services. On the other hand, how the lawyers themselves classify their work is important for issues of job satisfaction, morale, and recruitment.

In what areas did law reform activity take place? Lawyers report that much of their own law reform activity (65% in 1967, 59% in 1972) was spent on housing, welfare, and consumer affairs, in that order (see Table 3.2). Law reform activity in welfare would be on behalf of welfare rights organizations against state welfare departments; in housing, on behalf of tenant organizations against landlords and housing authorities; in consumer affairs, against merchants and other business persons. In the years between 1967 and 1972, there appears to have been a shift away from law reform work in housing and a diffusion of effort into areas such as employment practices and prison reform.

Lawyers were somewhat more likely to mention welfare in connection with law reform than with service work (18.1 versus 12.2%), but the biggest difference was in the family law area; although this area accounted for a great deal of service work, there was very little law reform effort in it.

Although the proportion of law reform work as reported by the lawyers was high (30%, on the average) and probably increased rather than declined over the years, we need to know the distribution of law reform work among the various programs. In the early years of Legal Services, larger programs sometimes had special law reform groups, at times staffed principally by Reggies. Over time, these arrangements became less common as problems emerged. In some instances, those who did not do law reform work resented the glamour law reformers seemed to have. In other cases, law reform activities by a special group were thought to cause awkward relations for other lawyers in their

Table 3.2

Law Reform Work Done by Legal Services Offices and Legal Services Lawyers

| | Percentage of law reform work | | | |
| | Offices | | Legal Services lawyers | |
Type of law reform work	1967	1972	1967	1972
Welfare	23.0	24.4	20.3	18.1
Housing, public housing, urban renewal, landlord–tenant	27.1	21.3	31.6	24.4
Consumer affairs law	17.9	16.7	13.5	16.1
Education	3.7	7.7	3.5	6.2
Family	4.2	1.7	4.6	2.6
Employment practices, discrimination	2.2	4.3	1.7	5.2
Prison reform	2.1	3.0	1.5	4.2
Civil rights, desegregation, civil liberties	1.3	4.3	1.0	4.2
Juvenile	5.0	3.8	6.3	4.2
Mental health, health	.6	2.6	.4	2.1
Other areas mentioned (each less than 2%)	12.9	10.2	15.6	12.7
Total	100.0	100.0	100.0	100.0

dealing with administrative agencies. By the end of the first decade of the program, most offices had evolved different law reform strategies. Larger offices often divided attorneys into specialty areas, with the understanding that they would develop and pursue the law reform issues as well as handle the service caseload. Smaller programs, rather than handle law reform work, tended to refer them to larger Legal Services offices with more specialized expertise.

What kinds of correspondence exist between the quality of an office and its involvement with law reform work? National and regional Legal Services directors were asked to rate the programs as excellent, medium, or poor.[4] We also compared the directors' ratings with evaluation studies of OEO Legal Services and found that there was a fair amount of congruence (Auerbach Corporation, 1971; Kettelle Corporation, 1971). There was a direct relationship between the quality of the

[4] A former national director and more than half a dozen Legal Services regional directors were asked to rate programs as excellent, medium, or poor. Unrated programs were assumed to be of medium quality.

program (by these measures) and the amount of law reform activity reported by the lawyers, both for the offices and for themselves. In general, we find that the greater the proportion of time spent in law reform, the higher the quality of the program both for 1967 and 1972. In 1967, for example, the amount of time spent in law reform by lawyers in excellent programs was 33.3%; in medium programs, 18.7%; and in poor programs, 14.1%. In 1972, the respective figures were 27.8, 24, and 17.7%.[5]

There are considerable differences in the evaluative ratings given to programs at different times. In 1967, only 10 to 15% of the programs were rated excellent; by 1972, about 35% were so rated, and the differences in the amount of law reform work performed among programs of different quality were considerably less. Over time, excellent programs have modestly reduced the percentage of time spent in law reform work, while medium and poor programs have increased it. As national and regional offices in Legal Services have asserted their influence and as there has been more opportunity for development of standards, there have been a variety of changes; small programs have been merged or closed, and statewide programs have become much more common. Similarly, the creation of more specialized back-up centers meant additional resources for various programs. Legal Services, in its early years, passed through the business of organizing a decentralized bureaucracy, with weaker units slowly being strengthened or weeded out. This has meant the emergence of a more homogeneous program.

Several other conditions were associated with more law reform work. In 1967, approximately the same amount of law reform was carried on in cities of all sizes and in all geographical regions. The organizations in existence prior to the initiation of OEO funding did more service work than did the new organizations (81% versus 74%), but the difference was not large. By 1972, these patterns had shifted only slightly; service time was lower in the largest cities (72% versus 76%), and higher in the South (81% versus 72% in the Northeast and West). Clearly, law reform work has become common throughout programs and is not confined to a few; and whereas programs newly established with OEO funding were somewhat more attuned to law reform work, neither city size nor geographical region had much effect on its amount.

The important finding is that, nationwide, participants report that a fairly uniform proportion of their time was spent on law reform—on the average about 30%—and if anything, this amount has even increased slightly over the years.

---

[5] At the time, the preferred ideology was law reform, so that we would expect programs that reportedly did the most law reform to be rated more highly.

During the 1967–1972 period, strategies other than law reform and service were highlighted by national and regional directors—community organization, economic development, legislation, and lobbying. Some have argued that law reform is an inappropriate strategy in that it is not concerned with building a power base and that community organization would be a far more fruitful line of endeavor in ensuring the access of the poor to the legal system (Bowler, 1973; Salsich, 1969). On the other hand, community organization is time consuming, requires the use of skills not unique to lawyers, and may incur hostility from local groups.

From the field perspective, how much community work was done? Legal Services neighborhood lawyers were asked: "In community work, how many hours a month—if any—do you personally spend (a) speaking to neighborhood client groups; (b) helping organize client or neighborhood groups; (c) counseling, for example, about welfare or consumer problems?" About one-half of the lawyers did no organizing at all. Lawyers were more likely to report speaking to neighborhood client groups or counseling. The average amount of time per month spent speaking was 4.1 hours; in organizing, 4.5 hours; and in counseling, 8.5 hours. An average, then, of 17 hours per month per lawyer went into such community activities. Reggies did more community work than other Legal Services lawyers, speaking to client groups 5.1 hours per month, organizing 6.8 hours per month, and counseling 14.5 hours per month for a total of 26.4 hours per month. This total is about 50% greater than the time Legal Services lawyers spent, on the average, another indication of the special mission of the Reggie fellows.

For Legal Services staff lawyers, community work in 1967 was somewhat greater than in 1972: 21.4 hours per month compared with 17 hours. Furthermore, there was a change in the kind of community work being done; in 1967, there was more speaking to client groups (7.2 hours versus 4 hours) compared to counseling, which remained the same. There are two likely explanations for the change. In 1967, the programs were newer, and more introductory public relations work was needed; there was less need when offices became inundated with cases. In addition, as the political troubles of Legal Services increased, lawyers might have been more reluctant to speak than to counsel; counseling is lawyer's work, whereas speaking is more akin to political activity.

It is not unexpected that there is an inverse relationship between the three kinds of community work and service work; the more service work a lawyer reports doing, the less community work he or she reports. When we look at the offices in terms of the directors' ratings, we find a consistent relationship between community work and reputed quality of program; that is, lawyers in higher quality offices also did more community work. On the whole, though, vigorous community work was never a significant part of OEO Legal Services, even in the elite offices; and most of community work consisted of counseling rather than organizing or speaking. Thus, most of the work called community work by Legal Services lawyers was rather traditional. Although an occasional lawyer helping those arrested in riots made headlines, such events were uncommon. Given the shortage of resources and caseload problems, most programs found it difficult to broaden activities to new areas such as community organization even if they so desired. Some few programs have been involved with active fostering of new organizations, but most have worked with existing community groups. Relationships between some programs and community groups (such as housing councils) have been quite close.

As Legal Services programs have put down roots in their communities, establishing ongoing relationships with political leaders, social service and voluntary organizations, bar groups, and state and local officials, much of the early distrust of the programs has been displaced and cooperative arrangements have emerged. Legal Services programs have become a resource to varieties of community groups. They have expertise for tapping federal and state funds, controlling unfair business practices, and allaying court challenges by assisting with the drafting of regulations and legislation. In most communities, Legal Services organizations have established legitimacy and recognition. This has made their day-to-day work somewhat easier.

Another aspect of the work of Legal Services lawyers is their court activity. In 1972, two-thirds of the lawyers report spending more than 20% of their time in court; an increase over 1967. Why would there be an increase? With the decline in family law matters, one might have expected a decline in court cases. We think the answer lies in the gradual transition of former legal aid offices to the Legal Services approach.

As noted in Chapter 2, in the initial years of Legal Services, some offices were legal aid offices that applied for and received federal funding. These legal aid offices did not do much court work; in fact, this was one of the major criticisms of legal aid (Levitan, 1969, Chapter 6; Carlin and Howard, 1965). Between 1967 and 1972, former legal aid programs recruited new personnel, the national office of Legal Services established directions, and there was a proportionate rise in litigation. Court time was related to service work; the more service work, the more time spent in court. This meant that the bulk of the court time was spent in the lower state and local courts. Only about 20% of the courts that lawyers mentioned were federal courts or state appellate courts (see Table 3.3). Overall, an important aspect of court work in Legal Services is that with the passage of time an important body of case law has emerged in several substantive areas of poverty law.

Legal Services lawyers also deal with government agencies; 86.7% report spending some time with government agencies, and 63.4% report a substantial time (more than 20%). As with court time, time spent with government agencies also increased between 1967 and 1972. One reason for this is that welfare increased considerably in the 5 years as a proportion of caseload. Almost one-half (47.9%) of all the agencies mentioned by lawyers spending a substantial amount of time before government agencies were welfare or related agencies, such as Social Security, and social services (see Table 3.4). Despite the large volume of housing cases, only 12.2% of the agencies mentioned were housing authorities, indicating that probably most housing matters involved private landlords.

Most of the work in Legal Services, then, was service work focused mainly in the four areas of family, welfare, housing, and consumer problems. Legal Services lawyers reported that the average number of open files they had at any one time was about 100; this varied, though, with how much law reform work was being done (see Table 3.5). Throughout its history, the Legal Services program has been virtually inundated with clients; and as we show, case pressure is perceived by Legal Services lawyers as a serious problem (Levitan, 1969, p. 186). There was a tradeoff between law reform work and the number of open files: the more law reform, the smaller the number of open files. Reggies

Table 3.3

Courts in Which Legal Services Lawyers Spent Time, 1972

Courts [a]	Percentage of time spent
State and county trial courts, including family and juvenile	57.5
Municipal, small claims	14.6
State appellate courts	6.2
Federal district courts	10.8
Federal appellate courts	2.9
Other	8.0
Total	100.0

[a] Courts mentioned only by those spending substantial time in court, defined as 20% or more of their time in court.

Table 3.4

Governmental Agencies with Which Legal Services Lawyers Dealt, 1972

Agencies[a]	Percentage of time spent
Welfare agencies, social service departments	33.4
Social Security	14.5
HUD, Model Cities, housing authorities	12.2
Unemployment offices, commissions	8.2
Prison authorities	2.4
Other federal agencies, including Bureau of Indian Affairs, HEW, OEO, Department of Justice	9.4
City, county government	2.1
Local, state law enforcement, district attorney, prosecutor	1.5
Other state agencies	7.9
Other county, local agencies (school board, Selective Service)	6.1
Other (public service commissions, state legislatures, labor relations)	2.3
Total	100.0

[a] Agencies mentioned only by those spending substantial time in an agency.

Table 3.5

Average Distribution of Lawyers according to Number of Open Files, 1972

Number of files	Percentage of lawyers
None	2.3
1–49	17.9
50–100	31.8
101–174	26.6
175 or more	21.4
Total	100.0

handled fewer cases, averaging 79 files. There was no systematic variation in case volume and program quality, however; the offices that
received the highest marks from regional and national directors were
able both to do law reform and to manage a volume of cases as large as
offices that were evaluated as lower in quality and did less law reform
work.

With 2000 Legal Services lawyers averaging 100 cases at a time, it is reasonable to estimate that at any given time Legal Services lawyers are handling about 200,000 cases. We do not know the number of clients they serve, but other sources have estimated about 900,000 clients per year (Scheindlin, 1974). This would mean that, on the average, a file stays open for 3 months.

Whatever strategies for efficiency and routinization have developed, caseload problems have been extremely serious in Legal Services. Although estimates of caseload have varied up to a high of 800 per lawyer, the generally accepted figure is in the neighborhood of 400 cases a year. In contrast, it has been estimated that the average private practitioner handles 50–100 cases per year (Auerbach Corporation, 1971). Even public defenders have much smaller caseloads, and NLADA suggests that 100 cases is the maximum load for adequate professional work for defenders. Cost data about Legal Services are imprecise and open to challenge, but the best estimates are that costs run $10–15 an hour (Auerbach Corporation, 1971). Allowing for inflation, this is still much less than private practitioners charge. Such savings result from a variety of factors, including the low salaries of the lawyers and the enormous caseloads.

In order to deal more effectively with caseload pressures, many programs have instituted office specialization programs to provide more routine and structure to services. Still, given the current ratio of Legal Services lawyers to poverty population, caseload problems remain overwhelming. A recent study has estimated that the 17 million poor people ostensibly covered by Legal Services have approximately 4 million legal problems a year, and Legal Services is able to handle just over a million cases (Goodman and Walker, 1975, p. 14): "And there is but three-fourths of a Legal Services staff lawyer's position for every 10,000 poor persons in the United States, or one lawyer for every 13,239 poor persons [p. 23]." It has recently been estimated that 12 million poor people have no access whatsoever to Legal Services attorneys.

Who are the clients of Legal Services offices? Nationwide, most of them were white, followed closely by blacks; far fewer Chicanos, Puerto Ricans, and native Americans are served. The racial and ethnic composition of the clients, of course, varies with the location of the office. Clients in the smaller cities and rural areas are white; in the large urban centers, they are mostly black; in the Southwest and Southern California, Chicano; and in New York City, Puerto Rican (see Table 3.6). New York City lawyers, for example, said 32% of their clients were Puerto Rican.

The conclusion that emerges from the data on work activities is that

Table 3.6

Percentage of Racial Distribution of Clients

	Large cities (over 600,000)		Medium cities (100,000–600,000)		Small cities (under 100,000)		All cities	
	1967	1972	1967	1972	1967	1972	1967	1972
Black	45.3	43.7	44.1	36.7	31.6	26.5	41.9	34.5
White	28.8	28.4	35.6	39.3	49.2	50.3	35.9	40.9
Other (Chicano, Native American, etc.)	25.9	27.9	20.3	24.0	19.2	23.2	22.2	24.6
Total	100.0	100.0	100.0	100.0	100.0	100.0	100.0	100.0

Legal Services lawyers are busy; at any one time, each handles about 100 open cases, primarily in family law, consumer affairs, housing, and welfare. This is not only office work; the lawyers spend a substantial amount of time in court and before government agencies. In addition, their work is not all routine; about one-fourth to one-third of their time is spent on law reform work.

JOB SATISFACTION AND MORALE

Lawyers in Legal Services in 1972 liked their jobs and thought well of their programs. Almost 90% said they were either satisfied (59.3%) or very satisfied (27.9%) with their jobs. Among the 1967 Legal Services lawyers, the replies were essentially the same. Very probably, an important reason for their satisfaction was their estimation of the quality of their programs. About 70% of the 1972 respondents said that their programs were either very good (41.1%) or excellent (28.6%); only 7% rated their programs fair or poor. There was some variation in these responses. Lawyers in large cities were somewhat more favorable in their judgments than lawyers in smaller cities and rural areas; programs in the Northeast and West were rated slightly higher than those of the North Central area and the South. Programs rated higher by the regional directors also received higher marks from staff lawyers. The most important determinant in program evaluation, however, had to do with the amount of time spent in law reform work; lawyers who spent proportionately more time in law reform were inclined to view their programs more favorably than lawyers who spent more time in service work. One should not get the impression, however, that program excellence meant doing mainly law reform work; lawyers in excellent programs (as rated either by participants or by regional directors) still spent an average of more than 60% of their time in service work.

Those favorable attitudes did not mean that the programs were without stress. In 1972, the first effort to form an independent Legal Services Corporation had failed, and the program was still under heavy attack for too much concern with class action and law reform work. Fred Speaker had resigned as director of Legal Services in February 1972, and many felt that the days of Legal Services were numbered. Pressures to weaken the program were very strong, at both local and national levels; and morale was reported to be low. On the other hand, by 1972, Legal Services had survived regionalization threats, and the very fact of the effort to form an independent corporation was a good omen to some.

While these national concerns were real and pressures were felt in the neighborhood offices, day-to-day pressures on the neighborhood lawyers were of a different sort, and far less dramatic. For example, it is often thought that neighborhood Legal Services offices operated in a hostile environment, primarily resulting from the opposition of local bar associations. For the program as a whole, this was not true. In 1967, most lawyers said that the local bar associations were either helpful (59.4%) or indifferent (25.5%) rather than hindering (15.5%). In 1972, there was somewhat of a shift: Bar associations were said to be less helpful (down to 40.2%) and more hindering (19.5%); but the biggest increase came in indifference—from 25.5% to 40.2%. The more time a program spent on service work, the more likely lawyers were to say that the local bar group was helpful. Also, in the offices that were rated high by regional directors, there were more negative feelings about local bar association attitudes.

After programs had been in operation for several years, it also became fairly clear that governing boards (sometimes highly responsive to bar associations) for the most part had only formal roles and inputs. It was the program director and the staff who ran the program, with some input from client representatives.

Aside from general feelings about bar association attitudes, there were pressures from the environment. For example, 60.3% of the lawyers reported outside pressure to do less law reform work. The most frequently mentioned sources of this pressure were local bar groups or private attorneys, although federal, state, and local government units were also mentioned. Fewer than one-third (31.2%) of the lawyers said that there was pressure from outside sources to do more law reform work; the major sources of such pressure were client groups, federal authorities, and OEO national and regional offices. About 44% said that their offices had been criticized on issues of legal ethics, mostly dealing with solicitation or questions about violating client eligibility guidelines. A high proportion of lawyers (79%) also said that they personally received objections about the types of cases they handled or the manner in which they handled them. Most of the objections had to do with issues of the financial eligibility of clients, law reform cases, or cases against government authorities. The incidence of these criticisms also varied with the amount of law reform work that was being done; lawyers doing more law reform work encountered more criticism. There was some shift over time in concern over outside pressure. Pressures from the outside for more law reform were greater in 1967 than in 1972; the outside was less favorable to law reform in the 1970s. In 1967, lawyers reflected less concern over outside pressure than they did in 1972, which probably reflected change in the political climate concerning Legal Services.

It was not unexpected that there were also internal pressures or concerns. Most of the lawyers (81.8%) worked in programs with branch offices; and about one-half (46%) were assigned to these offices, with about 30% in the main offices (the remainder had dual assignments). The sizes and structures of the branch offices varied. In some programs—for example, in major metropolitan areas and in California Rural Legal Assistance—the branch offices were usually large and enjoyed a great deal of autonomy; in other programs, the branch offices were small and sometimes open only a few days a week. Of the attorneys in branch offices, most (60.8%) mentioned problems between the branch offices and the main offices, the most common (most mentioned only one problem) being lack of communication, uneven caseloads, red tape, interoffice rivalry, and matters of personnel. Commentators on Legal Services have pointed to the friction created when central office staffs invest energies in law reform and expect branch offices to do service work almost exclusively (Carlin, 1970; Brill, 1973).

There was also internal pressure to do more law reform work; in fact, approximately the same proportion (60%) of the lawyers reported internal pressure to do more law reform as mentioned outside pressure to do less law reform. In short, the strains within the program for more law reform work were just the reverse of the strains from outside to do less reform work. Internal pressure for law reform was reported more than twice as often as outside pressure. Pressure from the national Legal Services office and OEO was, to the lawyers, less notable than the pressure of colleagues for more law reform. Internal pressure for more law reform work was reported most often in small cities and statewide programs in the South and West, but there were no differences according to ratings by the regional directors.

That there were complaints and strains in OEO Legal Services, then, is not unexpected. By and large, however, these were relatively minor. As stated before, overall job satisfaction and morale were high, and continued so throughout the 5 years. When asked specifically what they liked about their jobs, about two-thirds of the lawyers focused on the substantive aspects: helping people, working with the poor, the kinds of cases and issues, the nature of the work, the opportunity to work for social change, and contact with people. About a third mentioned professional working conditions: independence and responsibility and relations with colleagues. On the other hand, working conditions figured prominently in the things the lawyers disliked about their jobs: too many cases, too hectic a schedule, problems of administration, bad leadership, low pay, and insufficient funding. Comparatively few lawyers (8.8%) objected to restrictions on professional work. Legal Services lawyers were more likely to emphasize the positive aspects of their experiences than the negative.

Nevertheless, despite their job satisfaction and favorable image of program quality, Legal Services lawyers for the most part viewed their positions as temporary. Only 35% said that they planned to stay in the job at the time they took it, and another 20% said they had not known whether or not they would stay at the time of taking the job. The reasons they gave for planning not to stay varied: the desire to earn more, reservations about the nature of the job, getting burned out, and the desire to be in private practice or some other kind of job. As lawyers reported the conditions associated with their entering Legal Services, neither financial nor family considerations were important (60%). They had other job options available at the time they entered Legal Services; usually in private practice, another Legal Services program, or government work, in that order. But they chose Legal Services, usually not planning to remain. Their impression is that program attorneys have only short tenures. Asked how long attorneys usually stayed in the program, their average estimate was 20 months.

Although doubt about remaining in Legal Services and an estimate of 20 months average service seem to point to great personnel turnover, the picture is somewhat mixed. Looking at the 1972 Legal Services lawyers who had left the program by the time they were interviewed, we find that the average time in the program was 2.3 years. Those still in the program at the time of interview had 3.2 years of service. Among 1967 Legal Services lawyers, the average term of service was 3.9 years. Although this may have resulted from staffing large numbers of administrative positions in the early years of the program, the evidence indicates that 3 years is the time lawyers stay in Legal Services, not 20 months. Lawyers in Legal Services in 1967 who graduated from law school between 1965 and 1967 stayed 3 years; but lawyers from those same graduating classes who did not enter Legal Services tended to stay in their 1967 jobs only a bit longer—3.8 years. Thus, not only is turnover, or attorney retention, less of a problem than many believe, but it may be more an aspect of the career mobility of young lawyers than of the Legal Services organization itself.

Variations in length of the stay for those who left and those who stayed were not related to the amounts of service work they did or by the quality of their programs. Information and analysis about exit patterns are more fully presented in Chapter 8. The reasons they gave for leaving were similar to those they gave for planning not to stay: the desire to earn more, getting burned out, dissatisfaction with job (boring, not challenging), the availability of a new job, and the desire to be in private practice. Low salary levels were not commonly mentioned as a reason for leaving. For the 1967 Legal Services lawyers, reasons for leaving were much the same: dissatisfaction with job, wanting to be in private practice, and the availability of a new job. Among 1967 lawyers in Legal Services, directors stayed longer than staff attorneys, and those in medium quality programs stayed longer than attorneys in excellent or poor programs. Thus at the same time that Legal Services lawyers said they liked their jobs and evaluated their programs as high in quality, they said they left because of job dissatisfaction; many tired of their jobs in a couple of years and moved on. Subsequent career choices and how they relate to particular program experiences are also discussed in Chapter 8.

CONCLUSIONS

We have seen that as far as the participants in Legal Services are concerned the announcements of its decline or demise are premature. The same amount of law reform work is still being performed. Indeed, according to the lawyers themselves, there seems even to have been a slight increase. There has been somewhat of a shift away from family law, but most other areas of practice have remained constant. Job satisfaction and morale have remained high. Nor has quality of program suffered; according to the regional directors, although the percentage of poor quality programs has remained the same, many programs moved from the medium to the excellent range between 1967 and

1972. There are stresses and problems in working for Legal Services, but lawyers continue to enter the program with high ideals: Many view their jobs as short term, but they are satisfied with their jobs and their programs, and their morale is high. High morale and job satisfaction augur well for continued recruitment of well-qualified and motivated lawyers. At least, according to the participants, Legal Services is alive and well—in the field. The program continues to offer a desirable, structured opportunity for lawyers to engage in legal rights activity on a full-time professional basis.

4

Public Interest Law

Public interest law has emerged in a variety of forms. This chapter discusses those public interest law firms that are supported primarily by charity.[1] A subsequent chapter discusses other kinds of law firms that are sometimes labeled public interest.

In Chapter 2, we noted that the predecessors of present public interest law were the NAACP, the NAACP Legal Defense and Education Fund (the Inc. Fund), and the ACLU. Starting about 1970, new varieties of public interest law firms began to emerge. The impetus for the change was the decision of the Ford Foundation to begin funding law firms that would engage in law reform in a variety of substantive areas other than traditional civil rights and civil liberties (see Ford Foundation, 1973). Subsequently, many other foundations began supporting law firms, but Ford, by far, has been the principal benefactor in the field, in terms of both total dollars and number of firms it supports.

This chapter presents a cross-sectional view of charity-supported public interest law firms. However, because public interest law is still in a formative stage, descriptions tend to become dated. At the conclusion of the chapter, we try to assess future trends.

---

[1] By charity, we mean law firms that are supported by funds from charitable foundations, memberships, and other forms of solicited contributions and by court-awarded attorney fees pursuant to Internal Revenue Service guidelines. These firms qualify as charitable organizations under the Internal Revenue Service law. We exclude firms that call themselves public interest law firms but receive support from fees paid directly by clients and thus fail to qualify as charitable organizations. These firms are discussed in Chapter 6.

STRUCTURE, SIZE, AND DISTRIBUTION

Public interest law firms can be distinguished in terms of organizational structures. Some firms are formally affiliated with stable, ongoing organizations; thus, Consumers Union, the League of Women Voters, the Sierra Club, Common Cause, and Ralph Nader have their own law firms. The parent organization is usually the main or sole client of the firm. The funding of these firms is mixed. Some (e.g., the League of Women Voters and the Sierra Club) are supported in varying amounts from foundations (principally Ford); others are supported primarily or even exclusively by their parent organizations. The number of lawyers in such firms is small, and the firms are few in number.

Other law firms are formally independent. They are not attached to organizations, but usually deal with organizations as clients. A few of these firms support themselves in part through membership contributions, but the bulk of support for the formally independent law firms comes from foundations. In numbers, independent law firms are the dominant type of public interest firms.

The affiliated and independent law firms rely primarily on full-time staff. There is yet a third structural arrangement: a full-time staff with a wide network of participating lawyers. This is the Inc. Fund and ACLU model, which has been followed by some of the newer public interest law firms as well (e.g., the Sierra Club Legal Defense Fund, the Mexican-American Legal Defense and Education Fund). Usually the participating lawyers are engaged in private practice and take cases on behalf of an organization as part of their pro bono activities. Relationships between the central offices of these firms and their participating lawyers vary considerably. Instances are reported in which participating lawyers, as members of local chapters, select and prosecute cases with or without the consent, assistance, or cooperation of the central offices. The funding of these law firms, which are few in number, also varies between membership and foundation support.

In 1973, there were about 40 charity-supported public interest law firms. About half are located in Washington, D.C. and another quarter in New York City. The West Coast has the next largest number (4), and the remainder are scattered throughout the country. Several firms have branch offices in other cities; most are small or medium sized by national professional standards, with between 4 and 8 full-time lawyers. A few firms have between 15 and 25 full-time lawyers, but overall the average size is 10 lawyers. In addition to the full-time lawyers, some of the firms employ nonlawyer professionals. These may include various social and natural scientists, research analysts, and lobbyists. Public interest law firms are very small in comparison with their adversaries, who are, for the most part, the largest and most prestigious law firms, often numbering over 100 lawyers. Moreover, quite often public interest lawyers are suing multiple defendants, each one represented by a large law firm. In this discussion of public interest law firms, it is important to keep their relative size in mind. Despite what looks like generous foundation support, these firms are small and have slender resources for the type of work they do in comparison with the resources of their opponents.

ACTIVITIES

Subject Matter

There are a number of ways to describe the activities of public interest law firms, none of which is completely satisfactory. Lawyers were asked to list the major areas in which their firms specialized (see Table 4.1).[2] The areas mentioned most often by the lawyers were environment, voting rights, race discrimination, employment discrimination, and consumer protection, in that order. However, environmental cases accounted for only 15.5% of the areas mentioned, and many other subject matter areas were mentioned as areas of specialization. Most of the law firms prepare periodic listings of their activities called "docket sheets." The docket sheets for almost all of the firms list about 30 different subject matter areas in which the firms do at least some work. According to the number of docket item entries by subject matter, most activity is reported for education, employment discrimination, environment, criminal justice, and minorities, in that order (see Table 4.2).[3]

The differences between the areas of firm specialization and the docket sheet totals are attributable to differences in firm size, in that firms using large numbers of participating lawyers list an enormous number of cases. The Inc. Fund alone accounts for almost one-third of all the docket sheet entries. Docket sheets make no allowance for differences in amounts of time spent on individual cases; each item has an equal value, which of course is not the true situation. On the other hand, the lawyers listing areas of firm specialization are all full-time

---

[2] The sampling and interviewing of public interest lawyers is described in Appendix A.

[3] Docket sheets were tabulated for 35 firms as part of *Public Interest Law: An Economic Analysis* (Weisbrod, Handler, and Komesar, 1978). Additional materials for this chapter were obtained from semistructured interviews with 25 firms between 1973 and 1975 and from the reports of firm monitors (1972–1975).

Table 4.1

Major Areas in Which Public Interest Law Firms Specialize

Area	Percentage specializing[a]
Environmental, land use	15.5
Race discrimination, voting rights	10.8
Employment	9.3
Consumer protection	8.5
Civil rights	7.0
Health, mental health	7.0
Civil liberties	5.4
Education	4.6
Constitutional rights	3.8
Communication	3.8
Other (each 3.1% or less, including sex discrimination, housing, prisoner rights, poverty)	24.3
Total	100.0

[a] Three possible responses per lawyer; $N = 110$.

lawyers; and they indicated only major areas of specialization, not all areas of work.

Despite the deficiencies in the tabulations, a few generalizations about subject matter activity can be made. When the new charity-supported public interest law firms began to emerge, they attracted a great deal of publicity, not all of it favorable. Most of the publicity attended environmental and consumer litigation; and even today, public interest law is often identified primarily for work in those two areas. While these were considered important, it was charged that public interest law represented an abandonment of the poor and minorities by elite lawyers in favor of middle- and upper-class concerns. We see from the subject matter listings that although environmental work is prominently mentioned, public interest law firm work covers a wide spectrum of subjects. When environment accounts for only 15% of the firm specialties mentioned and consumer affairs 8%, it can hardly be claimed that public interest law is either heavily specialized or concentrated in these two areas. Nor can it be said that public interest law necessarily represents an abandonment of the poor and minorities. No matter how the subject matter tabulations are examined, much public interest work is undertaken on behalf of the poor. Activity in employment and voting discrimination, education, criminal justice, and health and mental health is mostly for the poor. Some of the activity in

Table 4.2

Subject Matter of Docket Entries for Public Interest Law Firms

Subject matter	Percentage of time spent[a]
Education	17.6
Employment discrimination	15.6
Environment	15.2
Criminal justice	12.4
Minorities	11.7
Electoral reform	4.5
Government reform	4.6
Housing	4.0
Communication	2.7
Consumer	2.9
Women	2.1
Health	3.6
Other	3.2
Total	100.1

[a] Based on 2347 entries from 35 firms.

housing, communications, and matters involving women is also for the poor.

There are, however, differences in subject matter in terms of organizational structure. The law firms where large numbers of participating lawyers account for most of the work usually concentrate their efforts on minority and poverty problems. The independent law firms, particularly those supported primarily by the Ford Foundation, do proportionately more environmental work and less poverty and minority work; but even this is changing. The first firms established were primarily environment oriented; new firms are stressing areas related to poverty and minorities more strongly. In comparison to OEO Legal Services, there is little welfare law reform work, but it cannot be said that public interest law represents an abandonment of the disadvantaged.

We obviously cannot describe in detail the specific kinds of activity engaged in by public interest lawyers in each of the subject matter areas. Instead, to give some flavor of their work, we present a brief synopsis of work in several important areas: environment and consumer affairs, employment discrimination, education, and race discrimination and minorities.

In the environmental field, a great deal of litigation during the past 5 years has sought to enforce provisions of the National Environmental

Policy Act (NEPA) and similar state statutes. Much of the litigation has been concerned with who must file environmental impact statements and what the contents of the statements must be. A great many of these cases have been won by environmental groups. It is reported that there is a new climate about responding to environmental considerations and that many government agencies are now taking the impact statement requirements of NEPA much more seriously. Clearly, without the lawsuits, NEPA would certainly have been a dead letter.

Public interest lawyers have also sought to enforce the provisions of other protective legislation, such as the Multiple Use Act, the Wilderness Act (excessive cutting of trees in the national forests), and pure water and clean air legislation. One important action secured a Supreme Court ruling that minimum standards of air quality are not intended to permit degradation of air of higher quality. A long campaign has been waged to ban DDT and other pesticides. Public interest law firms have become actively involved in a number of lawsuits that focus on the issues of the disposal of highly toxic radioactive waste materials in the construction and development of nuclear power. As a result of public interest law litigation, private land use development is increasingly being subjected to environmental control. In California, for example, land development and local zoning practices must comply with state environmental statutes and comprehensive long-range planning. In a recent case, as a result of public interest law pressure, plans for an enormous coal-burning power plant in Utah have been shelved; the environmentalists claimed that the project would result in the degradation of air quality in important scenic areas.

Consumers also benefit from much environmental litigation: for example, curtailing the use of poisons, protecting water quality, stimulating certain kinds of energy conservation practices, banning leaded paint, restricting hormone additives to meat, and otherwise improving the safety and quality of products. Also in the consumer area, litigation has been used to improve procedures for testing the safety of experimental drugs and removing worthless drugs from the market. Discriminatory credit pricing and import restrictions have also been under attack. Continued efforts are being made concerning the truthfulness of advertising. Public interest lawsuits are seeking to reverse the traditional rate structures of utilities, which now favor larger users, in favor of rate structures that will discourage waste and reduce demand.

In the fair employment field, suits have been brought to end racial and sexual discrimination in both public agencies (e.g., police and fire departments) and private businesses. Relief sought has not only been injunctive, against discrimination and for back pay, but primarily for affirmative action plans to assure minority hiring and equal treatment while employed. Sometimes, public interest firms join with public enforcement agencies to bring pressure on discriminators and to use their investigative resources. In other situations, the law firms sue public enforcement agencies that are reluctant to proceed or enter into "sweetheart" agreements. Having established its credibility in the employment discrimination area, one public interest law firm was able to negotiate industrywide hiring agreements in banking, savings and loans, and several utilities in California.

Public interest law firms have been involved in suits to equalize school financing. Other efforts have sought to obtain support for the educational needs of the handicapped and the retarded and for bilingual education for the Spanish-speaking community. Efforts are also being made to protect minorities from discriminatory placement. Standard IQ and other forms of testing are being questioned; and in some parts of the country, IQ testing has been suspended. There have been attempts to rid textbooks and curriculums of racial stereotyping. In addition, due process protection has been extended to students. These include the development of standards for punishment, access to records, and the expunging of certain kinds of information from records. Public interest law firms have also continued earlier traditions of protecting minorities from racial discrimination in voting and in the enjoyment of public benefits and facilities.

As these summaries of activity indicate, most of the efforts of public interest law firms have been directed against government. In addition, a great deal of the litigation is cast in terms of procedure: opening government administration to public scrutiny, providing methods by which the public can be involved in government decision making, improving the internal procedures of administration, and forcing government agencies to enforce the law. Not only are most of the lawsuits cast in procedural terms, but also much of the justification of public interest law is based on procedural due process grounds: Public interest law is to provide the unrepresented in American society an opportunity to be heard and to participate in decisions that affect them, and operates from the premise that our system of government works better when all relevant interests have an opportunity to be heard (see Rabin, 1976a, pp. 207, 230; Halpern and Cunningham, 1971, p. 1095).

Procedural reform is important to public interest lawyers, but it would be a mistake to assume that it is an end in itself. Many of these lawyers are interested in substantive results: a cleaner and safer environment; honest and economical commerce; better jobs, education, and health for the poor and minorities. Public interest lawyers are social reformers who also happen to be lawyers.

Strategies and Tactics

In private practice, lawyers attend to a great deal of work that is not done in the courtroom or in hearings before government agencies: Lawyers negotiate, draft documents, lobby, and so forth. Much of the work is also nonadversarial—for example, estate or business planning, tax advice, etc. In contrast, most public interest law work is adversarial, and as compared with most other legal work, disproportionately litigious. Some public interest work is analagous to nonadversarial planning: For example, public interest lawyers work on tribal affairs for Native Americans or do business planning for community groups; but this is relatively rare. Most public interest law work consists of seeking to change the behavior of others (usually government officials) on behalf of clients, chiefly through litigation.

There are a number of reasons why public interest lawyers tend to litigate more than private practitioners. One reason has to do with the particular historical position of the various public interest law firms. They are new; they are seeking to establish and define new rights; and they have to establish their credibility. The NEPA litigation in the environmental area is a prime example. In the initial years, government agencies resisted the notion that NEPA applied to them and refused to alter their behavior according to the demands of newly formed public interest law firms or the environmental organizations that the firms represented. After many lawsuits in which the courts halted government activity and defined the terms of NEPA, the agencies seem to have changed their behavior. There now seems to be more willingness to listen to public interest law firms and less controversy over whether NEPA applies. Similar experiences have occurred in other areas. In employment discrimination, a few very active public interest law firms have been able to rely more on negotiations with large employers and less on litigation, but only after the firms established their credibility in court. These are not isolated examples; and after the laws become settled and the firms have established their credibility, we expect that public interest law firms will do less litigation and more negotiation.

However, there are other reasons why public interest law firms have a litigation bias. One factor is the relative powerlessness of the clients. Public interest law clients, for the most part, turn to the law because they lack the resources to press their interests in the market or the political arenas. In many circumstances, litigation is the only tactic available with which to increase their bargaining positions and publicize their causes. Halting a giant project, even if only for a short period, has this effect. Lawsuits are newsworthy, especially if filed on behalf of several different community groups against a government agency or a large corporation. It may be true that in a great many of these cases, after the initial splash, public interest law firms and their clients lack the resources to sustain the struggle, but the point is that when dealing from a situation of powerlessness, quite often a lawsuit and a temporary injunction are all that the lawyers can get for their clients.

Other reasons why public interest law firms tend to favor litigation concern the relationships of firms to the funding sources, the structure of the firms, and their staffing. Public interest law firms, as test-case, law reform institutions, deal in highly controversial areas; they and their sponsors are frequently subject to attack by opponents who question their legitimacy and their motives. There is great pressure on them to establish their legitimacy, and the best form of legitimacy comes from the highest organs of government: courts, legislatures, or administrative agencies. For reasons we discuss later, the firms do best with the courts. Winning a favorable ruling from a high court does double duty: It advances the client's interests and serves as ammunition against the critics of public interest law. If the court agrees with the public interest law firm that the government agency has been acting illegally, then it can hardly be maintained that the public interest law firms are opportunistic obstructionists. Their opposition is put in the position of favoring lawlessness.

Why, though, would the firms favor courts rather than the other organs of government? The clearest way of answering this question is to contrast the litigating firm with the lobbyist. Good lobbyists stay with particular agencies or legislative committees for years, working quietly behind the scenes, cultivating personal contacts, supplying information, and so forth. Perhaps the most successful lobbyist is one who is able to get an agency or a committee to adopt the lobbyist's position, thinking that it is the agency's or committee's position. Public interest law firms are not well suited for this kind of work. By law, they are prohibited from lobbying, and although there are ways of avoiding the technical prohibition, it does hamper their efforts.[4] But even if there were no prohibition, they still would not favor these kinds of activities. Public interest lawyers consider themselves part of a movement—either

---

[4] The lobby prohibition relates to their retaining their tax exempt status as defined by the Internal Revenue Service. It has recently been somewhat relaxed.

the public interest law movement, or substantively oriented movements (e.g., environmental protection, consumer affairs, and civil
liberties). There is a great need for publicity: It is important for the law
firms, their supporters, and their clients; and it leads to increases in the
legitimacy and effectiveness of challenges raised by the organization
and to confidence on the part of financial supporters. As one public
interest lawyer put it, "A case which has no publicity value is our 'pro
bono' work." Lawsuits against giant corporations and government
agencies have great publicity value; lobbying and participating in administrative decision making are low-key and far less newsworthy.
Court victories, in the eyes of donors, lend sanction to public interest
efforts.

A final factor tending toward litigation is the size and staffing of the
firms. As stated earlier, the firms are small—fewer than a dozen
lawyers, on the average. These lawyers are young and fairly new to the
substantive areas with which they are dealing. Their professional training and orientation are toward litigation; they often lack the resources,
expertise, and probably the temperament to engage in lobbying activities. Although public interest law firms are too new to draw quantitative conclusions about subsequent career paths of the lawyers, it is
probable that these are relatively short-term jobs—2 to 4 or 5 years—in
contrast to the long-term staying power of lobbyists.

For these reasons, then—the need for public interest law firms to
establish credibility, legitimacy, and publicity; the unsettled areas of
the law; and firm size and staffing patterns—litigation is the preferred
strategy for public interest lawyers. Given the differences in public
interest firm structure, there is some variation in choice of legal
strategies and tactics. The opportunity to use nonlitigation techniques
would be strongest among firms affiliated with organizations such as
Consumers Union, the Sierra Club, Ralph Nader, Common Cause, or
the League of Women Voters. These firms have available to them the
nonlawyer resources of their organizations to which they can turn if the
problems they encounter are more amenable to nonlawyer skills. The
organizations themselves are experienced in nonlitigation techniques,
especially lobbying; they recognize their importance and do not need
the legitimation that litigation brings. A countervailing influence, however, may be the fact that a newly created law office within the organization will tend to favor litigation as a way of proving its value and
uniqueness to the organization.

Public interest law firms with participating lawyers are likely to
litigate the most. There are several reasons why lawyers in the field tend
to be litigators. As stated earlier, some are zealots, taking cases without

central office direction or approval. The participating lawyers take these cases as part of their pro bono work and usually lack the capacity to engage in nonlitigation activities, particularly if they are not located at a state capital. There is also the historical reason that the largest participating law firms have been concerned with race, civil rights, and employment discrimination—areas which have been defined and extended mainly by a great deal of litigation by essentially volunteer lawyers, often against local authorities. The tradition of litigation in these organizations is strong, although as central office staffs grow larger, alternatives to litigation become more feasible.

The public interest law firms that are formally independent also have a strong propensity to litigate. On the other hand, many are located in Washington, and they do have resources to engage in nonlitigation techniques, such as investigations, studying, reporting, testifying, and participating in administrative rule-making proceedings. Some of the lawyers who go into these firms have a more academic orientation, which leavens the desire to litigate; and to some extent funding sources have expected more diversified activities.

Table 4.3 lists the types of legal action tabulated from the docket sheet entries. As the table shows, litigation predominates as the preferred strategy of public interest law firms. Administrative complaints are

Table 4.3

Types of Legal Action by Public Interest Law Firms

	Percentage of activity			
	Participating firms	Affiliated[a] firms	Independent firms	All firms
Litigation	85.3	80.8	54.4	73.8
Administrative complaints	.2	.4	2.5	1.0
Administrative petition	1.7	15.0	16.1	8.4
Negotiation, participation	1.4	0	6.7	3.1
Investigation, reports, etc.	11.5	3.8	20.2	13.6
Total	100.1	100.0	99.9	99.9
N	1174	266	788	2228

[a] The Sierra Club is both an affiliated and a participating law firm. We have included it in the affiliated category although it could just as easily fit in the participating category.

brought before administrative agencies and thus equivalent to court cases. Administrative petitions may or may not be litigation; they could represent participation in agency rule-making proceedings and may or may not supply information as do studies and reports. On the other hand, administrative petitions could also be one stage in a sharply drawn adversary proceeding in which the public interest law firm is representing a client. In this type of situation, an administrative petition would be equivalent to a complaint in a litigated contest. Negotiations and participation, as well as investigations and reports, do not account for much public interest law activity, at least as revealed by the docket sheets.

As far as variation among firms is concerned, firms with participating attorneys are almost exclusively in litigation. We note also that the independent firms do more studies, investigations, reports, and administrative petition work. Lawyers in affiliated firms report that problems not amenable to litigation are filtered out before they reach the firms or are referred to the organization without appearing on the firm's docket. These specialized legal units of the organization, therefore, tend to list only litigation. The independent law firms cannot refer their problems; they have to do their own investigating and lobbying and tend to list everything.

The responses of the lawyers themselves further support the data indicating a propensity to litigation. Over 40% of the lawyers report they spend a substantial amount of time in court, and over 75% report a substantial amount of time spent in administrative agencies. Public interest lawyers, in contrast to the private bar, are not office lawyers. The courts and agencies before which public interest lawyers appear stand in sharp contrast to the courts and agencies confronted by Legal Services lawyers, reflecting the differences in the work. The public interest lawyers' courts are primarily federal, and more than half are appellate; the agencies are also federal (see Table 4.4).

Although primarily concerned with litigation, public interest law firms also engage in a variety of other activities. Some firms engage in publicity campaigns and in speaking, produce pamphlets, and write articles. Others manage to lobby by obtaining invitations to testify. Some firms also do official lobbying. A few firms work closely with community groups; a common activity of these firms is to conduct workshops on legal problems and strategies.

Since the strategies and tactics of all practicing lawyers, including public interest lawyers, vary with structural conditions, we would expect changes over time in the strategies and tactics of public interest lawyers. The propensity to litigate would decline for those firms work-

Table 4.4

Courts and Agencies in Which Public Interest Lawyers Spend Time[a]

Court or agency	Percentage of time
Federal Supreme or circuit court	28.0
Federal trial	49.3
State appellate	4.0
County, circuit, or local trial courts	17.3
Other	1.3
Total	99.9
Federal agencies	78.3
State agencies	9.7
County or local agencies	12.0
Total	100.0

[a] Two possible responses per lawyer for courts; three possible responses per lawyer for agencies.

ing in areas where the law has become settled, credibility and legitimacy have been acquired, more nonlitigation skills have been developed and proved valuable, and funding sources have changed. We would expect the litigation bias to be present as new firms are formed and new areas are explored. This process is analogous to that experienced by Legal Services programs as they have established respected roles in their communities. Of course, growth and change in public interest law depends on its most important structural condition—financial solvency, a subject we take up at the conclusion of this chapter.

CLIENTS: CASE SELECTION

In private practice, the client seeks out the lawyer and presents his case, which the lawyer is free to accept or reject. The lawyer's role is passive in client and case selection: The client pays the lawyer and exercises some control over the case; the lawyer is prohibited from advertising or soliciting. At least this is the model. In public interest law, the attorney–client relationship and the case selection process are very different. Public interest lawyers, in the process of organizing a firm and obtaining support, define their subject matter and priorities. The development of the firm's program, the need to litigate and to obtain publicity and legitimation, cannot be left to walk-in trade. The firm has to select clients that will further these goals. The ideal client, from the point of view of a public interest law firm, is a group that is newsworthy and either a hierarchical or a paper organization, so that the lawyers only have to deal with the leadership rather than a restless membership. Lawsuits generate a lot of excitement, but after the initial burst of publicity, they become technical and protracted. One of the problems of litigation is that it is hard to maintain the support and interest of the rank and file. Hierarchical and paper organizations lessen these problems.

Although public interest law reform cases can be taken on behalf of either individuals or groups, in fact, most plaintiffs (68.6%) are groups.[5] Some law firms have client groups fairly close to the ideal type, in that the organizations are strongly hierarchical or paper. In such instances, the services of the public interest firm are virtually a free good to the organization, giving it needed publicity at no cost; and the leaders are readily induced to go along with the agenda of the law firm. The benefits to the firm are that they have almost complete control over the strategies and tactics of the lawsuit. In other instances, firms deal with highly organized groups with knowledgeable and articulate leaders who know how to deal with lawyers and carefully assess the litigation in terms of their organizations' goals and needs. Generally speaking, attorney–client relations vary with the social status of the client group. Law firms affiliated with Ralph Nader, Common Cause, etc., or who have as clients higher prestige groups and persons, such as organizations of scientists, medical professionals, or women's groups, have different attorney–client relationships from those of law firms that deal with minorities and poor people. Even as they can rely on clients for more input, they are constrained by them and obliged to be responsive. With new, powerless groups or lower status groups, the lawyers usually have greater options in defining issues and strategies.

There is great deviation from private practice in the generation of cases. Practically all public interest law firms report that the lawyers think up at least some of the problems and seek out clients. There is variation as to how much case generation comes about in this manner. With some firms, practically their entire docket comes "out of the lawyers' heads." With other firms that are well known within subject areas, cases are constantly pressed upon them, in approximation of the private practice model. Some firms have developed close relationships with strong client organizations, and as a result of many dealings,

---

[5] Based on docket sheet tabulation and analysis.

informal conversations, etc., it would be difficult to determine where particular cases originated. The important point is that public interest lawyers are entrepreneurs: They seek to develop programs and establish career specialties, and they select clients and cases to further these goals.

Few conflicts of interest are reported by public interest law firms. About a third of the lawyers said their firms have general policies designed to avoid situations that would produce conflicts. In some cases, the firms may represent multiple plaintiffs, so clients may differ as to strategy and tactics. For example, in environmental litigation some clients will oppose any development whatsoever, whereas other clients would be willing to allow development under certain conditions. There is also a conflict between environmental groups that want to ally themselves with private concerns that have similar interests and environmental groups who oppose such alliances. In general, however, lawyers and firms do not encounter very many or serious conflicts of interest.

JOB SATISFACTION AND MORALE

Given the fact that public interest law firms provide the opportunity for young lawyers to work in small firms, pick their cases and clients, and control strategy and tactics, it is not surprising to find job satisfaction and morale quite high. Over 90% of the lawyers are either satisfied or very satisfied with their job; over 75% think they are making high or very high use of their special skills as lawyers. Aspects the lawyers particularly liked about their job are presented in Table 4.5. They are about evenly divided between working conditions (e.g., freedom, challenge, responsibility) and subject matter. In explaining why they took the jobs, lawyers mentioned subject matter considerations more prominently than working conditions. They tended to stress such things as "wanting a chance to do something worthwhile, wanting to do environmental–consumer–civil rights work." Generally speaking, neither family nor financial considerations were very important for lawyers choosing public interest work.

Overall, public interest lawyers were young. They were usually from high quality law schools (78.9% attended the 23 best law schools in the country), and class ranks were high. Most said they had other job alternatives at the time they joined a public interest law firm, usually not in private practice. The job opportunities matched their work experience prior to joining the public interest law firm. The public inter-

Table 4.5

What Lawyers Particularly Liked about Their Jobs[a]

Job feature	Percentage of responses
Freedom, challenge, responsibility, independence of work	35.7
Public service, social importance of issues	12.6
Subject matter of cases—types of cases (civil rights, etc.)	12.6
Type of work—litigation, etc.	11.0
Could see success, was exciting, satisfying, novel	11.0
Staff lawyers worked with	7.7
People worked with, unspecified	4.9
Clients worked with	3.8
Other	2.7
Total	100.0

[a] Three possible responses per lawyer.

est law firm was a first job for fewer than 20%; others came from a variety of jobs (see Table 4.6), but it is interesting that only about 25% of these lawyers came from private practice.

At the time of the interviews, the average length of time that public interest lawyers held their jobs was 2.8 years. Since most of the firms came into being and began to grow after 1970, there was not much of a

Table 4.6

Previous Jobs of Lawyers in Public Interest Law Firms

Type of practice	Percentage of responses
Private firm	23.1
Solo practice	3.3
Legal Services or Reggie program	13.2
Office for the poor (other than Legal Services) or public defender	8.8
Another public interest law firm	9.9
Mixed public interest–private practice law firm	7.7
Nonlaw job	4.4
Other law jobs (teaching, government work, house counsel, etc.)	29.7
Total	100.1
N	91

chance to experience much turnover. Still, some have left.[6] They have, for the most part, chosen other legal rights jobs (27%) or teaching or government work (43%), with less than a fifth entering private practice. Reasons for leaving, which are presented in Table 4.7, do not reflect poor work conditions (as, for example, was the case with Legal Services) or dissatisfaction with the type of work being done, but rather different or better opportunities to move on.

Table 4.7

Reasons for Leaving Public Interest Jobs[a]

Reason	Percentage of responses
Part of career plans to move on, to gain more experience	17.8
Dissatisfied with job, not challenging	13.3
Offered new, attractive job	20.0
Family, personal reasons	8.9
Wanted to be in private practice	6.7
Salary too low	6.7
Other reasons	26.6
Total	100.0
N	37

[a] Two possible responses per lawyer.

Lawyers in public interest jobs have average earnings 37% lower than those of their age cohorts in private practice. The average earnings for public interest lawyers was $21,120 per year, compared to $33,292 for the private bar. Naturally, the older the lawyers, the greater the discrepancy between the earnings of the two groups.

Because of the short period of time that most public interest law firms have been in existence, it is difficult to predict trends in the career paths of public interest lawyers. We would guess that lawyers do not view their public interest law firm jobs as permanent careers. The firms are young, and the future of public interest law, as we discuss shortly, is uncertain. The lawyers themselves are young and do not seem to be in the private practice stream; that is, public interest law is not an interlude from private practice but part of a different career line—government, teaching, other kinds of public interest law work. These

[6] Thirty-seven lawyers had left their public interest jobs at the time of interview, or 33.6% of the sample.

lawyers seem to be restless, confident young people not yet ready to settle down.

Although job satisfaction and morale are high in public interest law firms, this does not mean that there were no dissatisfactions. The most serious problems had to do with the nature of the law they were practicing. These were social reformers who sought to accomplish results for their clients and their causes. Many complained of the difficulties in translating court or government agency decisions into meaningful results. Quite often, there seemed to be interminable delays caused by appeals, evasions of judgments, or other kinds of foot dragging. Most of the decisions won by public interest lawyers involved long-term projects, ongoing administrative programs, or orders involving individualized decisions for large groups of people (e.g., voting, employment discrimination, education, etc.)—all of which require post-decision monitoring, which puts great strains on the resources of the public interest law firms and their clients.

Other problems were mentioned by the lawyers: They generally lacked the capacity to engage in complex factual litigation, since most firms could not attract experienced litigators. They complained of the lobbying restrictions.

In addition, there was concern about the uncertain financial future of the firms. Foundations have a reputation of being fickle; but in any event, it was also made clear to recipient firms that foundation support would not be long term. In the concluding section of this chapter, we discuss the financing of public interest law, but note here that it was a worry for the lawyers. In addition, one or two lawyers per firm were required to spend a considerable amount of time seeking financial support. These lawyers recognized the necessity for this kind of work but found it disagreeable.

THE FUTURE OF PUBLIC INTEREST LAW FIRMS

How likely are public interest law firms to survive? At this stage, there are a great many uncertainties; all we can do is point out a number of factors that are part of their future.

Although public interest law firms are staffed by elite lawyers, who in a sense seek out problems, define issues, and find clients, the causes they represent are not removed from the reality of social conditions. Despite severe pressures brought about by the economic recession, the environmental and consumer movements have not died. Great concern remains over protecting environmental amenities and establishing and institutionalizing consumer protection. Other public interest causes are less controversial (e.g., health, civil rights, etc.) and continue to command some measure of public support. There have been setbacks, and the outcomes of these struggles are by no means clear; but it is evident that the causes that public interest law represents do have a certain measure of staying power in the political arena. The presence of a political base is important in assessing the likelihood of increasing the public and private support measures that are now being tried. Without such public support, efforts to find means of securing the future of public interest law will be doomed. Whether there is sufficient public support remains to be seen.

It was always understood that foundation support, at least in its present form, would be temporary and that if public interest law firms were to survive, they would have to obtain alternative sources of support. At the present time, foundation support has leveled off and begun a phasing-out period. The foundations, led by Ford, are doing this in a number of ways. With few exceptions, grants to existing firms are slowly being reduced, and not many new grants are being made. This phasing-out period, however, will be fairly long term—at least 5 years, and perhaps as much as 7 or 10. In the meantime, the foundations are actively exploring other means of support; for example, they have established a special project called the Council for the Advancement of Public Interest Law, which is a consortium to pursue alternatives.

One principal alternative source of support was the awarding of counsel fees. Under the American rule, each party pays his own counsel fees. There were, however, some well-known exceptions. The most important exception, and the one that had the greatest relevance to public interest law, was the "private attorney general" exception under which the defendant would pay the winning plaintiff's counsel fees if the court determined that the plaintiff was vindicating a general public right that otherwise would not have been enforced. A good example is a public interest lawsuit forcing an administrative agency to comply with NEPA before proceeding with a project. The government agency is defaulting on its obligation to fulfill the public rights by complying with the law; and, for a variety of reasons, it is unlikely that individual citizens or organizations have the resources to pursue this kind of costly litigation. In these situations, more than two dozen federal courts and some state courts have awarded victorious public interest law firms counsel fees; and in many cases, these fees have been substantial (several hundred thousand dollars). However, in 1974 the United States

Supreme Court held that the federal courts lacked the power to grant fees under the private attorney-general theory.[7] Other theories are still intact, but they are of less importance.

Counsel fees can also be paid pursuant to specific statutes: some civil rights statutes, employment discrimination acts, air and water legislation, and recent amendments to the Federal Trade Commission Act. Several of these statutes are of recent origin; other statutes providing for the payment of counsel fees have been introduced, along with a general statute overruling the Supreme Court's *Aleyeska* decision. It is obviously too early to tell whether this indicates a trend in Congress or not. There is also the possibility that some provision for public interest law might be made in the Legal Services Corporation program. In any event, the most one can say is that there is legislative support for public interest law, but whether it will materialize, and in what form, is hard to say.

There is also a great deal of professional support for public interest law. As stated earlier, an ABA special committee strongly endorsed public interest law (ABA, 1971c; 1973), and the ABA House of Delegates endorsed the committee report in 1975. The ABA cannot provide financial assistance to public interest law firms, but it can help in other ways. It can encourage state and local bar associations to set up public interest law firms. The ABA has influence in Congress, both for general support and to protect public interest law from attacks. Clearly, without ABA support public interest law would be in a far weaker position.

In addition to that provided by the ABA, support comes from a variety of sources. Scholarly opinion has generally been favorable and also supported attorneys' fees. In the early 1970s, a prestigious group called the American Assembly, composed of judges, prominent lawyers, and ABA and law school representatives, issued a ringing endorsement of public interest law.

Finally, other developments, which do not technically affect public interest law firms, are related in basic philosophy and serve to support the general idea. For example, New Jersey has created an office of public advocacy to do a variety of public interest work. Several government agencies have established structures to facilitate citizen input on public interest law models. And, as we see in a later chapter, there are a variety of arrangements in private practice similar to those found in public interest law practice.

Some public interest law firms have tried to establish a membership base in the community at large to support their activities. The results so far have been mixed. The most successful firms have been those active

[7] *Aleyeska Pipeline Service Co.* v. *Wilderness Society.* 1975. 421 US 240.

in protecting the environment, which have attracted support from the elites. Firms which have less clearly defined missions or specialize in lower-social-class issues have had much more difficulty in obtaining membership funds. One reason for this difference in fund-raising results is that for lower-class problems, especially in the discrimination area, there are established competitors, both legal and nonlegal, for liberal support. The environmental area is new, with fewer nationally known organizations. The public interest law firms got in on the ground floor. There are probably other reasons for the success of environmental public interest law firms. At this time, it appears that even if other public and private sources of support falter, some of the major environmental firms will probably be able to make it on their own.

What does all this add up to? Each strand or part of public interest law endeavors should not be looked at in isolation. Taken together, they seem to be representative of a diverse and probably fairly broad view that underrepresented people and groups should have better access to public and private decision making procedures and that law is a useful mechanism for accomplishing these goals. Although public interest law in its present form is new, the ideals are traditional in American society, which explains in part its establishment support. The roots of public interest law and the present variety of social causes and interests that look to public interest law suggest that it will gradually become established in our institutions, although its future form may be considerably different from what presently exists.

5

The Private Bar

Taken together, all of the lawyers engaged in legal rights activities described in the two previous chapters represent about 1 or 2% of the legal profession; most lawyers, by far, are in the private practice of law. In order to assess the range of legal rights activities, as well as the prospects for change within the profession, we must turn to the private bar. First, we describe the extent and nature of legal rights work presently being performed by the private bar; and second, we must analyze who among private practitioners are making the various contributions. With better information on these questions, we can more adequately address the need for different types of specialized legal rights organizations and the extent to which changes within the ranks of private practitioners carry implications for the availability of legal rights and services for the underrepresented.

Legal rights activities of the private bar are more complex and require more careful definition than the work of lawyers in the settings previously discussed. Private practitioners perform pro bono or, as the American Bar Association now calls it, public interest activities. This usually means professional services for reduced fees or for none at all. At its core, this definition will not present many problems, except for the possibility that lawyers may classify as pro bono cases for which they initially expected to be paid but about which they have given up any such hope. Pro bono work is performed by lawyers during regular practice (billable hours) or off-hours (nonbillable). There is also some systematic effort among the private bar to provide pro bono services. Organizational structures, including pro bono departments of large law firms and the efforts of bar association groups, are discussed in Chapter 6.

In addition to pro bono work, the legal rights activity of the private bar is reflected in the types of paying clients represented and in areas of practice. Many poor and minority clients have legal needs that generate some fees. Service to these clients is important because their needs are often ignored. We wish to include as a type of legal rights activity the efforts of lawyers who engage in a practice that differs from the norm in terms of distribution of professional services.

In the first part of this chapter, we present the range and nature of pro bono activities of the private bar, and the distribution of professional services across income and ethnic groups as such patterns of service bear on the underrepresented. In the second part, we examine which lawyers in the bar are doing pro bono work and providing professional services to underrepresented individuals and groups.

PRO BONO AND PROFESSIONAL SERVICES FOR THE UNDERREPRESENTED

Pro Bono Activities

How much pro bono practice is being done, and for whom? The following question was asked of all lawyers in a nationwide sample:

> Do you spend any of your billable hours doing pro bono work? (If yes), roughly what percent of your billable hours in the past twelve months did you spend doing pro bono work? Without naming names, would you give me some examples of the kinds of groups or individuals you do pro bono work for, the kinds of problems you are working with, and what you have done.

Table 5.1 shows that about three-fifths of the lawyers responding to our survey spent less than 5% of their billable hours doing pro bono work—and almost half of these spent no time at all. The average for the entire bar was 6.4% of billable hours per lawyer.[1]

The value of pro bono work can be roughly estimated on the basis of the lawyers' reported annual earnings from the practice of law. This measure does not capture indirect costs or benefits from colleagues or clients pleased or displeased by pro bono activity, the value of advertising and contacts, or the redefining of work as pro bono because of the failure of clients to pay. Nor does it capture the value of the work to the clients. At the time of our survey, of the lawyers who reported doing pro bono work, the average dollar amount of their work was about

---

[1] The sampling procedures are described in Appendix A.

Table 5.1

Billable Hours Spent in pro Bono Work by Lawyers in Private Practice

Billable hours (%)	Percentage of lawyers
0	30.3
1–5	32.0
6–10	18.4
More than 10	19.2
Total	99.9
N	881

$3019 per lawyer per year.[2] For the private practice bar as a whole, the pro bono contribution was approximately 6% of their billable time, or $2126 per lawyer. Both income and pro bono time were, of course, self-reported. Both the figures seem quite large (income averaged over $35,000), but it should be stressed that undertaking pro bono work does not necessarily mean refusing to take a paying client because of time spent on a pro bono client. In some firms, a certain amount of pro bono work is expected without professional earnings being adversely affected. In other words, the dollar amount reportedly spent on pro bono work may or may not represent foregone income.

Pro bono activities also take place outside of billable hours: Some firms may not permit pro bono work; lawyers may prefer to use their business hours for business purposes only; or pro bono work may encompass both billable and nonbillable time. The following question was asked:

> Outside of working hours, during the past two years, have there been any groups or individuals for which you have done free, or reduced-fee, legal work—like the Scouts, a charitable agency, a neighborhood association, a hospital, volunteer work in a ghetto law office, advising a legal aid office, etc.? (If yes), what groups or individuals—or what type of groups or individuals—have you done law work for? What kind of law work or law problem did you work on? About how many hours of your time altogether was involved?

In all, 62% of the bar reported doing pro bono work during nonbillable hours. Among those doing such work after hours, more than 90% spent

---

[2] In calculating the value of billable hours of pro bono work, the following method was used: The lawyer's earnings, treated as the midpoint of the category he had selected, were multiplied by the percentage of time in pro bono work indicated, treated as a category midpoint. Earnings were adjusted for those with more than one job.

2 hours or fewer per week, and 70% spent 1 hour or less per week. The average effort for these lawyers amounted to 47 hours per year. Including those lawyers who did no pro bono work in nonbillable hours would bring the average to 27 hours—about one-half hour per week.

Perhaps lawyers who do no pro bono work during billable hours make up their charitable contribution after hours. We found no such relationship: Lawyers who did little or no pro bono work during the working day were not more likely to do more pro bono work during nonbillable hours. In fact, the greater the amount of billable-hours work, the greater the afterhours work.

If we value the afterhours pro bono work at the same rates that lawyers charge clients during billable hours, then the average annual cost was $924 per lawyer for those who did afterhours pro bono work and $540 for all lawyers.[3] Comparing the billable hours and afterhours pro bono time, we see that much more work was reported in professional hours (125 billable hours versus 27 nonbillable hours).

Who are the clients of the lawyers who do pro bono work? Are they individuals or groups? More than 73% of the work reported during billable hours was done for individuals. Matters handled most frequently for these clients were matrimonial, family, and criminal. Housing, credit–consumer problems, and small claims were also mentioned, but much less frequently. Very few lawyers mentioned working for individuals in the areas of welfare, employment, poverty, Social Security, mental health, or health law.

Slightly more than one-fourth (26.5%) of the pro bono work reported during billable hours was done for organizations. The groups most often represented were churches, legal aid or Legal Services, and nonpolitical community groups (women's clubs, garden clubs, Masons, Jaycees). More than 50% of the organizations represented were churches, community groups, charities like the United Fund, or educational institutions. Very few lawyers mentioned peace, consumer, or welfare–poverty groups. The types of organizations for whom lawyers worked are shown in Table 5.2.

One question often raised about pro bono work is the extent to which it is a traditional or an aggressive legal rights activity. To what extent are lawyers working for individuals or groups that are traditional

---

[3] To determine the value of nonbillable hours pro bono work, the method used was to set the earnings of the lawyer equal to the midpoint of the earnings category indicated. The actual number of hours in nonbillable pro bono work was considered as a fraction of 1920 hours of professional work annually (40 hours weekly for 48 weeks). The mean figure for those doing pro bono work in nonbillable hours was slightly reduced by this method of calculation.

Table 5.2

Distribution of Organizations among Clients of Lawyers Doing pro Bono Work during Billable Hours

Organizations	Percentage of all organizations mentioned	Percentage of all clients mentioned
Traditional organizations		
Churches	16.6	4.4
Community groups (nonpolitical): women's clubs, garden clubs, Masons, Jaycees	9.8	2.6
United Fund and similar kinds of charities	8.9	2.4
Colleges and universities	3.8	1.0
Government agencies	3.1	.8
Union groups	1.9	.5
Community groups (political): e.g., Urban League	1.6	.4
Hospitals	2.6	.7
Nonprofit groups—unspecified	1.8	.5
Other groups mentioned—law reform, political, professional	each less than 1.3	each less than .3
Subtotal	55.8	14.8
Change-oriented organizations		
Civil rights and civil liberties	7.8	2.1
Neighborhood groups	3.6	1.0
Ethnic groups: Native Americans, Chicanos, blacks	4.3	1.1

95

Table 5.2 (*Continued*)
Distribution of Organizations among Clients of Lawyers Doing pro Bono Work during Billable Hours

Organizations	Percentage of all organizations mentioned	Percentage of all clients mentioned
Environmental groups	2.8	.7
Voluntary action, drug, or crisis centers	1.8	.5
Tenant groups	.9	.2
Peace or antiwar, consumer, economic development, welfare–poverty, co-ops, and commune groups	each less than 1.3	each less than .3
Subtotal	29.4	7.8
Legal aid and defender		
Legal aid and Legal Services	14.3	3.8
Defender	.4	.1
Subtotal	14.7	3.9
Total	99.9	26.5

objects of charity as opposed to individuals or groups that are controversial and challenging to the existing order? To answer this question, we have classified pro bono clients in the following categories:

1. Individuals—standard civil work
2. Individuals—standard criminal work
3. Individuals—civil rights, politics, drugs, draft, police misconduct work
4. Traditional organizations, such as churches, hospitals, the United Fund, and colleges and community groups, such as Jaycees, Masons, garden clubs
5. Change-oriented organizations primarily concerned with civil rights and civil liberties, peace, consumer affairs, and environmental problems
6. Legal aid, Legal Services, and defender programs

The results appear in Table 5.3.

It is clear that the overwhelming majority of lawyers are not working for individuals or groups seeking to upset the status quo. It is possible that work for legal aid, Legal Services, and defender programs involves test cases or law reform, but this is uncertain. If we exclude legal aid, Legal Services, and defender work, we find that fewer than 10% of the responses lawyers gave about pro bono clients and cases handled during billable hours involved individuals or groups that challenge the status quo. And if we include legal aid and defender work, the figure is still only about 13%.

Table 5.3

Clients for Whom Lawyers Do pro Bono Work during Billable Hours

Clients	Percentage	N
Individual—standard civil	53.9	559
Individual—standard criminal, juvenile	18.2	193
Individual—such as civil rights	1.4	16
Subtotal	73.5	
Traditional organizations, such as churches, community groups	14.8	159
Change-oriented organizations, such as civil rights groups, environmental groups	7.8	88
Legal Services, legal aid, and defender programs	3.9	44
Subtotal	26.5	
Total	100.0	1059

What kind of work did lawyers say they were doing for their pro bono clients during billable hours? The results are shown in Table 5.4. More than three-quarters of the work mentioned was either general practice—drafting, filing, representation—or general advice and counseling. Only about 17% of the work mentioned was litigation, and this was far more common for individuals with standard criminal offenses. In other words, very little pro bono work was done by lawyers for clients oriented toward social change, and most of the work was general practice or advice—not litigation.

For whom do the lawyers work in their nonbillable time? In contrast to the pro bono clients served during billable hours—who were primarily individuals—more than 80% of the clients lawyers mentioned serving afterhours were organizations. One-third of the individual clients or cases mentioned were relatives and friends. Among organizations, 82% of the clients mentioned were churches and community groups, 5% were legal aid and defender programs, and only 13% were change-oriented organizations, such as civil rights, ethnic–minority, or environmental groups (see Table 5.5). In terms of the extent to which pro bono work in nonbillable hours is concerned with individuals or groups challenging the status quo, the pattern is the same as that for billable hours (see Table 5.6). As with pro bono work done during billable hours, the type of work done for the organizations was, for the most part, general practice, advice, and counseling; there was very little litigation.

Why were the pro bono clients of lawyers during nonbillable hours so predominantly organizations whereas their clients during billable hours were so often individuals? Our data do not permit an answer. However, we suspect that three factors are important. First, individuals needing low-fee legal work seek lawyers during billable hours (rather than after the business day), and some of these clients are redefined as pro bono work when they fail to pay. Second, we suspect that lawyers consider work for civic and charity organizations as nonbillable hours work, whereas they think of individual clients as part of their billable hours responsibilities. Finally, lawyers probably feel they can exert greater discretion over their selection of nonbillable hours clients and are more likely to choose organizations with which they have some relationship; thus, approximately one-third of the lawyers were officers of the organizations for which they did pro bono work in nonbillable time. They were more likely to be officers of church and community organizations than of civil rights and minority groups. But regardless of the precise process, the important point is that even though nonbillable hours clients are predominantly organizations, they are mainly status

Table 5.4

Pro Bono Work Classified by Type of Client

				Percentage of work			
Type of work	All clients	Individual, standard civil	Individual, standard criminal	Individual, such as drug, draft	Traditional community organizations	Change-oriented organizations	Legal aid, Legal Services, defender
Advice	37.8	42.8	19.4	37.4	43.4	37.3	35.6
General practice	39.3	39.4	38.7	41.4	45.1	33.2	31.5
Litigation	16.3	11.7	39.5	15.8	5.7	16.4	11.5
Other	6.5	6.0	2.4	5.5	5.8	13.1	21.4
Total	99.9	99.9	100.0	100.1	100.0	100.0	100.0
N	1052	555	193	16	157	87	44

Table 5.5

Distribution of Organizations for Which Lawyers Do pro Bono Work during
Nonbillable Hours

Organizations	Percentage of all organizations mentioned	Percentage of all clients mentioned
Traditional organizations		
Church groups	18.8	15.3
Social, fraternal, benevolent organizations	35.5	28.9
Schools, colleges	4.5	3.7
Museums, libraries, arts councils	2.0	1.6
Hospitals	4.6	3.7
Neighborhood associations	8.6	7.0
Other	8.4	6.8
Subtotal	82.4	67.0
Change-oriented organizations		
ACLU, civil liberties	1.1	.9
NAACP, SCLC, local civil rights groups	.3	.2
Housing–tenants groups	1.7	1.4
Welfare rights groups	.4	.3
Environmental protection groups	1.7	1.4
Consumer protection groups	.3	.2
Minority groups	1.0	.8
Economic, business development	.9	.7
Planned Parenthood Association, family planning groups	.4	.3
Other	5.2	4.2
Subtotal	13.0	10.4
Legal aid, defender programs	4.6	3.7
Total	100.0	81.1

quo organizations. Lawyers are just as little social activists in their pro
bono work after hours as during billable hours.

Summarizing the data from the bar as a whole, we find the following.
The amount of pro bono work of the entire bar is approximately 6% of
the average lawyer's billable time, based on lawyers' own reports. If
anything, the figure is probably inflated. Most pro bono work is done
in billable hours for individuals who make up almost three-fourths of
the clients mentioned. One-third of the individual clients are friends or
relatives. Virtually all of this work is of a traditional nature. Insofar as
nontraditional work is done, it is mainly for organizations, but the
effort here is minimal in comparison with the pro bono work offered

Table 5.6

Clients for Whom Lawyers Do pro Bono Work during Nonbillable Hours

Clients	Percentage	N
Individuals, friends, relatives	18.7	180
Traditional community organizations such as churches, social organizations	67.0	691
Change-oriented organizations such as civil rights groups, environmental groups	10.6	117
Legal aid, Legal Services, and defender programs	3.7	43
Total	100.0	1031

traditional organizations. Overall, it is quite obvious that the overwhelming majority of lawyers are not working toward fundamental change of representation in the legal system. There is practically no litigation connected with pro bono work. The lawyers' contributions consist mainly of general advice and counseling. What is being offered by the practicing bar is essentially legal services for the poor, without litigation, and to a lesser extent, legal services for civil and charitable organizations. Overall, it is clearly at the traditional end of the spectrum.

The Distribution of Professional Services

Previous studies of lawyers conclude that the legal profession works primarily for the upper-class individual, business, and commercial interests; lawyers are high-income professionals employed by the high-income segments of society, and presumably unresponsive to the needy. We now examine to what extent these findings apply nationally. Since income and wealth vary according to location, we control for city size; that is, lawyers in smaller cities and rural areas will be compared with one another rather than with lawyers in the largest cities. The aspects of practice with which we are mainly concerned are work with poor and minority clients and area of practice.

Although all social classes are represented by lawyers, the common impression that the legal profession primarily serves the upper classes is correct (see Table 5.7). For example, at approximately the time of the survey, 15.7% of the population reported incomes of $15,000 or more per year, but more than half of the lawyers' clients were in these income

Table 5.7

Comparison of Wealth of Businesses and Individuals with Wealth of Lawyers' Clients

Individual income categories	Percentage of population	Percentage of individual clients of private practice lawyers
Under $5000	34.1	9.8
$5000–14,999	50.2	37.3
$15,000–34,999	13.3	30.2
$35,000 and over	2.4	22.7
Total	100.0	100.0

Businesses, by receipts categories	Percentage of all proprietorships, partnerships, and corporations[a]	Percentage of time with business clients reported by private practice lawyers
Units with receipts of less than $100,000	87.3	29.3
Units with receipts of $100,000 and over	12.7	72.7
Total	100.0	100.0

[a] U.S. Bureau of the Census, 1974, Table 778.

brackets. Conversely, more than a third of the population had incomes of less than $5000, but these individuals accounted for fewer than 10% of the individual clients. A similar distribution applies to business clients; 12.7% of all business have receipts of $100,000 or more per year, but these businesses account for more than 70% of the business clients of the profession.

Only a relatively small amount of professional time (5.8%) is spent with the poorest individual clients and with the smallest businesses (13.8%). These results varied somewhat by city size, as shown in Table 5.8. Overall, only 22% of lawyers spend 30% or more of their time with poor individuals, small businesses, or both; and 31% spend less than 10% of their time with such clients.

In addition to clients, another important aspect of the distribution of professional services is area of practive.[4] To a considerable extent, a lawyer's area of practice defines the clients to be seen, matters to be handled, roles in bar groups, etc. In Table 5.9 the major areas of practice

[4] The method for making area of practice designation is explained in Appendix A.

Table 5.8

Professional Time Spent with Low-Income Individuals and Small Businesses

	Percentage of time	
City size	Individuals with incomes under $5000	Businesses grossing $100,000 per year or less
Under 100,000	7.2	15.4
100,000–600,000	3.2	13.7
Over 600,000	5.5	11.1
All cities	5.8	13.8

are shown by city size. In larger cities, business and litigation were more common, and the areas of family, civil, and criminal less common. In small cities, lawyers are more evenly divided among areas of practice; the client base does not support much specialization, especially in the business area (Handler, 1967). Lawyers more often said they had specialties in larger cities, and business as a specialty was more commonly named. Regardless of city size, however, only rather small percentages of lawyers had as their major area of practice criminal, family, or general civil work. These are the areas of practice which, along with injury work, are most likely to bring lawyers into contact with the less well-to-do. In the largest cities, about one lawyer in ten names an area of practice likely to involve working with poorer people on a continuing or regular basis.

Table 5.9

Major Areas of Practice, by City Size

	Under 100,000		100,000–600,000		Over 600,000		All cities	
	N	%	N	%	N	%	N	%
Business	57	13.8	58	26.3	103	34.3	218	22.9
Wills, estates	82	21.2	23	10.1	30	12.2	135	15.9
Real estate	81	20.0	32	15.7	38	11.6	151	16.4
Litigation	36	7.6	30	16.0	37	12.3	103	11.0
Injury	52	12.0	29	12.8	31	11.7	112	12.1
Criminal	46	10.3	11	5.1	13	5.1	70	7.5
Civil	32	8.0	12	5.1	9	3.4	53	5.9
Marital	17	4.5	9	4.0	8	2.8	34	3.9
Other	12	2.6	11	4.8	17	6.5	40	4.3
Total	415	100.0	215	99.9	286	99.9	916	99.9

As another measure of the distribution of legal services, lawyers were asked what percentages of their clients came from minority groups. The average was 15.3%, with blacks, Chicanos, and Puerto Ricans mentioned most commonly. In small cities, 13% of the clients were minority; in middle-sized cities, 15%; and in large cities, 19%. Higher percentages of minority clients were reported by lawyers in criminal, injury, and family practice, who had more individual clients than business clients. This finding was essentially the same in cities of all sizes. About 20% of the lawyers reported that more than a quarter of their clients came from minority groups.

In terms of the distribution of professional services, the extent to which lawyers work for the lower social classes is modest. The overall picture is much the same as for pro bono work: A small percentage of lawyers do a considerable amount of work for the poor and for small businesses, or are in criminal–marital–civil practice, or have sizable percentages of clients from minority groups. Most lawyers do very little work for the poor, small business, or minorities; they may spend their time with business clients. About a fourth of the lawyers do no poverty, small business, or minority work at all.

PROVIDERS OF PRIVATE PRACTICE LEGAL SERVICES

We are concerned with who among the private bar are performing what we call "private practice legal services," which includes both pro bono activities and the distribution of professional work. The six indicators of private practice legal services we use are (a) percentage of billable hours in pro bono work; (b) total nonbillable hours in pro bono work; (c) aggressive pro bono work; (d) percentage of clients who are minority; (e) percentage of time working for small business clients or individuals with incomes under $5000; and (f) areas of practice. In this section, we show that the private practice legal services measures are related to important aspects of private practice, such as firm size, professional income, and client wealth. We ask the following question: To what extent are lower-status lawyers doing a disproportionate share of private practice legal services work?

Turning to firm size as one aspect of private practice, we find a mixed relationship between firm size and indicators of private practice (see Table 5.10). There is a strong relationship between firm size and time spent in pro bono or minority work and with small business or poor clients. Solo lawyers do more work with these clients than firm lawyers, and much more work than lawyers from large firms.

Table 5.10

Relationship of Solo Practice and Firm Size to pro Bono Work and Private Practice
Legal Services

| | All Cities | | | | |
	Solo	Small firms[a]	Large firms[a]	All firms	Firms and solo
Percentage of pro bono in billable hours	9.5	5.2	4.1	4.9	6.8
Total nonbillable hours in pro bono work	23.6	28.2	32.2	29.2	27.5
Percentage of clients who are minorities	18.6	16.1	6.6	13.7	15.4
Percentage of clients who were small business or had incomes under $5000	25.3	18.8	15.9	18.2	21.0
Percentage of aggressive pro bono work[b]	18.1	24.5	32.2	26.5	23.8
N	283	448	185	633	916

[a] Small and large firms were determined separately for each size of community, then pooled. Small firms are those at or below the average size for the community; large firms are above the average.

[b] This refers to pro bono work, done in either billable or nonbillable hours, for individuals with drug, draft, political–radical problems, for organizations concerned with social change work, and for legal aid–Legal Services programs.

Firm lawyers do more nonbillable pro bono work, and aggressive pro bono work that challenges traditional institutions. When firm lawyers are divided into small and large categories, further differences are shown. Lawyers from large firms do the most nonbillable pro bono work and the most work challenging traditional institutions, but the least billable-hours pro bono work, minority work, and work for the poor. Whereas even large firm settings seem to be supportive of some kinds of legal rights and services work, it should be recalled that the overall amount of both nonbillable and aggressive pro bono work is very small. Solo lawyers are doing more work in time costs, but work that may be traditional.

For the sixth measure of private practice legal services, area of practice, Table 5.11 shows how differently firm and solo lawyers are distributed. Firm lawyers do more business work, much less wills work, and

Table 5.11

Relationship of Solo Practice and Firm Size to Areas of Practice

| | Percentage of practice | | | |
	Solo	Small firms[a]	Large firms[a]	All firms
Business	17.5	19.7	40.1	25.4
Wills	23.2	12.3	12.6	12.4
Real estate	19.0	16.7	11.4	15.2
Litigation	4.6	13.3	16.3	14.2
Injury	12.0	14.3	6.7	12.2
Criminal	8.8	7.8	4.9	7.0
Civil	7.1	6.3	3.1	5.4
Family	5.1	4.3	.4	3.2
Other	2.6	5.3	4.5	5.1
Total	99.9	100.0	100.0	100.1
N	283	448	183	631

[a] For small and large firms, see note [a] to Table 5.10.

more litigation than solo practitioners. When the large–small firm distinction is introduced, differences are even more striking. Forty percent of large firm lawyers do business work, and the percentages of large firm lawyers in family, civil, and criminal work are negligible. Firm lawyers, especially lawyers in large firms, do not work mainly in areas that direct their services to the poor and unrepresented. Tables 5.10 and 5.11, taken together, indicate that firm size does carry fairly strong implications for private practice legal services. Aside from small amounts of aggressive, nonbillable pro bono activities, lawyers from large firms are the least likely to deliver private practice legal services. The work is done, to the extent it is done, by solo practitioners and lawyers from small firms.

Another aspect of practice traditionally considered is professional earnings. The professional incomes of lawyers vary considerably. The larger the city, the higher the average professional earnings, with the average income $33,000 in small cities, $34,500 in medium cities, and $39,000 in large cities. But professional earnings are unrelated, or related at a low level, to the private practice legal services measures with two exceptions: Lower income clients and earnings are associated ($r = .23$), as are earnings and areas of practice.[5]

On the sixth private practice legal services measure, the lower earn-

[5] Other correlation coefficients were .13 or lower.

ings lawyers are those who work in the areas of family, criminal, civil, and wills–probate (see Table 5.12). Overall, firm size is more consistently associated with variations in private practice legal services than with professional earnings.

To ascertain how wealth of clients was related to measures of private practice legal services, we have computed a set of indexes: business client wealth, individual client wealth, and total client wealth. The methods by which these indexes were created are described in Appendix A. Tables 5.13 and 5.14 show how the various client wealth measures are related to the other private practice legal services measures.

Table 5.13 shows virtually no relationship between client wealth scales and the total hours of pro bono nonbillable time and whether lawyers do aggressive pro bono work. On the other hand, the greater the wealth of clients, the less pro bono work done in billable hours and the smaller the percentage of clients from minority groups.

When we turn to the other measure of private practice legal services, we see that the clients of lawyers in some areas of practice are clearly less wealthy (see Table 5.14), particularly criminal, family, and civil lawyers. Clients of those in wills, injury, and real estate are only slightly better off. The most well-to-do clients are those of lawyers specializing in business, litigation, and areas of practice not listed separately in the table.

Status of Practice Scale

We have combined the customary indicators of status of practice—practice setting, income, and client wealth—to form an index.[6] High, medium, and low categories of status have been related to private practice legal services measures in Tables 5.15 and 5.16.[7] Not only are there differences in the status of lawyers' practices and in their private practice legal services work, but the two types of measures are related. As Table 5.15 shows, those with high status practices do considerably fewer billable hours of pro bono work, more nonbillable hours of pro bono work, and much less work with minority clients; lawyers with low status practices do just the opposite. Doing aggressive pro bono work was unrelated to practice status. High-status lawyers are dispro-

---

[6] Client wealth scales and the Status of Practice Index are explained in Appendix A.

[7] The percentage of clients who were small businesses or individuals with incomes under $5000 is not shown, inasmuch as it is related to the client wealth indexes and thus to the Status of Practice Index.

Table 5.12

Relationship between Average Professional Earnings and Areas of Practice

Areas	Average income in dollars
Business	39,620
Wills	31,650
Real estate	35,410
Litigation	38,390
Injury	36,800
Criminal	29,600
Civil	30,290
Family	27,980
Other	44,200
All	35,670

portionately involved in business and litigation; low-status lawyers are disproportionately involved in injury, criminal, civil, and family work.

Lawyers who are low in status are doing more pro bono work and minority work; the overall tone of their practices is oriented toward low-income individuals. To some extent, their greater pro bono work may be for minority clients. Poor clients and minority clients probably more often have to be redefined as pro bono work when they do not pay. On the other hand, poor and minority clients probably know more needy individuals whom they can refer to lawyers for pro bono assis-

Table 5.13

Correlations between Client Wealth and Private Practice Legal Services Measures

	Zero-order correlation coefficients		
	Business client wealth scores	Individual client wealth scores	Total client wealth scores
Percentage of billable hours in pro bono work	−.19	−.13	−.18
Total nonbillable hours in pro bono work	.01	.02	.02
Challenging traditional institutions in pro bono work	−.02	.02	.01
Percentage of minority clients	−.27	−.30	−.32

Table 5.14

Relations between Average Client Wealth Scores and Areas of Practice

Areas	Business client wealth[a]	Individual client wealth[a]	Total client wealth[b]
Business	2.3	3.0	3.3
Wills	1.6	2.6	2.7
Real estate	1.7	2.7	2.8
Litigation	2.3	2.7	3.2
Injury	1.8	2.4	2.7
Criminal	1.4	2.4	2.4
Civil	1.6	2.6	2.6
Family	1.5	2.5	2.5
Other	1.9	2.9	3.1
All	1.8	2.7	2.9

[a] 4 = high, 1 = low.
[b] 5 = high, 1 = low.

tance. Finally, simply being known as an injury, criminal, or family lawyer in a community may be sufficient to attract people needing aid with problems of those types; they would tend not to go to lawyers in large firms (Lochner, 1975; Carlin, 1962).

The high-status lawyers tend to do more afterhours pro bono work. It will be recalled that most of this work is for organizations rather than individuals; that most of these organizations are traditional charities and community groups; and that many of the lawyers are officers or directors of the organizations.

Table 5.15

Status of Practice and Private Practice Legal Services Measures

	High	Medium	Low
Percentage of billable hours in pro bono work	4.8	6.8	7.4
Total nonbillable hours in pro bono work	37.2	26.7	24.2
Percentage challenging traditional institutions	23.7	23.5	24.2
Percentage of clients who are minority	7.5	15.4	25.0
N	143	587	139

Table 5.16

Status of Practice Categories and Area of Practice

Area	High		Medium		Low	
	N	Percentage	N	Percentage	N	Percentage
Business	56	39.1	134	21.5	12	9.3
Wills–probate	18	12.7	85	15.8	24	19.4
Real estate	17	11.8	108	18.4	22	15.5
Litigation	22	15.0	65	10.5	11	9.2
Injury	12	9.5	75	12.5	24	15.7
Criminal	1	.8	46	7.7	18	12.0
Civil	4	2.0	35	6.7	13	8.3
Family	2	1.2	19	3.6	13	9.0
Other	11	7.9	20	3.3	2	1.5
Total	143	100.0	587	100.0	139	99.9

Although there are relationships between aspects of practice and the various private practice legal services measures, one should not assume that the various measures are equivalent. For example, low-status lawyers do more billable hours pro bono work, whereas high-status lawyers do more nonbillable hours pro bono work; but the differences in time spent in these two activities are very great. Over the course of a year, high-status lawyers do about 13 more hours of pro bono work in nonbillable hours than low-status lawyers. On the other hand, with conservative figures (a 40-hour work week for 48 weeks), low-status lawyers do about 50 more hours per year of pro bono work during billable hours than high-status lawyers. There are other differences between the measures, although they are not susceptible to quantitative comparisons. As pointed out, billable hours pro bono work tends to be for individuals, and afterhours work tends to be for organizations; thus, the pro bono work of low-status lawyers is done for individuals (including minorities), and that of high-status lawyers is done for organizations, most of which are charities and communities. In sum, different types of lawyers are doing different kinds of private practice legal services work. Overall, the level of pro bono work is low, and the distribution of professional services is strongly skewed in favor of the prosperous. Within these parameters, proportionately more of the legal rights activities work is being done by the lower-status lawyers.

6

Organizations of the Private Bar

In Chapter 5, we examined the pro bono work of private practitioners as part of the everyday practice of law. In this chapter, we look at more systematic attempts of private practitioners to organize pro bono work. As we shall see, there is considerable variation, ranging from organized pro bono departments of elite large firms to law communes. They all share two distinguishing characteristics that merit separate treatment. With relatively minor exceptions, the pro bono work is financed out of private practice; thus, in contrast to the legal rights activities discussed in Chapters 3 and 4, there is little or no foundation or government support. The lawyers pay for the charitable work out of their own pockets. On the other hand, as distinguished from the data presented in the previous chapter, the pro bono work discussed here is organized. Presumably, the very fact of organization implies different kinds of commitments, which should result in different kinds of pro bono work.

AGGRESSIVE LEGAL RIGHTS ACTIVITIES

As noted in Chapter 2, analogues of the foundation-supported public interest law firm are found within private practice.

Public Interest Firms Funded by Bar Groups

The Beverly Hills Bar Association Law Foundation was the first bar-funded public interest law firm. Because it has been cited so often and yet had few imitators, its history and problems bear close remark: For example, how realistic is the model of public interest firms funded by bar groups in view of the experiences of the Beverly Hills Bar Association Law Foundation (Marshall, 1975; Handler *et al.*, 1975)?

Founded in 1971, the foundation received half its funding from the bar organization and half from large private law firms, small businesses, and individual lawyers. The foundation employed two full-time staff attorneys and had four clinical law students. Committed to aggressive legal rights activities, the foundation provided legal services only for groups or individuals with "high social impact cases." Some of the issues with which the foundation had been involved included testing the constitutionality of the death penalty in California, challenging laws against private possession of marijuana, arguing for the right to counsel at parole hearings, challenging the constitutionality of the misdemeanor bail system in Los Angeles County as discriminatory against the poor, and representing the Chicano residents of Los Angeles in a case contesting the reapportionment of the city council. Sometimes the foundation had worked as cocounsel with other California public interest firms.

However, conflicts of interest developed between the types of cases the foundation represented and clients of firms which funded the foundation. Concern over this matter on the part of supporting firms led to financial insecurity and tension between the bar and the foundation. At one point, the foundation was without a professional staff because of financial and morale problems and it finally terminated.

The model of the Beverly Hills foundation has been widely discussed, particularly in other large cities, inasmuch as it offers a structured way of mobilizing financial resources of the private bar on behalf of those who otherwise would not obtain representation in the legal system. For lawyers who cannot or do not wish to give their own time for public interest work, support of public interest firms by bar groups provides an opportunity for broadening access to the legal system. It has been presumed that lawyers in such bar-supported public interest firms would have less conflict of interest than lawyers in regular practice settings and would thus be much more willing to undertake challenging and time-consuming cases. On the other hand, as the Beverly Hills foundation indicates, conflicts of interest do occur and questions of allegiance—to donors or to clients—are serious.

Mixed Public Interest Private Firms

Another expression of aggressive legal rights work has been the emergence of private firms mixing regular paying clients with a substantial number of public interest clients who often pay reduced rates for legal services. The number of these firms is small. Their size and number will be limited by the number of public interest clients who can make some payment, the extent to which the regular paying clients can be attracted by firms that identify themselves with substantial amounts of public interest work and are willing to subsidize such work, and the extent to which the lawyers themselves are willing to subsidize their commitments (Marks et al., 1972). Fewer than 100 lawyers to date have been identified with these mixed firms; 59 were interviewed as part of this study.

Most of these firms are in the nation's largest cities, in the Northeast and in Washington, D.C.; but there are mixed public interest firms in all parts of the country. Our data indicate that the firms are usually small; the average is 5 full-time lawyers. No firm had more than 10 lawyers, and most firms are staffed entirely by full-time lawyers.

Both the firms and the lawyers in them divide their time between public interest and regular cases in about the same way—roughly 60% of their time is spent on what they consider public interest work (see Table 6.1). However, about 30% of the lawyers spend at least 80% of their time doing only public interest work while others handle regular cases; lawyers seem to have mixed caseloads, roughly like the overall distribution of cases undertaken by the firm.

The areas most often mentioned as those in which the firms do public interest work were consumer protection and environmental work, but employment discrimination, housing, criminal, and civil rights work were also mentioned fairly often (see Table 6.2). The main areas in which firms did regular work were personal injury (20.4% of the types of work mentioned), labor (16.3%), corporate–commercial–business

Table 6.1

Time Spent in Public Interest Work by Lawyers in Mixed Public Interest Private Firms

Percentage of time	Percentage of lawyers
0–19	6.4
20–39	10.6
40–59	27.7
60–79	23.4
80–99	8.5
100	23.4
Total	100.0
N	47

Table 6.2

Public Interest Cases of Mixed Public Interest Private Firms[a]

Types of cases	Percentage of firms
Environmental	16.0
Consumer protection	16.0
Housing, urban renewal	7.6
Civil rights	7.6
Employment	6.9
Criminal	6.1
Civil liberties	5.3
Welfare	3.8
Race discrimination, voting rights	3.8

[a] Based on three responses per lawyer. Also mentioned, but each less than 2.5%: education, Indian affairs, sex discrimination, antitrust, prisoner rights, poverty, health and mental health, constitutional rights, law reform, general indigent work, community organization, Title 7 employment discrimination, and land use planning.

(12.2%), real estate (9.2%), family–domestic (9.2%), and general civil (9.2%).

Lawyers were somewhat more likely to go to court for their public interest clients than for regular clients (66% versus 50%). In addition, they go to more elite courts for their public interest clients. Almost 70% of the courts were federal, state supreme, or appellate versus 31% for the regular clients. Work for public interest clients is much more likely to involve government agencies than is work for regular clients (66% versus 21%). Usually government agencies involved with both public interest and regular clients are federal (about 70%).

Among regular clients, lawyers indicated that about 70% of their time is spent on individuals; 18% on small businesses; and very small percentages on medium, large, or major national or international businesses. Of all the lawyers, 88% said they spent a third or more of their time with individuals. Lawyers who spent 35% or more of their time with individuals were asked about the incomes of the clients. They indicated that most of their individual clients were in the $5,000–15,000 range of income (see Table 6.3). Individuals of fairly modest means and small businesses, then, are the major types of regular clients for mixed public interest firms—clients who would not pay large fees. On the other hand, they are also clients who would not exert much pressure about types or amounts of public interest work. In their regular practices, mixed public interest law firms resemble small private practice firms. Only to a modest extent do regular clients subsidize public

Table 6.3

Income Groups of Regular Individual Clients of Mixed Public Interest Private Firms[a]

Client incomes	Percentage
Less than $5,000	26.0
$5,000–15,000	46.4[b]
$15,000–35,000	17.4
More than $35,000	10.3
Total	100.1
N	34

[a] Only for lawyers with 35% or more of their time with regular clients spent with individuals.

[b] Individuals with incomes from $5,000 to $15,000 make up approximately one-third of regular clients of mixed firms. Fourteen lawyers did not spend as much as 35% of their time with individual regular clients.

interest clients; they make up 46.2% of firm income from clients and take up just under 40% of firm time.

Only about a sixth of the lawyers in mixed firms said that they encountered conflict of interest problems between their regular clients and public interest clients. Usually these conflicts revolved around refusing such clients as landlords or coal companies because of previous connections with tenants or coal miners. About half the lawyers said their firms had policies for dealing with conflicts of interest: The policies most often mentioned were staying with the first client handled, discussion and compromise, or not allowing conflict of interest. Conflict of interest problems are, as already suggested, not of much concern for these mixed firms so long as they are able to depend on small business or moderate-income individual clients.

Although over three-fifths of the firms were supported wholly by their regular and public interest clients, others received money from grants and, less commonly, from private individuals, consulting fees, private foundations, contributions by lawyers in the firm, and colleges and universities. Only 15% of the lawyers said their regular clients or sponsors had tried to influence the types of public interest cases the firm took.

At the time they entered mixed firms, most lawyers had other job options—27% mentioned private practice; 11%, staying in former job; 15%, government work other than Legal Services; and 11%, Legal Services. Since 71% were from national or high quality regional law schools, other job options were probably good ones. Only a tenth of the mixed firm lawyers were in their first jobs. In deciding to enter a mixed firm, about half the lawyers said family and financial considerations were not important at all; and 90% said they intended at the time they took the job to stay in that kind of work.

The mixed firm lawyers were overwhelmingly satisfied or very satisfied with their work (95.7%). The reasons usually given for liking their work were the social importance of the issues involved and of performing a public service, the freedom and challenge of the job, and the success and excitement of the work. A few lawyers also mentioned liking the people they worked with. The main objections to the job were the low income and problems regarding firm policy and personnel. Income for the lawyers in these firms was low, especially when compared with that of their peers in private practice. About a third earned less than $12,000, a third between $12,000 and $20,000, and a third over $20,000. Overall, the lawyers in the mixed firms earned only 54% as much as their age-matched counterparts in regular private practice.

Most lawyers (58.3%) are in firms formed in 1971 or later. Usually, they are quite optimistic about the future of their firms, predicting success or stability. On the other hand, in private practice there is a large amount of instability in small law firms, generally caused by changes in clientele. Perhaps the public interest commitments of the lawyers in these mixed firms will counteract some of the forces of instability. At the present time, it is too early to tell.

Communes

Another aspect of aggressive legal rights activity in the private bar has been the emergence of the law commune. The overriding aim of communes has been political activism, not legal work as such. The law has been regarded by commune participants as a means of educating people and heightening their awareness of what those lawyers see as grave inequities in the American legal system. Communes have usually been identified by their preference for working with radical clients; by their determination to work mostly for those with whom they sympathize (since their clients frequently have limited resources, communes do some "straight" fee work, often minor matters for neighborhood people, to provide some support); and by their decision to give legal workers and secretaries voices equal to those of lawyers in policy decisions (New York Times, 1971). Salaries or allowances are often low; law commune members may share housing to minimize financial outlays and to express their philosophical solidarity. The most famous communes—the ones that have given so much visibility to the term *movement lawyers*—are the now-defunct Law Commune in New York City, the Bar Sinister in Los Angeles, and the communes in Newark, New Jersey and Cambridge, Massachusetts. Since the definition of a commune is, to some extent, a matter of taste, it is unclear how many lawyers are or have been members of law communes or how many communes have existed. The most reliable figures suggest that perhaps there have been as many as two dozen communes, involving about 100 lawyers at one time or another (Naitove and Nichols, 1972). The following findings are based on a random sample of 53 lawyers interviewed in 1973.

Virtually all commune lawyers interviewed were found in groups that originated in 1970 or later (88.7%). Most commune lawyers were in the Northeast (43.6%) or the West (39.6%), with only a few in the North Central or Southern states. Commune lawyers were not concentrated in large cities; 24.5% were in cities of under 100,000; 39.6% in cities between 100,000 and 600,000; and 35.8% in cities of over 600,000. Communes have had small numbers of lawyers—the average number is five. Communes usually had two or three legal workers, though a few had none and a few had eight or more. Since communes stress group discussions and decision making, having many participants has posed morale problems. Sheer size was one of the reasons Robert Lefcourt gave for the break-up of the New York Law Commune (Lefcourt, 1971).

Traditional work brings in the bulk of the fees but takes only a relatively small part of the commune's work effort. On the average, 37% of the cases were "straight," but 74% of the income of communes derived from these cases. As with mixed public interest firms, most lawyers combined straight cases with others, and there was not a system in which some lawyers did only straight cases or only other cases (see Table 6.4). Some commune lawyers have complained that in

Table 6.4

Straight Cases of Commune Lawyers

Percentage of cases	Percentage of lawyers
1–20	27.1
21–40	12.5
41–60	52.1
61–80	6.2
81–100	2.1
Total	100.0

fact there was such a system—that in a small group, if one or two lawyers were tied up with a major radical case, the other lawyers in the group had to do bread-and-butter work (Lefcourt, 1971; Naitove and Nichols, 1972). Almost a third of the lawyers did have fewer than 20% regular cases.[1]

Regular clients were almost always individuals. Only an average of 7.8% of straight clients were businesses. Usually the business clients were small businesses, such as health food stores and "hip" capitalists; nonprofit corporations and daycare centers were also mentioned. Most of the individual clients had rather modest incomes, as Table 6.5 indicates. The work done for straight clients is shown in Table 6.6. Criminal, family, and personal injury matters made up three-quarters of the regular caseload of communes.[2] Many of these clients would seek a lawyer only once and probably pay only modest fees. Commune lawyers have said they often preferred to take paying cases from those whose problems were not very different from those of their low-fee or no-fee cases. The paying criminal and marital cases would have brought rather modest fees, but communes did not expect to earn much money.[3]

Most commune lawyers said they placed limitations on the types of straight cases they took. The most common limitations were no landlords, rape, hard drug or drug dealer cases, businesses, banks, insurance companies, or "oppressor types."

Very few commune lawyers said their communes had income other than client income. A few mentioned money raised through political work or donations, however. Over 60% of commune lawyers reported that sources of income did result in pressure about types of cases, and

Table 6.5

Income Brackets of Individual Straight Clients of Commune Lawyers

Client income	Percentage
Under $5,000	36.1
$5,000–15,000	46.9
$15,000–35,000	9.0
Over $35,000	8.0
Total	100.0

[1] Of 53 lawyers, 6 indicated that 7% of their cases were regular.

[2] In contrast to our findings, several articles about communes have mentioned middle class drug and draft work as major types of paying cases (see Braudy, 1971; *Newsweek*, 1970; *Washington Post*, 1970).

[3] Commune charges for divorces, for example, are usually lower than the charges of other lawyers (see *New York Times*, 1971).

Table 6.6

Main Types of Straight Cases Handled by Commune Lawyers[a]

Cases	Percentage
Criminal	30.6
Family, marital	29.0
Personal injury	16.9
Employment discrimination	4.8
Labor	4.8
Civil	4.8
Other	9.9
Total	100.0

[a] Three possible responses per lawyer.

the specific problem they mentioned was almost exclusively the need to make money. Clearly, the need to attract and keep enough straight cases to make the commune viable poses problems.

One type of problem commune lawyers did not appear to have was conflict of interest (77.8% of the lawyers reported no problem), and the conflicts that were mentioned were between nonstraight clients. No lawyer mentioned problems between straight and nonstraight clients.

One of the main attractions of the law commune has been the opportunity to work on cases of one's choice. Communes handled a wide variety of public interest cases (see Table 6.7), but concentrated mainly

Table 6.7

Main Kinds of Nonstraight Cases Handled by Commune Lawyers

Cases	Percentage
Criminal defense	20.2
Political cases, political criminal	16.0
Labor cases, labor law	15.1
Prisoner rights, prison reform	9.2
Antiwar, antidraft	7.6
Discrimination, civil rights	5.9
Employment discrimination—Title VII	5.0
Marital, family	5.0
Landlord–tenant	4.2
Other (each less than 3%)— police brutality, sex discrimination, women, community groups, drug addicts, abortion	11.8
Total	100.0

in criminal, political, and employment discrimination cases, prison work, and antiwar activities.

Commune lawyers overwhelmingly (71.2%) said they had spent a substantial amount of time in court. This follows from the large number of criminal cases, both straight and nonstraight. The courts most often mentioned were state or county trial courts (41.3%), federal trial courts (25%), and municipal courts (17.4%). Little appellate work was done by commune lawyers. Although commune lawyers did a lot of court work, only 34% spent more than 20% of their time appearing before government agencies. Agency contacts were fairly evenly divided among county, local, state, and federal agencies. Little work was done with the Internal Revenue Service or major regulatory agencies.

Most commune lawyers said they took their jobs because they liked the type of work the commune did; they liked the other attorneys or people in the office; or because they wanted to engage in social reform and social conscience work. A few lawyers mentioned being attracted by the independence they could have in their work, the interesting aspects of the work, and the opportunity to start a new type of law group. For most (68–72%), family and financial considerations were not important in their job choices.

Commune lawyers usually had other job alternatives at the time they joined the commune; 18.5% mentioned private practice, 21.9% said they could have retained a previous job. About 10% said they did not consider other options, but only 4.6% said they had no other choices.[4] Since commune lawyers disproportionately were recruited from the nation's best schools (81.1% were from the top 23 schools) and from the upper halves of their classes (88.9%), it is very likely that they had a considerable range of job choices.

Overwhelmingly, commune lawyers liked their work; 49% said they were very satisfied, and 37% said they were satisfied. The specific reasons why they liked their jobs are shown in Table 6.8; and the reasons why they disliked their jobs are shown in Table 6.9. Money problems loomed large for commune lawyers; indeed they were far and away the greatest concern. Most (53.1%) said that need governed the division of money in the commune, with 38.8% saying money was divided evenly, and only 8.2% mentioning salaries. Professional earnings for commune lawyers were low, as shown in Table 6.10. The main reason lawyers gave for leaving communes was money, but organizational problems were also mentioned often (see Table 6.11).

---

[4] A variety of other options, including government work, defender work, Reginald Heber Smith fellowships, another commune, and nonlaw jobs, were also mentioned.

Table 6.8

Reasons Commune Lawyers Liked Their Jobs[a]

Reasons	Percentage
Independence, freedom, responsibility of work	22.0
Working conditions	13.8
Clients and staff	12.8
Work atmosphere	11.9
Type of practice	11.0
Doing social good or reform	7.3
Political potential	5.5
Interesting work	4.6
Other (relationship with community, lack of hassle with clients about money, using skills, courtroom work)	11.0
Total	99.9

[a] Three possible responses per lawyer.

Table 6.9

Reasons Commune Lawyers Disliked Their Jobs[a]

Reasons	Percentage
Financial uncertainty, inadequate money, having to charge clients	35.2
Administrative problems, can't take certain cases	8.5
Frustrations, opposition from outsiders	8.5
Nothing	7.0
Complaints about colleagues	7.0
Long hours, hard work, small staff	7.0
Court problems	4.2
Specific types of cases	4.2
Other (including tension, boring work, objections to clients, lack of respect, political pressure, poor working conditions)	18.2
Total	99.8

[a] Two possible responses per lawyer.

Table 6.10

Professional Earnings of Commune Lawyers

Earnings	Percentage
Under $5,000	51.9
$5,000–10,000	36.5
Over $10,000	11.5
Total	99.9

Table 6.11

Reasons Commune Lawyers Left Commune[a]

Reasons	Percentage
Inadequate money, financial insecurity	20.8
Partner left, commune broke up	16.7
Dissatisfaction with work or colleagues	16.7
Personal reasons (family, wanted new location)	16.7
Wanted to be in another type of practice	12.5
Other (offered new job, wanted to teach, etc.)	16.6
Total	100.0

[a] Two possible responses per lawyer.

Communes have primarily recruited lawyers who finished law school in the last year or two (73.1%). Still, most commune lawyers have held other jobs (66%). Images of commune lawyers as predominantly young are correct, but they usually were not neophytes to law work.[5] Since communes are so new, it is difficult to judge their staying power, but a variety of indicators suggest considerable turnover among commune lawyers. For example, those who have left the communes (19 lawyers) were there an average of only 1.6 years. Lawyers burned out or became discouraged for a variety of professional, financial, and personal reasons. Communes disband, fragment, or turn to more traditional clients and cases.

Although there is a great deal of difference between bar-supported

[5] Other writers have stressed that many lawyers have entered communes after being in Legal Services.

public interest law firms, mixed public interest law firms, and law communes, all represent aggressive legal rights activities. All engaged in extensive amounts of litigation which challenged the status quo. Indeed, in the Beverly Hills Bar Association Law Foundation, it was the conflicts of interest that proved so troublesome to the firm. Although conflicts of interest have not been serious for the mixed public interest law firms and the law communes, financial uncertainty poses serious problems for all three types of organizations.

PRO BONO DEPARTMENTS OF LARGE LAW FIRMS

As stated in Chapter 2, some law firms began to organize pro bono departments during the 1960s. In part, this was a response to the social activism of that decade, and allegedly the large firm response to the competition of OEO, Legal Services, and civil rights work. It is also claimed that as the glamour of law reform in the 1960s faded and competitive pressures lessened, law firms cut back on their commitments to organized pro bono programs. Faced with a tight market, applicants were less demanding for pro bono work, and law firms were under less pressure to cater to such tastes.

It is difficult to get precise measures with which to examine these assertions. There seemed to be a rise in organized pro bono departments during the 1960s, but there is no way of tabulating accurately how many firms organized programs or of what size. Similarly, it is difficult to measure any presumed decline. There are reports of such declines, but no figures. At any rate, at the time of the interview of this study (1973), we were able to identify 24 such programs and obtain interviews with 86% of the universe.[6] In addition, in-depth interviews were held with lawyers in charge of several programs.

Organized pro bono departments are usually found in very large firms in the largest cities. The average law firms of the interviewed lawyers numbered 98, and 96% of these firms were located in cities with more than 600,000 people. Firms had various arrangements, the three most common being (a) a firm committee handled or reviewed intake of pro bono cases, and individual lawyers associated themselves with cases of interest; (b) the firm committed itself to release lawyers for full-time public interest work or maintained a separate office for legal aid work; and (c) individual lawyers determined their own amounts

---

[6] All lawyers identified as associated with pro bono work in target firms were included in the sample. Some had done their pro bono work in the late 1960s; others were carrying on structured pro bono work at the time of the interviews.

and types of public interest work and felt that the firm supported and encouraged pro bono work.

Data from our interviews indicate that the pro bono programs of large law firms are staffed, in the main, by younger lawyers who have graduated from the best law schools. Of these lawyers, 60% were under 35; another 27% were between 35 and 44. More than 80% graduated from the nation's top 23 law schools. Most (about 60%) are associates. Their main areas of practice are either litigation (40.9%) or business (37.4%).

Does working in pro bono departments help or hinder a lawyer's career in these large law firms? Because of the relatively recent origin of the pro bono programs, we lack the data on subsequent career paths of these lawyers. However, 95% of the lawyers who have been identified with pro bono responsibilities in firms (as partners or committee members, in separate departments and offices, on loan to other organizations) were, at the time of the interview, still associated with the firms, although not always in a structured pro bono setting (these lawyers will hereafter be referred to as pro bono lawyers).

Lawyers in structured pro bono arrangements reported doing much more pro bono work than the average firm lawyer (see Table 6.12); the average proportion of their time in pro bono work (17.7%) was about three times the average for the private bar (see Handler *et al.*, 1975). However, this figure is open to interpretation in that it does not take account of specialization within the large firm. For example, in one of the largest Washington, D.C. law firms, and one that enjoys a national reputation for being a leader in the pro bono field, the pro bono department is staffed by 4 full-time lawyers. Yet, since this firm has about 100 lawyers who refer most of their pro bono work to the pro bono specialists, the average pro bono time per lawyer for this very large law firm is only about 5%, which is about the average for the entire bar. The contribution of this firm is even less when one considers the age, status, and salaries of the pro bono department staff—three are young associates, and only one is a partner. The analysis of this firm raises questions about other firms that support pro bono programs. To what extent do the other lawyers in the firms thereby reduce their contributions?

The types of clients pro bono lawyers in large firms worked with are shown in Table 6.13. Unlike the rest of the private bar, the pro bono department lawyers spent much more time with groups seeking to challenge the status quo and with Legal Services programs. Their work is also much more concerned with those two types of clients than that of other lawyers in large firms in major urban areas. However, the pro

Table 6.12

Comparison of Billable Hours in pro Bono Work for pro Bono
and Private Practice Lawyers

Percentage of billable hours pro bono	Percentage of pro bono lawyers	Percentage of private practice lawyers
None	4.4[a]	30.3[a]
1–5	28.3	32.0
6–10	19.5	18.4
More than 10	47.8	19.2
Total	100.0	99.9
N	113	881
Average pro bono time for partners	16.0	5.0
Average pro bono time for associates	18.7	4.3
Average pro bono time for all firm lawyers	17.7	4.8

[a] Evidently these lawyers' pro bono responsibilities in firms involve no actual work time.

Table 6.13

Comparison of pro Bono Clients in Billable Hours for pro Bono
and Private Practice Lawyers[a]

Clients	Percentage of billable hours		
	Pro bono lawyers	Large urban firm lawyers	Private practice lawyers
Individual standard civil	14.3	38.0	53.9
Individual standard criminal	11.2	12.8	18.2
Individual civil rights, politics, drug, draft	1.2	4.5	1.4
Traditional organizations	21.1	19.9	14.8
Change-oriented organizations	36.2	18.9	7.8
Legal Services and defender programs	15.9	5.9	3.9
Total	99.9	100.0	100.0

[a] Three possible responses per lawyer.

bono department lawyers did relatively little litigation (17.3% of work mentioned) and usually said their work was general advice or counseling (22.5%) or general practice work (43.8%).

In their nonbillable hours, these lawyers spent about the same number of hours with pro bono clients as did members of the private bar. Pro bono lawyers reported 26 hours per year; private bar lawyers reported 27 hours. Again, the clients differed; pro bono lawyers did much more work with change-oriented groups and much less traditional community organization work than private bar lawyers who did pro bono work in nonbillable hours.

The pro bono lawyers were asked whether they thought they were doing too much, about the right amount, or too little pro bono or social reform work; whereas 58.8% thought they were doing the right amount, 36% thought they should do more. By modest amounts, pro bono lawyers were less satisfied with the amount of pro bono work they did than were members of the private bar, even though they did much more such work. Almost three-quarters of the pro bono lawyers thought their participation in this kind of work had not made any difference in their professional earnings, although 20.4% thought they were worse off as a result of such participation.

Professional earnings for pro bono lawyers are shown in Table 6.14; the average professional earnings for these lawyers was $41,010. This figure compares favorably with the average earnings of all private practitioners ($35,540). On the other hand, these lawyers were in very large firms, in which partners' earnings would be very high. The pro bono lawyers who were partners earned $63,670; the associates earned $25,040. Large firm, big city partners in the contrast group earned $70,510; associates $25,040 (for both partners and associates the average was $43,980). Compared to an age-standardized contrast group of

Table 6.14

Professional Earnings of pro Bono Lawyers in Traditional Firms

Earnings	Percentage of lawyers
Under $20,000	19.8
$20,000–30,000	30.6
$30,000–50,000	20.7
$50,000–75,000	12.6
More than $75,000	16.2
Total	99.9
N	111

lawyers in large firms in cities over 600,000, the pro bono lawyers earned about 7% less. The differences between earnings of pro bono lawyers and those of comparably situated firm lawyers are not large, but they are real for partners, at least.

The picture that emerges from the data is that within a relatively few law firms, large and influential by national standards, there are small subunits of lawyers who have somewhat different commitments to pro bono work than their colleagues. They have usually publicly identified with a particular part of the law that sets them apart from their peers and superiors. Although most of their pro bono services are office practice rather than litigation, they do handle a different pro bono clientele from the average private practitioner or other large urban firm lawyers.

The viability of this form of legal rights activity depends solely on the discretion of the law firms. The members of the pro bono programs are young and, for the most part, without much influence in their firms. The arrangement is convenient for the lawyers who run the firm. They may be excused from doing pro bono work themselves; yet their professional obligations, in their own view, are more than satisfied. On the other hand, maintaining structured pro bono opportunities does cost firms money. The pro bono program lawyers have opportunities to engage in legal rights activities, but obviously they must steer a prudent course. As we see from the data, some feel that they have suffered financially, and comparative income data seem to confirm this view, to a modest extent. In sum, the pro bono departments of large law firms represent a larger commitment to legal rights activity than is found in most of the private bar, but their work and attitude seem less aggressive than those of public interest law firms.[7]

TRADITIONAL LEGAL RIGHTS ACTIVITIES

Offices for the Poor

Chicago Volunteer Legal Services Foundation (CVLSF) was the first volunteer effort of the private bar to staff neighborhood legal service clinics. CVLSF, initially sponsored by the Church Federation of Greater Chicago, grew from 6 clinics in 1964 to 19 in 1975, including the Civil Legal Aid and Social Service Project of the Cook County Department

[7] Marks *et al.* (1972, Chapter 13) discuss some of the constraints on large firm sponsorship of public interest programs.

of Corrections, better known as the "jail project." CVLSF's pool of volunteer attorneys who staff the clinics has grown from 15 to 250. In the past, most of the volunteer lawyers came from large law firms, but recently CVLSF has been attracting attorneys from smaller firms and solo practice as well. The clinics are funded by donations from churches and businesses, the Legal Assistance Foundation of Chicago, and the Law Enforcement Assistance Agency (LEAA), which supports the jail project. The jail project provides civil legal aid to inmates and in the past was involved with research supporting juvenile law reform.

The CVLSF program encourages volunteers from private law firms who are not involved in other types of legal rights work to respond to the legal needs of the poor. CVLSF believes that a large voluntary organization stands a better chance of avoiding both an overwhelming caseload and the problems of unpleasant communication within the bureaucracy. In addition, CVLSF believes that client choice among different competing forms of available legal service is necessary for quality legal aid. For the most part, the services provided by CVLSF are fairly traditional.

Volunteer attorneys come to the clinics once a month and are expected to follow up any cases they take. There are 11 staff attorneys to coordinate the volunteer lawyers and assist in matters requiring experience in poverty law. There are no restrictions on the types of cases that may be taken at the clinics, except for prohibition of any cases that recover more than $500. Eligibility standards for legal assistance are based on the Chicago Bar Association's rules. The majority of cases deal with divorces and other kinds of family problems.

New York's Community Law Office (CLO) program is similar to CVLSF in many respects. CLO is a volunteer legal assistance program that staffs offices in East Harlem and Central Harlem. Established in 1968, CLO's objectives were to combat some of the problems that the Legal Aid Society in New York encountered, such as large caseloads and bureaucratic red tape. CLO has attempted to increase participation of private firms and eventually would like to see them assume responsibility for financing the program. CLO began with 30 volunteer lawyers in 1968 and had 230 volunteers in 1971.

CLO has been funded by private foundations and the federal Model Cities Program and sponsored by the Legal Aid Society of New York City and the larger elite Manhattan firms (contributing primarily volunteer attorney time). The two offices in Harlem serve as continuing contact points for clients and as coordination centers and clearinghouses for volunteer attorneys. The full-time staff contains attorneys experienced in poverty law who function as special advisers for volunteer lawyers. The staff provides training workshops in legal services for volunteer lawyers.

More than 60% of CLO's cases are service cases, of which the largest proportion are marital disputes and other family problems. In this respect, CLO resembles CVLSF. Other typical cases CLO handles concern landlord–tenant controversies, consumer problems, and difficulties with administrative agencies. CLO has done research and supplied legislative testimony regarding various law reform issues such as rights of criminals, correctional reform, community development of daycare facilities, and consumer rights. In this regard, CLO is more active in law reform issues than CVLSF.

A somewhat different type of office for the poor is the Legal Rights Center of Minneapolis, which receives 60% of its financial support from the Minnesota Crime Commission, private foundations, and LEAA. Contributions from five large Minneapolis law firms make up the remaining 40% of the center's budget. The center has a staff of four attorneys who handle only criminal defense cases; their clients are indigents from racial minorities (blacks and Indians). Between 70% and 80% of their work is service work, but the center has also been working in juvenile penal law reform.

There are other offices for the poor that have the private sector as their main resource, its money and its time. Some cities still have legal aid offices that depend on private support. But aside from CVLSF and CLO offices, aid programs are small, like the Minneapolis Legal Rights Center. CVLSF and CLO are unusual both in their size and in their combination of staff attorneys with large numbers of volunteers.

Interviews with a small number of staff attorneys in these two programs indicate effective utilization of volunteer attorneys is a serious problem. Volunteer attorneys are often inexperienced, sometimes incapable, difficult to control, and pressured to subordinate their volunteer work to firm (private practice) matters. Even so, staffs in both organizations hope for more volunteers. Staff lawyers usually found their own work satisfying and rewarding, mentioning the opportunity to aid the poor and work with clients as the job aspects they liked best. Before taking positions as staff lawyers in offices for the poor, most respondents had other professional experience, half in private practice and half in other legal rights work.

Lawyer Councils and Clearinghouses

The primary purpose of the Council of New York Law Associates is to serve as an informal clearinghouse for legal problems of groups and not-for-profit corporations that cannot afford to retain private counsel. Some of the organizations for which the council has obtained volunteer legal services are

1. Crime Victims Service Center of the Albert Einstein College of Medicine, to establish a panel of volunteer lawyers to answer questions posed by victims of violent crimes about their rights
2. Riverside Church, to establish a bond system to provide bail for persons who otherwise could not afford the costs involved
3. The Sierra Club, to aid in its challenge of the Metropolitan Transportation Authority's refusal to make public information relevant to the proposed rail spur through Forest Park
4. Prospect Lefferts Garden Neighborhood Association, to provide the help of lawyers in a variety of areas as part of its fight to maintain a stable integrated neighborhood
5. Citizens Union Committee on City Planning and Budget, to provide volunteers to work on studies of various low-profile city agencies [Council of New York Law Associates, 1974, p. 5].

Acting in the capacity of a clearinghouse, the New York council coordinates volunteer legal services much as a referral agency. The council's *Newsletter* publishes requests for legal assistance for groups seeking volunteer help.

In addition to the council's clearinghouse function, it has been active in educational programs to encourage lawyers to do public service work. The council's 1974 project (in conjunction with the Association of the Bar of the City of New York) monitored behavior of judges sitting in the New York courts to promote high quality performance.

The council is funded by membership dues and contributions from law firms in New York City. Although the council is independent from the Association of the Bar of the City of New York, it is given free office space by the bar association, with which it often cosponsors educational programs. Furthermore, council staff members have been employed by the New York Bar Association in the past. The council's membership includes 1600 young lawyers, two-thirds from large law firms and one-third from small firms, solo practice, and government agencies.

The Chicago Council of Lawyers (1969) is an independent bar association and local affiliate of the Illinois State Bar. The Chicago council perceives itself as a reform-minded professional organization. The council's 1200 members are its largest source of financial support. In addition, the council has received foundation support for specific projects they have undertaken, such as the police misconduct lawyers' referral service. The council's two full-time staff members publish a newsletter once a month and coordinate educational programs sponsored by the council. Active in current court reform issues, the Chicago council is attempting to be a counter bar association.

CONCLUSIONS

We find that the organizations engaged in legal rights activities which are supported by private practitioners fall into a number of different categories. The bar-supported public interest law firm(s), the mixed public interest law firms, the communes, and the pro bono departments of firms account for very few lawyers working in a few locations. The offices for the poor and the councils, on the other hand, are quite large, and in their localities they account for a great number of lawyers and cases. If coverage and volume are the criteria of success, then these latter organizations seem to be the model.

The different organizations do different things. The offices for the poor and the councils in the main duplicate legal aid. This parallels, in rough fashion, the pro bono work of the practitioners and consists of traditional legal rights activities. There are distinct advantages to this approach: The sponsors of these offices and councils argue that there should be an alternative to publicly supported legal aid. Although the record of private charity legal aid is not enviable, Legal Services also has not been without its troubles. The poor need legal services for the problems that beset them—family, consumer, landlord and tenant—and, subject to other considerations discussed shortly, it is better if they have options as to the types of legal services available. The question is the cost of the private bar's duplicating legal aid. Will the bar be satisfied with this form of contribution in lieu of other kinds of legal rights activities? It may be that this is all that one can reasonably expect of the private bar.

If we view the private bar legal rights organizations on a continuum of traditional to aggressive, we would place them in the following order: legal aid offices, which involve the least challenge except in the very unlikely event that they become massive in scope; offices for the poor and the councils that did some law reform work; and pro bono programs of private law firms. These programs, it will be recalled, did take some social change organizations as clients. The lawyers did a bit more litigation than the private bar in their pro bono activities, but nevertheless the pro bono department lawyers were under the considerable constraints of the law firm. Next in line would be the bar-supported public interest law firms, which seem to be the favorite model of the most public interest minded of the private bar. The record of the Beverly Hills bar public interest law firm is not unblemished. The firm suffered from pressures from private law firms arising out of complaining clients. Perhaps this is the lot of a pathbreaker. It was also true that adversaries of foundation-supported public interest law firms tried to intimidate the firms and their sponsors. It may be that if these bar-supported law firms caught on and traditions of noninterference were developed, the legal rights activities of the private bar would take on a qualitative difference. Support, diffusion, and noninterference, however, remain important conditions that thus far have not been met.

In their very different ways, the mixed public interest law firm and the law communes represent the other end of the spectrum. At the risk of oversimplification, the mixed firms challenge parts of the existing economic order or at least the customary way of doing business. The communes represent more of a political and social challenge. Both types of organizations, however, tend to be very small and, it seems, to be in precarious financial situations. They operate on very slender resources, especially in the case of the mixed firms, in view of the resources of their adversaries.

It is not surprising, then, that those organizations of the private bar that are the most aggressive and seek the most social change are the weakest by far. Those that are most traditional and represent the least challenge to the status quo are the strongest. Evaluative judgments and adoption of policy alternatives depend on one's assessment of the capacity of the private bar. If the bar is considered really incapable of supporting vigorous, independent public interest law firms, then it should be encouraged to support offices for the poor and councils. This is worthwhile activity, and half a loaf is better than none. Some of the leadership of the organized bar, however, are thus far not willing to settle for a duplication of legal aid. They are calling for a public interest responsibility of the private bar more oriented toward social change and specifically, for adoption of the Beverly Hills model in other states. In light of the data in these two chapters on the private bar, this would represent a significant change. Whether it will transpire remains to be seen.

III

CAREERS IN LEGAL RIGHTS ACTIVITIES

7

Lawyers in Legal Services

By 1967, Legal Services was established as a major part of the social reform efforts of the period. Who are the lawyers who would participate in such a program? As noted in Chapter 1, a good deal of literature suggests that the lawyers would be young, perhaps mostly new law school graduates. Youth, after all, seemed to have dominated the reform movements of the 1960s, as well as those efforts directed at more radical social change. "Never trust anyone over thirty" was the battle cry of the movement, at least until its participants began approaching that point in their lives themselves. The literature on activist professionals in general also suggests that Legal Services lawyers of the late 1960s were disproportionately drawn from high status, relatively liberal families, from top law schools, and from student activists; in short, that they were part of the "young intelligentsia" that was making waves all through society (see, for example, Gross and Osterman, 1972).

At the same time, there were other factors which ran counter to the young intelligentsia expectation. Zald and McCarthy (1975) and others have pointed out that social reform organizations attract personnel with a variety of backgrounds, political interests, and reasons for joining. This is especially likely to be true in a large-scale, government-sponsored effort such as Legal Services. For example, we would expect women and ethnic minorities to be overrepresented because of the attractiveness of government employment. Although the federal government has had a mixed record on its stated commitment of offering an

A slightly different version of this chapter has been published as Howard Erlanger, "Lawyers and Neighborhood Legal Services: Social Background and the Impetus for Reform," *Law and Society Review*, in press.

equal opportunity work setting, its record, particularly in the mid 1960s, was clearly better than that of the private sector. Similarly, for the young professional, a governmental social action program can offer an attractive opportunity to gain practical experience in the field.

Legal Services put the young lawyer into direct contact with clients and offered immediate court experience. Although much of this experience occurs with clients of low social status and in lower-level courts, it still may offer good opportunities to get one's feet wet and prepare for a future career. Large-scale government programs can also be attractive to older professionals. For example, for an older activist professional a program like Legal Services is offered an opportunity to be involved in social reform on a larger scale than he could on his own. For an older struggling professional, such a program can offer an opportunity for more stable employment, perhaps with largely the same clientele as he or she was serving before.

The first part of this chapter examines the composition of Legal Services staff in the early stages of the program, focusing on lawyers participating in 1967, the first full year in which the program had a large number of local offices operating.[1] The composition of staff in 1967 is also briefly compared to that of 1972 staff. The second part of the chapter considers variations within Legal Services, comparing lawyers in different types of programs, lawyers involved in varying degrees of law reform work, and lawyers with differing degrees of administrative responsibility. Finally, we consider variations in length of service of staff and the possible implications of these variations for the program.

CHARACTERISTICS OF EARLY LEGAL SERVICES STAFF

Age

Of all the factors commonly thought to distinguish Legal Services lawyers from the bar as a whole, the one with the strongest predictive power is age. Table 7.1 shows that 40% of 1967 Legal Services lawyers were new or recent law school graduates (the large majority of whom were under 30 at the time), having graduated in 1965 or later: This compares to only 12% of the bar. Nonetheless, almost as many (37%) had graduated in 1960 or before, which is over 5 years before the formation of the Legal Services program in 1965.

---

[1] The analysis here pertains only to Legal Services employees, not to Reggies or VISTA lawyers assigned to Legal Services.

Table 7.1

Year of Graduation from Law School, Lawyers in Bar, and in Legal Services[a]

Year of graduation	Cumulative weighted percentages	
	Bar	Legal Services
1967	5	10
1966	9	29
1965	12	40
1961–1964	25	63
1956–1960	38	77
1946–1955	68	91
Before 1945	100	100
N	1017	285

[a] Of the respondents, 3% did not graduate from law school and were assigned a year of graduation equal to their year of birth plus 24 years. All of these respondents fell into the oldest category shown.

Race and Sex

Apart from age, the strongest predictors of participation in Legal Services are race and sex. For a variety of reasons, Legal Services would be expected to have much higher percentages of blacks and women than the bar as a whole. The usual barriers of discrimination would be weaker because it is a government program and because of its social reform nature; in addition, for both women and blacks, the financial rewards of private practice are more limited, so the income foregone would, on the average, be less for them than for white males. Women are also more likely to be socialized to social service roles, and blacks may be more likely to identify with underrepresented people because of their own experiences. Blacks and women were historically overrepresented in legal aid work and are overrepresented in government work in general.

Table 7.2 shows a striking heterogeneity by race and sex in Legal Services, compared to the bar as a whole, which in 1967 almost totally comprised white males; 99% were white, and 96% of those whites were male. In Legal Services, by contrast, only 74% of the lawyers were white males, with the remainder divided evenly between white females and nonwhites (most of whom were male).[2]

[2] These findings on the bar as a whole are comparable to those of the census for 1970. More recently there has been a major change in the recruitment patterns of law schools, which will eventually be reflected in the bar.

Table 7.2

Distribution by Race and Sex, Lawyers in Bar, and in Legal Services

	Weighted percentages	
Race and Sex	Bar	Legal Services
Whites		
Male	96	74
Female	3	13
Blacks		
Male	1	12
Female		1
Other nonwhites		
Male	0	0.4
Total	100	100
N	1017	284[a]

[a] Data on both race and sex are missing for one person in the Legal Services sample.

Readers should note that in spite of the marked differences between Legal Services and the bar on age, sex, and race, the analysis in this chapter does not control for these variables. This is because the popular accounts of Legal Services seem to be concerned with overall descriptive differences between people in the program and those in traditional employment, without regard to generational or other differences. The background characteristics analyzed do vary by race, sex, and age,[3] but except as noted extensive analysis controlling for these factors does not change the substantive conclusions reached in this chapter.[4]

[3] White women lawyers in Legal Services were much more likely than white males to have come from families with high social status or with a liberal orientation. They are also more likely to have attended a national law school and to have engaged in reform activity prior to Legal Services. Nonwhite male lawyers in Legal Services were more likely than white males to have come from professional or liberal families and much more likely to have engaged earlier in reform politics. They are, however, less likely to come from families with high incomes, to have attended national or major regional law schools, or to report that they ranked in the first quarters of their classes.

[4] Because of the small number of cases for these groups in the sample of the bar, race and sex were controlled by repeating the analysis for white males only, and by doing comparisons within Legal Services.

Social and Educational Background

Social Status of Family of Origin

Participants in Legal Services are already an elite, in that the college population is quite disproportionately drawn from families in the upper income and higher occupational strata, and the law school population is even more so (Warkov and Zelan, 1965). Various commentaries suggest that even within this elite, Legal Services lawyers would have higher status backgrounds (see, for example, Moonan and Goldstein, 1972). However, one could easily expect the opposite, since this type of practice would be one in which lawyers of less elite background would be more comfortable and feel less of a "step down." Prior to the War on Poverty, legal aid attracted lawyers with much less elite backgrounds (Katz, 1976).

Table 7.3 indicates that there was no difference between 1967 Legal

Table 7.3

Father's Occupation, Lawyers in Bar, and in Legal Services

	Percentage	
Father's occupation	Bar	Legal Services
Professional	25	24
Proprietor–manager	38	36
Other	37	40
Total	100	100
N	979	266

Services lawyers and other lawyers in 1967 in terms of father's occupation. Much the same finding emerges when mother's occupation, or father's or mother's education is examined (not shown); differences follow no clear pattern and are slight.

There is, however, a tendency for Legal Services lawyers to come from less wealthy families. Of the lawyers in the bar, 24% came from families with annual incomes over $20,000 (a substantial amount of money when these lawyers were growing up), as compared to 14% of lawyers in Legal Services.[5] This tendency is more pronounced for

[5] These figures are based on lawyers who estimated their family's income while they were growing up. About 25% of the respondents did not answer the question.

lawyers graduating after 1960. Legal Services lawyers are also less likely (49% to 70%; 58% to 71% for whites) to be of Northern or Western European heritage, a heritage generally considered to be of higher status (see, for example, Carlin, 1962; 1966; Ladinsky, 1963). Legal Services lawyers were also more likely to have foreign-born fathers.

Political–Religious Orientation of Parents

To the extent that participation in Legal Services was politically motivated, one would expect Legal Services lawyers to come from relatively liberal or reformist backgrounds. Several indications of parents' political orientations were examined, including religion, which several investigators have found to be related to political socialization in other contexts.[6] These studies have found Protestants to be the least active in social reform activities while Jews have tended to be most active.

Analysis of the data indicates that political–socialization variables are related to participation in Legal Services, but that when all indicators are considered together, the relationship is, at best, only of slight to moderate strength. Legal Services lawyers are more likely than other lawyers to report that when they were growing up their parents were liberal or moderate rather than conservative (see Table 7.4). But in spite of these differences, in absolute terms the percentage of lawyers from liberal families is small—only 27%. Differences by father's or mother's political party (not shown) are less pronounced than differences by political stance, although there is a tendency for parents of Legal Services lawyers to have been either Democrats, Independents, or supporters of third parties.

When parents' involvement in social reform activities is considered, an unexpected finding emerges: Parents of Legal Services participants are, if anything, slightly less likely than parents of other lawyers to have been involved. All in all, then, the data provide little evidence that the "red diaper syndrome" (Keniston, 1968) holds for Legal Services participants.

That fewer Legal Services lawyers have Protestant backgrounds than other lawyers is as expected. (Mother's religion is used as the indicator of religious background because research indicates that the mother is generally the more influential parent in religious matters.) For white males, the figures are somewhat different; 53% of members of the bar came from Protestant backgrounds but only 35% of Legal Services

---

[6] See, for example, these studies of student activists: Lipset (1968); Watts et al. (1969); Braungart (1971); Hunter (1968).

Table 7.4

Political–Religious Orientation of Parents, Lawyers in Bar, and in Legal Services

	Percentage	
	Bar	Legal Services
Father's political stance		
Liberal	18	27
Moderate	41	49
Conservative	42	24
Total	100	100
N	965	261
Parents' involvement in social reform organizations		
Very active	14	15
Somewhat	24	16
A little	22	27
Not active	40	42
Total	100	100
N	1008	277
Mother's religion		
Protestant	55	45
Catholic	25	27
Jewish	20	28
Total	100	100
N	983	275

lawyers. However, among younger lawyers, Catholic (rather than Jewish) lawyers were heavily overrepresented. Of the Legal Services lawyers who had graduated after 1964, 45% were Catholics, compared to only 21% of members of the bar in that cohort; for Jews, the comparable figures are 28% and 20%.

Prior Political Activity

When the prior political activity of the lawyers themselves is examined, the most striking finding is that lawyers report very little social reform type political activity in college or law school. Only 4% of the bar and 14% of Legal Services lawyers report such activity (see Table 7.5). For lawyers who graduated before 1965, fewer than 5% report having been involved in any kind of reform politics—such as civil rights marches, boycotts, ACLU work—prior to graduation from law school;

Table 7.5

Prior Political Activity in College or Law School, Lawyers in Bar,
and in Legal Services

	Percentage	
Political activity	Bar	Legal Services
Reform	4	14
Traditional only	14	13
None	82	73
Total	100	100
N	1017	280

and this does not vary between people in the bar and people in the
Legal Services program. Among the lawyers graduating in 1965 or later,
there were both an increase in reform activity and a greater tendency of
Legal Services lawyers to have engaged in such activity. A quarter of
Legal Services lawyers, compared to 10% of lawyers in the bar, report
that they were engaged in reform-oriented politics prior to graduation
from law school. (Note, however, that three-quarters of even this
youngest cohort of Legal Services lawyers report no such activity.) For
all years, blacks and women were much more likely than white males to
have been involved in reform activity.

Educational Background

Indicators of law school quality and of individual performance in law
school are those stressed most in the literature on the Legal Services
program. As stated earlier, there was a belief that Legal Services was
primarily staffed by lawyers from elite backgrounds. This was certainly
the belief at the national office, which, however, kept no records on the
matter. Burt Griffin (1967), an early national director of the Legal Services program, believed that overrepresentation of elites was bad policy
and argued strongly for increased recruitment from the night schools—a
traditionally disparaged source of talent.

Table 7.6 shows very little difference between Legal Services lawyers
and the bar in attendance at national law schools, and a slight tendency
for Legal Services lawyers to come from the major regional schools
rather than from less prestigious schools. (This is more pronounced for
lawyers graduating after 1960.) Legal Services lawyers are, however,
less likely to report graduating in the top quarters of their law school

Table 7.6

Type of Law School Attended, Lawyers in Bar, and in Legal Services

	Percentage	
Schools	Bar	Legal Services
Major national school	16	15
Major regional school	21	27
Other	63	58
Total	100	100
N	991	278

classes[7] (39% to 49%), and less likely to report that they had the opportunity to be on law review.[8] About the same percentage of each group clerked for judges.

Prior Job Experience

Although Legal Services lawyers in 1967 were predominantly recent graduates, only about a quarter of them were on their first jobs. This, combined with the relatively low discriminating power of social and educational background variables, suggests that prior job experience may be important in predicting who will join Legal Services.[9]

[7] The assessment of class standing is difficult because of problems of knowledge and recall and because of a tendency to exaggerate achievement. Even though it is true that lawyers in the bottom quarters of their classes are less likely to practice law, it is still highly unlikely that over 40% of practicing lawyers graduated in the top quarters of their classes while fewer than 25% graduated in the bottom halves, as our respondents report.

[8] Not all students offered the opportunity to participate on law review accept; the honor is in the offer rather than the acceptance by the student.

[9] One would expect that the relationships predicted would be clearest for lawyers choosing Legal Services as a first job, since their decision making would not be affected by prior job experiences. In general, this is the case. For example, when white male Legal Services lawyers with no prior experience are compared to other Legal Services lawyers who graduated in the same period (1965–1967), analysis shows that the lawyers without prior experience were higher on all educational measures except reputation of law school. They were also from families in which the fathers had higher occupational or ethnic status, but lower incomes. The lawyers with no prior experience were much more likely to be from families active in social reform or in which the fathers were not conservative. There was no difference in the percentage non-Protestant nor in prior political activity. Legal Services lawyers in their first jobs were also much more likely than other Legal Services lawyers in their graduating cohort to cite an explicit social conscience motivation for joining the program.

Much of what has been written on activist lawyers would lead one to expect that a substantial percentage of Legal Services lawyers with prior jobs may have been dropouts from elite practice, especially from the larger firms, which mainly handle corporate work. But this is probably an unrealistic expectation because, if nothing else, moving to Legal Services from a large firm would entail a fairly substantial cut in salary. The literature on legal aid work and on private practice with low-status clientele suggests that since serving the poor has always been seen as marginal work, since the type of clientele served by Legal Services is similar to that found in much of solo practice, and since solo practice may be financially precarious at times, Legal Services may offer a more stable employment.

Table 7.7 compares the immediate prior jobs of Legal Services lawyers with the jobs left by other lawyers who were changing jobs in the period 1965 to 1968.[10] Lawyers graduating after 1965 are shown separately because the pattern for them was quite different. Further controls for year of graduation do not affect the findings.

A major finding in the table, and one which cuts across the year of graduation, is the tendency for Legal Services lawyers not to come from firms of five or more members. This is especially noteworthy since a five-member firm would generally be considered small. Of lawyers graduating before 1965, 43% came to Legal Services from solo practice or from a firm of fewer than five members, compared to only 24% of other lawyers changing jobs in a comparable period. These are traditionally considered low-status forms of practice (Carlin, 1966). Legal Services lawyers were also more likely to have moved from jobs in the legal rights area. Most of these legal rights jobs were in legal aid or public defender programs, although some were with social reform organizations. Younger Legal Services lawyers were much less likely than either older Legal Services lawyers or other lawyers changing jobs to

[10] In this analysis, Legal Services lawyers who had prior jobs are contrasted with those lawyers in the bar who changed jobs in the period between 1965 and 1968. (This period was chosen to be roughly contemporaneous to the period in which lawyers were joining 1967 Legal Services; it is a little longer in order to increase the cell size. This control group is used instead of the whole bar because lawyers are rarely fired and tend, once established, to stay in particular jobs for long periods of time. Thus many lawyers were not really on the market at the time recruitment to Legal Services was taking place. Compared to other lawyers in the bar, the lawyers changing jobs between 1965 and 1968 were more likely to have graduated after 1955, and if they had jobs in 1965, to have been in salaried jobs rather than private practice. Those in private practice were less likely to have been in solo practice.

Table 7.7

Comparison of Prior Jobs of Legal Services Lawyers and Lawyers in the Bar Who Changed Jobs in the Period 1965 to 1968

	Percentage			
	Graduated before 1965		Graduated between 1965 and 1967	
	Bar	Legal Services	Bar	Legal Services
Solo practice	11	27	4	1
Firm of 2–4 lawyers	13	16	12	8
Firm of 5 or more lawyers	13	5	31	5
Legal rights field	1	10	6	16
Salaried business counsel	16	4	7	12
Other (mostly salaried counsel for government)	18	22	16	39
Nonlaw job	8	2	14	16
Combination of above types	19	14	9	3
Total	99	100	99	100
N	194	166	72	45

have come from any form of private practice; two-thirds came from salaried jobs, especially in the legal rights field or in government.

Lawyers moving into Legal Services also had lower incomes than other lawyers changing jobs. This could indicate their marginality to the mainstream of the profession or it could mean that only lawyers with relatively modest incomes could afford to move into low paying Legal Services work. The income difference was sharpest for lawyers graduating in 1960 and earlier, among whom only 25% of the Legal Services participants were making $15,000 or more, compared to 55% of other lawyers changing jobs.

THE COMPOSITION OF LEGAL SERVICES STAFF IN 1972

The popular account of Legal Services that holds that the quality and backgrounds of lawyers changed dramatically as a result of the political troubles of the late 1960s is incorrect. Basically, there was little change between 1967 and 1972 in the characteristics of lawyers participating in the program; if anything, their backgrounds were more activist in 1972. Thus, despite the turmoil at the top, there was a steady stream of lawyers who remained interested in legal rights work. The 5 years in question were difficult for Legal Services nationally, but they did not fundamentally affect composition of the staff in the program.

Over three-fourths of the 1967 Legal Services lawyers were gone by 1972, and this fact, combined with an expansion in the number of lawyers in the program, means that in 1972 perhaps as few as 10% of the lawyers were holdovers from 1967. Overall, there was little change in the backgrounds or educational characteristics of Legal Services staff. The biggest change was in the prior political activity of white male Legal Services lawyers; 34% (versus 14% in 1967) had engaged in reform-oriented political activity prior to graduation from law school, as compared to 12% in the bar (4% in 1967).[11] The other changes are smaller; staff included more white males (82% versus 74%) and became somewhat younger (81% of the white male lawyers had 5 years of experience or less, compared to 75% in 1967). One might have expected the organization to open up a bit in response to the equal employment push of the 1970s, but perhaps this push meant that blacks and women could more easily find jobs elsewhere.

STAFF COMPOSITION IN DIFFERENT TYPES OF LOCAL PROGRAMS

Within Legal Services, there has been enormous variation in reputed quality of local programs. Some programs have been very active, especially in law reform litigation, and even garnered national reputations outside of social reform circles. At the other extreme, some programs continue to be simply local legal aid programs that shifted funding but not ideology. Since the reform-oriented programs received most of the attention (from both supporters and critics), most people's images of Legal Services probably have in reality reflected their images of these programs. Thus, one might argue that ideas about who is in Legal Services are really ideas about personnel in the highly visible programs.

As discussed in Chapter 3, local programs were divided into three groups, based on their reputed quality.[12] Of all the variables analyzed

[11] This shift appears to be independent of political orientations of parents, which are not different in 1972 compared to 1967; it also appears to be independent of mother's religion, as the percentage of Catholics and Jews went down slightly over the period.
[12] See Chapter 3, note 4 for classification of programs.

in the previous discussion, only two—type of law school attended and political activity before graduation from law school—are significantly associated with the quality of the offices. Although Table 7.8 suggests a fairly strong relationship between these variables and program quality, several caveats must be made. First, the excellent programs were numerically dominated neither by lawyers from the major national schools

Table 7.8

Characteristics That Have a Statistically Significant Association with Reputed Quality of Local Legal Services Programs

	Lawyers in reputedly excellent programs	
Characteristic	N^a	Percentage
Type of law school attended		
Major national	43	42
Major regional	62	14
Other	173	17
Political activity in college or law school		
Reform oriented	41	35
Traditional only	48	30
None	190	11

[a] Weighted number on which percentage is based.

nor by those with prior political activism of a reformist nature. Recalculation of the data in the table shows that in these programs, fewer than a third of the lawyers came from the elite national schools and only about a quarter had been involved in activist politics. Second, as noted above, other indicators of law school performance and political orientation do not have statistically significant relationships to type of program, and some are even negatively related.[13] Third, regression analysis indicates that type of law school attended and prior political activity explain just 7% of the variance in program quality.[14]

Thus it does not appear that the high quality, reform-oriented programs were "captured" by activist lawyers to the extent previously

[13] Year of graduation, class standing, and parents' participation in social reform organizations are each somewhat positively correlated with reputed program quality; and high parental socioeconomic status, father's being liberal, and mother's being Jewish are each somewhat negatively correlated.

[14] In this analysis, program quality was indicated by a three-category variable: reputed quality "excellent," "medium," or "poor."

suggested (Finman, 1971). Lawyers with elite training and prior participation in reform politics did tend to be in these programs, but overall the activists formed a minority representation in the whole range of programs.

DIFFERENCES IN EXTENT OF LAW REFORM WORK

If, instead of looking at differences between local programs, we look at differences in types of work within local programs, similar findings emerge. Distinguishing among Legal Services lawyers in terms of the percentage of their time devoted to law reform activity, we find that three of the background variables previously discussed have significant associations with the dependent variable.[15] One of these (reported class standing) is an indicator of educational experience, and two (father's political stance and parents' involvement in social reform organizations) are indicators of prior political socialization. These data are shown in Table 7.9, but much the same caveats apply here as for Table 7.8. Together, these three variables explain only 5% of the variance in percentage of time spent in law reform work. These findings support Katz's argument (1976) that the impetus for law reform activity in Legal Services come from professional rather than political sources.

LOCAL PROGRAM DIRECTORSHIPS

Another way in which Legal Services lawyers are differentiated is in their relative access to policymaking within local programs. Broadly speaking, there are three tiers of authority in local programs: directors; assistant directors, senior attorneys, neighborhood office directors, etc.; and staff. Obviously the importance and policymaking power of the administrative positions vary greatly among the different local programs, which have ranged from large programs constantly in the limelight, such as San Francisco Neighborhood Legal Assistance (see, for example, Miller, 1973), to two-person offices in quiet towns. However, detailed analysis indicates that for 1967 Legal Services lawyers the

---

[15] Percentage of time spent on law reform work is a self-reported variable, originally coded into five categories, 0–20%, 21–40%, etc. For the analysis here, each respondent was assigned the theoretical mean for the category in which he or she was scored, i.e., 10%, 30%, etc. The means shown in Table 7.9 are thus only approximations of what were already only rough estimates.

Table 7.9

Characteristics That Have a Statistically Significant Association with Time Spent on Law
Reform Work

Characteristic	N^a	Average percentage of time spent on law reform
Reported class standing		
First quarter	102	36
Other	181	28
Father's political stance		
Liberal	71	36
Moderate	130	30
Conservative	63	26
Parents' participation in social reform organizations		
Very active	40	42
Somewhat active	43	38
A little active	75	28
Not active	116	27

^{a} Weighted number on which percentage is based.

background characteristics associated with being in an administrative
position were, by and large, the same across program type.

As Table 7.10 indicates, although 1967 Legal Services was numerically
dominated by recent law school graduates, the administrative responsibility was much more likely to be held by older lawyers, especially
those who came to Legal Services from some form of government
employment. (Often this employment was only part-time, and involved
legal aid or public defender work.) There were also differences by sex,
ethnicity, and religious background in the tendency to hold an administrative position at the local level. With the exception of the finding for
blacks, the tendency on these variables (and on those variables for
which the findings are not statistically significant) is for lawyers with
presumably more liberal or activist leanings to be staff rather than
administrators.

Some of the variables in Table 7.10 tap similar dimensions, and when
all are entered together in a regression analysis (with the dependent
variable, administrative responsibility, being an index ranging from 0
for staff to 2 for directors) some of the relationships change substantially. The difference between males and females increases; the tendency for blacks to be directors is erased; and there are no longer statistically significant differences by religion, although Jews are still least

Table 7.10

Characteristics That Have a Statistically Significant Association with Administrative
Responsibility in a Local Legal Services Program

Characteristic	N^a	Average score, index of administrative responsibility[b]
Year of graduation		
Before 1955	65	.97
1956–1960	39	.76
1961–1964	69	.94
1965–1967	110	.28
Sex		
Male	250	.72
Female	33	.30
Ethnic background		
White, Northwestern		
European	133	.71
White, other	112	.53
Black	37	.95
Mother's religion		
Protestant	122	.82
Catholic	75	.63
Jewish	78	.52
Prior job		
Government position	70	1.12
Other	135	.66
None	78	.29

[a] Weighted number on which index is based.
[b] Ranges from high of two (directors) to low of zero (staff).

likely to have administrative responsibility. Together, the variables in
Table 7.10 explain 27% of the variance (corrected for degrees of freedom) in the index of administrative responsibility.

LENGTH OF PARTICIPATION IN LEGAL SERVICES

Variables which have a statistically significant association with
length of participation are shown in Table 7.11. The most striking
finding in that table is a turnabout on age. The lawyers who stay the
longest tend to be older; this is especially noticeable for the lawyers
who graduated before 1955. Lawyers in that cohort are the least likely to

Table 7.11

Characteristics That Have a Statistically Significant Association with Length of Participation in Legal Services

Characteristic	N^a	Average years of service[b]
Year of graduation		
Before 1955	65	5.7
1956–1960	39	4.2
1961–1964	69	4.3
1965–1967	110	3.4
Father's political stance		
Liberal	71	3.7
Moderate	130	4.7
Conservative	63	4.0
Parents' participation in social reform organizations		
Very active	41	5.1
Somewhat active	43	3.5
A little active	75	3.6
Not active	116	4.7
Political activity in college or law school		
Reform oriented	39	3.5
Traditional only	37	4.7
None	203	4.4
Prior job		
Solo practice	40	6.2
Other	162	3.9
No prior job	78	3.9
Quality of local Legal Services office in 1967		
Excellent	54	3.9
Medium	198	4.5
Poor	31	3.5
Position in local program		
Director or assistant	125	4.8
Staff	158	3.8

[a] Weighted number on which average is based.
[b] Not all service is in same local program.

151

join, but the most likely to stay.[16] In addition, at least two variables indicating liberal or reform-oriented background (having a liberal father and having participated in reform-oriented political activities while in college or law school) are negatively associated with length of service.[17] Some of the variables in the table tap similar dimensions, and if all are entered together in a regression model, the average years of service are adjusted somewhat, but not enough to change the general thrust of the findings. Together, these variables explain 34% of the variance in length of participation.

The most striking finding in the analysis of who stays in Legal Services is that lawyers whose prior jobs were in solo practice were by far the most likely to remain. This persistence of solo practitioners lends a new dimension to the progressive bureaucratization of the solo practitioner envisioned by Ladinsky (1963), who noted that the work of solo practitioners is increasingly being taken over by trust departments, title insurance companies, accounting firms, and other, often large-scale, organizations. Thus, he argues, lawyers who went into solo practice to pursue a varied practice may find that they must specialize, taking a job with one of these lay organizations or concentrating on the work that is left over. Now it appears that the legal needs of the poor may be emerging as yet another specialty and yet another force leading the attorney away from the presumed independence of solo practice.

Varying implications can be drawn from the finding that the younger lawyers with more liberal political backgrounds and more elite educational backgrounds are most likely to leave. As we discussed in Chapter 1, critics have suggested that the urge to undertake social reform work was a passing fancy, a fad spurred on by the political climate of the 1960s and by a favorable economic situation for professionals. This argument suggests that there is a shake-out effect such that bright "do gooders" burn out from the often repetitious and demanding work and then leave to pursue more traditional elite careers. Older lawyers, especially those with prior day-to-day experience handling the affairs of the poor (e.g., former solo practitioners) would be more likely to stay, and the organization might become a variation of the traditional legal aid society. However, as an earlier chapter has shown, the organization remains alive and well, and this chapter has noted that the composition

---

[16] Length of participation refers to the total years of service between 1965 (the year Legal Services was started) and 1974 for lawyers who were in local programs in 1967. All service is not necessarily in the same local program.

[17] Variables indicating elite socioeconomic status or educational background also generally have negative correlations with length of participation in Legal Services. However, none of these correlations is statistically significant.

of staff did not change much between 1967 and 1972. Most important, the following chapter shows that lawyers who leave do not pursue the types of careers traditionally accorded high status. On the contrary, those who do leave often do other kinds of legal services or public interest law work or go into government. If they do go into private practice, they tend to avoid the types of careers that have traditionally been accorded high status, and to engage in nontraditional pro bono work.

CONCLUSIONS

The finding that the Legal Services program apparently was not dominated by activist lawyers of liberal backgrounds and elite social status and education suggests that the radical character of Legal Services was not simply a consequence of the personnel in the program but rather followed in large part from the task they were being hired to do: to represent individuals and groups who were virtually unheard from previously and who were often taken advantage of by others who had greater access to legal resources.

In addition, since the Legal Services staff apparently did not consist primarily of people with strong prior commitments to working with the poor, the impact of the program on the redistribution of professional services is potentially greater. The stronger the prior commitments of Legal Services lawyers, the more the role of the program would be to give an organizational base to reform-oriented lawyers. In the extreme case of strong prior commitments, the impact of the program would primarily be to free these lawyers from the need to worry about making a living wage while serving clients who generally could not afford to pay them. By recruiting instead from a broad spectrum of the bar, the program can serve to mobilize lawyers who, although they may have felt that there ought to be broader representation in the legal system, would not necessarily have been active on their own. These lawyers would come from a variety of backgrounds and join for a variety of reasons. They may have served low-income clients or other underrepresented groups not so much because of ideology but more as an incidental consequence of the types of practice they were in. The increase in reform effort is greater with this group because there is less borrowing from other efforts. There is also more potential for redirecting the lawyers' subsequent careers, the subject we turn to next.

8

Six Years Later

There has been a good deal of speculation about the fate of activist lawyers who join a bureaucratic reform organization like Legal Services. Many people believe that these new professionals burn out after a few years or that they "mature"—either judgment leading to the conclusion that the lawyer from a high-status family or elite educational background will not continue to represent clients traditionally accorded low status. Others believe that the new professionals move on to other reform-oriented work, continuing to do the type of work they did before, but in a different context.[1] A third view is that participation in a reform-oriented program can reinforce prior commitments and accentuate a career line.

What is neglected in these discussions is the wide variation in the characteristics of lawyers joining such an organization. The early Legal Services attorneys had both activist and nonactivist backgrounds, came from families of high and low socioeconomic status, went to both elite and proprietary schools; in all, they were as much like the bar as they were different from it. Thus, in asking what happened to Legal Services lawyers, we are asking about a diverse set of people who were in the organization.

This chapter is organized into two parts. The first is descriptive, seeking simply to compare the jobs held in 1973 by the 1967 Legal Services lawyers to the jobs held in 1973 by other lawyers who were in

---

[1] See, for example, Wilensky's discussion (1956) of the "program professional."

the bar in 1967.[2] The second part asks a specific analytic question: Given the diverse backgrounds of lawyers in the program, what can we say about the effect of the program on the careers of those lawyers who leave?

THE PROFESSIONAL POSITIONS OF 1967 LEGAL SERVICES LAWYERS IN 1973–1974

Table 8.1 is a description of the types of jobs held by the 1967 Legal Services lawyers at the time they were interviewed in late 1973 or early 1974. For comparison purposes, the 1973–1974 jobs held by lawyers who were in the bar in 1967 are also shown. There are no controls of any kind in this table. The table indicates that contrary to one popular impression most Legal Services lawyers do not enter private practice. Of the 1967 Legal Services lawyers, 27% were still in the program, 22% in the same offices as in 1967. Another 30% were in jobs outside the private practice of law, 5% were retired or unemployed, and only 38% (compared to 62% of the bar as a whole) were in private practice.

Table 8.2 repeats Table 8.1, but this presentation shows only the jobs held by white males, and in addition, the year of graduation of lawyers in the comparison group has been standardized to have the same distribution as that of the Legal Services lawyers. This procedure eliminates the substantial effects of race, sex, and year of graduation on the comparison and allows a better assessment of the extent to which Legal Services lawyers are really different from others in the bar. However, it also means that for lack of an appropriate control group, the subsequent careers of blacks and women cannot be analyzed.

Although the numbers are different,[3] the conclusion from Table 8.2 remains the same: Legal Services lawyers are much less likely to be in private practice—39% as compared to 67%. Even discounting the high

---

[2] All analysis of current job refers to the predominant job held at the time of the interview. Many lawyers hold more than one job simultaneously (one of our respondents reported holding four), and the predominant job was defined as the one in which the respondent spent 60% or more of his income. (Of all respondents having more than one job, 95% could be classified in this way; for the other 5%, a predominant job was designated on the basis of time and income shared among jobs.) Preliminary analyses indicated that concentration on the predominant job did not affect the conclusions drawn in this chapter.

[3] Given the change in N for the bar is small, the differences in the percentages in Tables 8.1 and 8.2 seem large. This apparent discrepancy results from the weights carried by the people omitted from Table 8.2.

Table 8.1

Professional Positions at Time of Interview

| | Percentage | |
	1967 Legal Services lawyers	Lawyers in bar
Private practice		
Solo	19	24
Firm of 2–4 members	14	19
Firm of 5–9 members	4	9
Firm of 10+ members	1	10
Subtotal	38	62
Salaried positions		
Counsel for business	2	8
University position	4	2
Activist government agency[a]	5	1
Legal rights work[a]	4	0
Other (e.g., district attorney, judge)	11	11
Subtotal	26	22
Legal Services		
Same legal services job	22	—
New legal services job	5	—
Other		
Nonlaw	5	10
Retired, unemployed	5	6
Total	101	100
N	283	1017

[a] Defined in text.

percentage who remain in Legal Services, former Legal Services lawyers are more likely to be in jobs oriented to legal rights or public service activity than are other lawyers. Table 8.3, which for Legal Services shows only the lawyers who left the program, illustrates this more clearly. Whether in private practice or not, lawyers no longer with Legal Services serve a different type of client and do a different type of work.

Former Legal Services lawyers who are not in private practice are heavily concentrated in nonbusiness pursuits. Of these, 15% have remained in legal rights work,[4] working with a public defender's office, a public interest law firm, or a social reform oriented foundation. Another 16% work for an activist government agency, such as the Civil

[4] The varieties of legal rights work are discussed in Borosage (1970) and Marks (1972).

Table 8.2

Adjusted Professional Positions at Time of Interview[a]

	Percentage	
	1967 Legal Services lawyers	Lawyers in bar
Private practice		
Solo	17	19
Firm of 2–4 members	17	25
Firm of 5–9 members	4	11
Firm of 10+ members	1	12
Subtotal	39	67
Salaried positions		
Counsel for business	1	9
University position	3	2
Activist government agency[b]	5	1
Legal rights work[b]	5	0
Other	13	10
Subtotal	27	22
Legal services		
Same legal services job	22	—
New legal services job	7	—
Other		
Nonlaw	4	9
Retired, unemployed	1	2
Total	100	100
N	228	981

[a] White males only; year of graduation standardized to that of Legal Services.
[b] Defined in text.

Rights Division of the U.S. Department of Justice or the Environmental Protection Agency. Another 10% are primarily employed as law professors, in general teaching at least one nontraditional course such as welfare law, consumer protection, etc. Only 13% are staff counsels for business corporations or working in nonlaw (usually business) jobs. As Table 8.3 shows, this distribution is very different in the bar, where 60% of lawyers not in private practice work either in nonlaw jobs or as salaried counsels to business corporations. The percentage of law faculty is similar in the bar, but the courses taught are different.

Former Legal Services lawyers in private practice also have practices oriented away from wealth and power. Of former Legal Services

Table 8.3

Professional Positions at Time of Interview for Lawyers Who Left Legal Services[a]

	Percentage	
	Former Legal Services lawyers	Lawyers in bar
Distribution within private practice		
Solo practice	43	27
Small firm (2–4 lawyers)	43	37
Medium firm (5–9 lawyers)	10	17
Larger firm (10+ lawyers)	4	18
Total	100	99
N	92	621
Distribution of other jobs		
Nonlaw job	13	30
Salaried counsel for business	3	30
Legal rights work[b]	15	2
Activist government agency[b]	16	2
Other salaried counsel (mostly government agencies)	43	30
University faculty	10	7
Total	100	101
N	77	306

[a] White males only; distribution year of graduation of lawyers in the bar standardized to that of lawyers in Legal Services.
[b] Defined in text.

lawyers in private practice, 86% (compared to 64% of the bar) are either in solo practice or in small firms and consequently deal almost exclusively with the affairs of individuals with low or moderate incomes or those of relatively small business. Only a very small percentage of former Legal Services lawyers are associated with firms of 10 or more members, and virtually none have moved into the major firms, which often have over 100 lawyers and handle the affairs of the major corporations and of wealthy individuals (Smigel, 1964). By contrast, 18% of the bar are in firms with 10 or more lawyers. Lawyers who had been in Legal Services not only chose smaller firms or solo practice, they also chose somewhat smaller communities to live in. But as Table 8.4 shows, former Legal Services lawyers have much smaller firm size, even when city size is controlled.

Table 8.4

Average Firm Size by City Size[a]

| | 1967 Legal Services lawyers | | Lawyers in bar | |
City size	Firm size	N^b	Firm size	N^b
Under 100,000	2.0	46	4.2	296
100,000–600,000	3.5	33	10.8	137
Over 600,000	3.0	13[c]	16.5	188
Total	2.7	92	9.5	621

[a] White males only, standardized by year of graduation; private practice only, solo practice counted as firm size of one.
[b] N indicates basis of average.
[c] An average calculated on such a small N is unstable.

Further Differences within Private Practice

Firm size is a traditional indicator of the type of work engaged in by a lawyer in private practice (Carlin, 1966; Ladinsky, 1963), but as such it is really a proxy for several aspects of practice such as types of clients (business rather than individuals; relatively wealthy business and individuals), income, types of courts appeared in (federal and state appeals rather than lower state and county courts), physical work setting, types of cases (corporate, commercial, or tax, as opposed to matrimonial, criminal, or personal injury). This section compares the former Legal Services lawyers and the sample of the bar on some of these and related dimensions, as well as on the composite status of practice index. (Here and throughout the rest of the chapter, the comparison is for white males only, with the year of graduation of lawyers in the bar standardized to the distribution of Legal Services lawyers.)

For all these indicators of professional work in private practice, former Legal Services lawyers show patterns different from those shown by lawyers in the bar. Major areas of practice are shown in Table 8.5.[5] Legal Services lawyers are much less likely to designate business or real estate as their areas of practice and far more likely to mention criminal or marital work. They also report less work in litigation or wills, trusts, and estates. Former Legal Services lawyers do different kinds of work because to some extent those are the types of work associated with small firms. Small firms do much less business work

[5] See Appendix A for methodology of grouping major areas of practice.

Table 8.5

Major Areas of Practice[a]

Areas	1967 Legal Services lawyers	Lawyers in bar
Business	8	29
Wills, trusts, estates	10	11
Real estate	12	16
Litigation	7	10
Personal injury	12	12
Criminal	17	8
Civil	15	4
Marital	17	4
Other	3	5
Total	101	99
N	91	621

[a] White males only, standardized by year of graduation; private practice only.

and more civil, marital, and criminal work in general. Nevertheless, former Legal Services lawyers do even more criminal and marital work than lawyers in small firms average.

We asked our respondents first how they divided their time between business and individual clients and then in more detail about the wealth of the businesses and the individuals. As Table 8.6 shows, former Legal Services lawyers said they spent much less time with business clients than the other lawyers did, regardless of whether firm or solo practice. When city size is controlled, the findings are similar. Although legal work for businesses increases with both firm size and

Table 8.6

Average Time with Business Clients[a]

Type of firm	1967 Legal Services lawyers		Lawyers in bar	
	Percentage	N[b]	Percentage	N[b]
Solo	22	41	32	226
Firm	35	51	55	395
All private practitioners	29	92	48	621

[a] White males only; private practice only; standardized by year of graduation.
[b] Numbers on which mean percentage is based.

city size, overall, compared with those lawyers who have not been in Legal Services, former Legal Services lawyers are much less oriented toward business work and business clients. In all city sizes, whether solo or firm, they work primarily for individuals rather than businesses.

Furthermore, the business clients of former Legal Services lawyers are less wealthy than the clients of other lawyers. The mean wealth of business clients (see Appendix A) is 1.5, while for the matched sample it is 1.9. The difference on the scale of individual clients' wealth is similar (2.2 to 2.6), while the difference in overall client wealth is 2.4 to 2.8 (Appendix A).

Given these differences in size of firms, major area of practice, and wealth of both business and individual clients, it follows that former Legal Services lawyers earn less from their practice than the other lawyers who graduated in their cohort. This is indeed the case; the average income for former Legal Services lawyers is $25,660, while for the lawyers in the bar, standardized for year of graduation, it is $37,100. Analysis indicates that although income rises with both city size and firm size, the substantial income difference between former Legal Services lawyers and the bar remains, even when these factors are controlled.

Firm size, client wealth, and professional earnings are variables that have traditionally been seen by both lay people and lawyers as dimensions of professional status. These variables are summarized in the status of practice index in Appendix A. Table 8.7 shows the distribution of this index, controlling for city size, and summarizes the differences in private practice discussed so far.[6]

Lawyers were asked what percentage of their firms' (or their own, for solos) clients were members of minority groups. White males who had been in Legal Services reported having more minority clients than did lawyers in the bar—24% versus 14%. (When blacks and women from Legal Services are included, the comparison is more striking—33% versus 14%.) As we shall see, this difference in percentage of minority clients is to a large extent a consequence of other facets of practice.

---

[6] Analysis also indicates that regardless of area of practice, the practice status of the former Legal Services lawyers remains lower. That is, former Legal Services lawyers do not have a lower practice status only because they tend to work in different areas of practice than the standardized sample from the bar; even when they work in the same areas, there are differences between the two groups of lawyers. In other words, a former Legal Services lawyer whose major area of practice is criminal or personal injury will have a poorer clientele, earn less money, and be in a smaller firm than a criminal or personal injury lawyer who had not been in Legal Services and who graduated in a comparable year.

Table 8.7

Average Score, Status of Practice Index by City Size[a]

	1967 Legal Services lawyers		Lawyers in bar	
City size	Percentage	N^b	Percentage	N^b
Under 100,000	3.1	46	4.4	296
100,000–600,000	3.4	33	5.4	137
Over 600,000	3.0	13[c]	5.6	188
All cities	3.2	92	5.0	621

[a] White males only; standardized by year of graduation; private practice only.
[b] Numbers on which mean percentage is based.
[c] Mean based on such a small N is unreliable.

In terms of pro bono activities, former Legal Services lawyers differ substantially from the matched sample. Those now in private practice report spending a greater portion of their billable hours doing pro bono work, regardless of whether they are in firms or solo practice. The average time spent by white male former Legal Services lawyers was 8.5% of billable hours, versus 6% for the bar. The pattern holds regardless of city size, but the difference was larger in the biggest cities. Former Legal Services lawyers in private practice are also likely to do more pro bono work in their nonbillable hours, reporting an average of 42 hours per year, as compared to 30 for the standardized sample of the bar.

More important, lawyers who have been in Legal Services are more likely to report pro bono work for underrepresented individuals and groups. This can be clearly seen in Table 8.8, which combines public interest activities in billable and nonbillable hours. As the table shows, former Legal Services lawyers are much more likely to do reform-oriented work in both billable and nonbillable hours.[7] Tables 8.9 and 8.10 show the breakdowns for billable and nonbillable hours in a manner analogous to that used in Chapter 5. The numbers (Ns) in these tables is the number of responses, running two or three per lawyer,

[7] The analysis in the text refers to lawyers in private practice only. Lawyers not in private practice do less pro bono work, but differences between the two groups are still evident. The major difference is in the clients served, with former Legal Services lawyers much more likely to undertake work with individuals or groups challenging traditional institutions or to work with Legal Services. In the types of work done for public interest clients, former Legal Services lawyers also assumed a more active role, doing much more litigation.

Table 8.8

Social Reform pro Bono Work[a]

	Percentage	
Type	1967 Legal Services lawyers	Lawyers in bar
None[b]	58	73
Billable hours only	16	14
Nonbillable hours only	12	9
Both	14	4
Total	100	100
N	92	621

[a] White males only, standardized by year of graduation; private practice only.
[b] Either no pro bono work or none oriented toward social reform.

rather than the number of lawyers, as in Table 8.8. These tables do not show the trend as clearly as does Table 8.8.

In sum, we have described the private practices of former Legal Services lawyers and how they differ from a standardized sample of the bar. Former Legal Services lawyers were more likely to be in solo practice or in smaller firms; to spend more time with individual clients;

Table 8.9

Pro Bono Clients, Billable Hours[a]

	Percentage	
Clients	1967 Legal Services lawyers	Lawyers in bar
Individuals		
Criminal	16	19
Reform oriented	13	10
Other	37	43
Organizations		
Traditional	12	17
Reform oriented	15	7
Legal aid–public defender	7	3
Total	100	99
N[b]	140	762

[a] White males only, standardized by year of graduation; private practice only.
[b] Indicates number of responses from lawyers doing pro bono work.

Table 8.10

Pro Bono Clients, Nonbillable Hours[a]

	Percentage	
Clients	1967 Legal Services lawyers	Lawyers in bar
Individuals	13	14
Organizations		
Traditional	53	70
Reform oriented	21	13
Legal aid–public defender	12	4
Total	99	101
N^b	135	722

[a] White males only, standardized by year of graduation; private practice only.
[b] Number of responses from lawyers doing pro bono work.

to have less wealthy business clients; to work in nonbusiness areas such as criminal and marital work; to earn less from their professional work; to have more minority clients; and to do more pro bono work, especially that oriented toward social change.

Perhaps an important part of the explanation of these differences is that former Legal Services lawyers have "lost" professional time as a result of being in Legal Services. The argument would hold that their Legal Services work would not give the same type of on-the-job training as being in private practice and that the relevant group with which to compare them would therefore be younger graduates. Accordingly, we adjusted the year of graduation of former Legal Services lawyers by subtracting their years of Legal Services experience and then re-standardized the year of graduation of the sample from the bar to match the new distribution of those formerly in Legal Services. Even with this adjustment, substantial differences remain between the law practices of those who have been in Legal Services and of those who have not. The former Legal Services lawyers are still more likely to be in solo practice or smaller firms, and to have more individual clients rather than business clients, less wealthy business and individual clients, more minority and public interest clients, etc. All of the differences already described between former Legal Services and the standardized sample from the bar remain, and they are about as large. The argument that lost time in Legal Services is largely responsible for differences in practice is not supported.

CONTROLS FOR BACKGROUND VARIABLES

Let us now turn to our second task, that of evaluating whether these observed differences in subsequent careers are attributable to the Legal Services experience or products of a predisposition to social reform work which would account for both the participation in Legal Services and the apparent effects of that participation.

The primary question to be addressed here is whether the operation of a government-sponsored social reform program such as Legal Services is essentially at the margin of the profession, with participants simply taking time out to "do good" for the indigent citizen; or, alternatively, whether such a program can act as a channeling mechanism, substantially redirecting the careers of those lawyers who pass through it, thus effecting a redistribution of professional services in society.

A variety of variables have been examined in the literature to predict the positions and work patterns of professionals. It has been argued that social background variables affect careers, in that people acquire different exposures as a result of variations in parents' occupations,

Table 8.11

Effect of Participation in the Legal Services Program on Characteristics of Private Practice (White Males Only)

	Dependent variables		
	Index of status of practice (range 0–18)	Percentage of minority clients (range 0–100)	Does social reform pro bono work (range 0–1)
Average score, lawyers in bar	5.02	14	.24
Average score, Legal Services Without controls	3.22	26	.42
Controlling for year of graduation and background and educational factors[a]	3.33	23	.40
Controlling for factors above,[a] plus status of practice index score	—	21	.39

[a] These factors are entered as sets of dummy variables.

education, and income; home environment; concern with politics and social issues; and personal experiences in law schools of different qualities (see, for example, Carlin, 1962, 1966; Ladinsky, 1964, 1967; Lortie, 1959). The type of job a lawyer accepts at the beginning of his career is similarly thought to be systematically related to later professional work characteristics. To separate the effects of these variables on current job from the effect of having been in Legal Services, we have used regression analysis, a statistical technique for specifying the strength of relationships when other variables are taken into account or controlled.

The analysis here will concentrate on three aspects of private practice: the status of practice index, the percentage of minority clients, and the propensity to do pro bono work oriented to social reform. Table 8.11 shows how these three characteristics are affected by simultaneous controls for family characteristics (father's political stance, parents' participation in social reform organizations, mother's religion, and father's occupation); educational characteristics (type of law school attended, reported class standing); political involvements prior to graduation; and year of graduation from law school.[8] (Several other control variables were analyzed, but did not affect the findings reported below.)

The table indicates that these control variables have little effect on the tendency for Legal Services lawyers to avoid those types of practice that have traditionally been accorded high status and to do more reform-oriented pro bono work.[9] Percentage of minority clients is reduced

---

[8] Although the relationships among these control variables and the direct and indirect effects of these variables on current job would be of some substantive interest, these considerations are not relevant to the task at hand. Rather, the analysis here seeks only to gauge the effect of participation in Legal Services on the lawyer's subsequent career, not of the effect of these controls. Hence in the analysis of spuriousness, control variables were for the most part entered into the model in one group. (When Legal Services lawyers are compared to the bar as a whole, prior job is omitted. For reasons explained later, prior job is added to the other controls only after lawyers with stable job histories are dropped from the control group.)

[9] Tables 8.10 and 8.11 are based on dummy variable regression (multiple classification analysis), a variant of the general linear model (Cohen, 1968). A global test for interactions in which each category of each control variable was interacted with the variable "participation in Legal Services" indicated that for each dependent variable addition of the interaction terms did not significantly increase the corrected R^2.

For the dichotomous variable "does social reform pro bono work," analysis was also done using a logit model (Theil, 1971), a log-linear model which yields more accurate estimates than regression when the dependent variable is dichotomous. This analysis yielded stronger findings than those reported in the text for the regression analysis; the Legal Services effect was actually somewhat greater with the control variables than without. The regression findings are presented in the table because they are more easily interpretable.

somewhat more than the other variables (from 26% to 23%) and an additional control for status of practice reduces it further (to 21%). At this point, however, the difference between participants and nonparticipants in the percentage of minority clients is still statistically significant ($p = .005$).[10] The Legal Services effect for the status of practice and pro bono variables seems to operate primarily in an additive fashion to the control variables.

Let us now consider the effect of control for prior jobs on the findings for the three characteristics of private practice. Prior job is a critical control variable, since about three-fourths of former Legal Services lawyers moved into the program from other jobs, and one would expect the contacts and experiences of those jobs to influence the types of jobs held subsequent to being in the program. To analyze the influence of prior jobs, the most appropriate control group to which Legal Services lawyers can be compared is one composed of other lawyers who changed jobs during the period from 1965 to 1968, a period roughly equivalent to the span of time in which Legal Services lawyers joined the program. Since lawyers are rarely fired and tend, once established, to stay in jobs for long periods of time, most lawyers are not on the market, and thus their careers cannot appropriately be compared to those of the more mobile lawyers.[11]

The job held by a lawyer prior to making a job shift in the period from 1965 to 1968 is a relatively good predictor of the job held in 1973–1974. Lawyers who were in solo practice in the earlier period are more likely to have a relatively low status of practice in the later period; lawyers who were in larger firms have higher status practices in the later period, etc. But the important point for the analysis here is that for two of the dependent variables (status of practice and reform-oriented pro bono work), the effect of participation in Legal Services appears to be independent of the effect of prior jobs (Table 8.12). However, when background, status of practice, and prior job are all controlled, the difference in the percentage of clients who are members of minority groups is no longer statistically significant (Table 8.12). With all the controls, the

---

[10] Fractional weights were used, so the significance level is not affected by any artificial increase in sample size. However, the significance level is not as accurate as with a true random sample because the weighting scheme used sacrifices some efficiency in sample design. Because of the relatively large N, rather small coefficients are statistically significant. Hence significance levels are not shown in the tables, but for small coefficients are reported in the text for reference by the interested reader.

[11] Ideally, the control group would be lawyers who changed jobs during the earlier period and then changed again in the late 1960s or early 1970s; but this criterion would yield too small an N for analysis.

Table 8.12

Effect of Participation in the Legal Services Program on Characteristics of Private Practice[a]

	Dependent variables		
	Index of status of practice (range 0–18)	Percentage of minority clients (range 0–100)	Does social reform pro bono work (range 0–1)
Average score, lawyers in bar	4.61	17	.24
Average score, Legal Services Without controls	2.98	27	.44
Controlling for year of graduation and background and educational factors[b]	2.94	23	.43
Controlling for factors above, plus job left 1965–1968[b]	2.96	23	.44
Controlling for all of the above,[b] plus status of practice index	—	19	.41

[a] Table includes only white male Legal Services lawyers who had prior jobs and other lawyers who changed jobs in the period from 1965 to 1968. N = 210.
[b] These factors are entered as sets of dummy variables.

difference between former Legal Services lawyers and lawyers in the bar is just two percentage points. The observed difference in percentage of minority clients is thus attributable partly to differences in background, education, and prior job and partly to an indirect effect associated with the lower status clientele served.

The Question of Self-Selection

Note that the argument above, which sees subsequent careers as being in part a result of the Legal Services experience, does not require the absence of self-selection. Rather, the argument is that in the case of self-selection, socialization, training, and especially the job market factors would tend to reinforce the decision. In short, lawyers join Legal Services for a variety of reasons, but overall, participation tends to decrease the probability that they will pursue the traditional routes to success.

The importance of program effects as opposed to self-selection effects can also be seen in a comparison of lawyers who stated different motives for joining the program. Legal Services lawyers gave three general types of reasons for joining: reasons that appear to have an explicit social reform content ("I felt I had a duty to help the poor, I wanted to work with these types of issues"); reasons that might include a social reform component (the types of cases would be "challenging," the job afforded "community contacts," etc.); and reasons that appear to include only personal factors (the desire to gain practical experience, the location of the office, the steady income). If the observed effects of participation in Legal Services were spurious, then one would expect that the effects would be strongest for those lawyers who report a reformist motivation for joining. However, there are no statistically significant differences among the three groups on the dependent variables. Moreover, insofar as there are differences, lawyers explicitly citing a social reform motivation for joining are actually somewhat lower than either of the other groups in both the percentage of minority clients served and the rendering of reform-oriented pro bono work.

The Effect of Variation in Experience

One important further consideration in the analysis of the effects of participation in Legal Services is the effect of variation in the experience of different participants. Probably the greatest difference in experience in Legal Services occurred between lawyers engaged in law reform and those doing service work. As noted earlier, from the outset Legal Services had dual aims: serving the immediate needs of individual clients through direct adjudication of their cases; and changing the laws affecting the poor, primarily through class action or test case litigation. Those lawyers who spent a significant amount of their time on law reform work experienced a very different milieu; in some local programs, they even worked in different offices (Carlin, 1970).

While doing law reform work, a lawyer had substantially less direct contact with clients than did other Legal Services lawyers. Most of the time on such litigation is spent researching the law, preparing lengthy briefs, appearing before the court, and (on occasion) preparing appeals to higher courts. In doing this work, the Legal Services lawyer may have undergone a different type of socialization and training from that of the lawyer doing service work exclusively. First, the political component of his or her work was different, being focused on change in the centers of power rather than change for discrete individuals. Second, lawyers in this type of work might be expected to put a premium on meticulousness, skill in legal research, and ability to draft complex briefs. For lawyers doing service work, the pressures were different. Our data indicate that these lawyers carried heavy caseloads, generally averaging over 100 open files at a time. With this type of workload, a lawyer, no matter how conscientious, was still in a situation in which he or she could not pursue every angle of a case or devote much attention to detail. The different combinations of socialization, training, and concomitant job information networks and employer preferences seem to lead to different subsequent careers for lawyers engaged in the two types of work in Legal Services.

The lawyer who worked on law reform may be expected to take one of two career paths. One would be to continue the same type of work, albeit in a different context. This would mean employment in an activist government agency, a public interest law firm, a reform-oriented foundation like the NAACP Legal Defense Fund, or possibly a university. The other would be to go into the type of private practice that has traditionally been accorded high status and in which one would have opportunities to deal with complex matters and delve deeply into the intricacies of the law. As a consequence of this type of private practice, these lawyers might be expected to continue to have low contact with minority clients. However, because of the type of cases handled in Legal Services, one might expect such lawyers to be more likely to engage in pro bono work oriented to social change.

Lawyers who basically spent their time on service cases might be expected to take rather different subsequent careers. If they remain out of private practice, they might be expected to move to some of the variety of agencies doing service work for groups underrepresented in the legal system, such as public defenders' offices (which handle criminal matters, as opposed to the primarily civil cases handled by Legal Services), other offices working with the poor, or to different Legal Services local programs that offered some amenities like directorships, better colleagues, or better places to live. If these lawyers went into private practice, we might expect them to be more likely to deal with lower status clients in general, and with minority clients in particular.

While this discussion is limited to socialization or training, consideration of the possible effects of the job information network and of employer preferences leads to similar expectations. Legal Services lawyers are likely to come in contact with lawyers in private practice working with similar kinds of clients and on similar cases. A lawyer doing service cases would be particularly unlikely to come into contact with an attorney from a major corporate firm and, for example, learn of an opening for a good tax lawyer there. In addition, in this example, the senior partner for tax matters is likely to view the Legal Services lawyer as untrained for work in the firm.

The lawyer engaged in law reform litigation would be much more likely than other Legal Services lawyers to come in contact with lawyers in federal agencies, universities, and (to a lesser extent) major firms, both through writing briefs and through appearances at higher level courts. And of course, the same skills that made the lawyer who worked on law reform interested in a higher-status practice involving more complicated affairs or in an elite position outside of private practice would also make that lawyer more attractive to such potential employers. If the lawyer were to go out on his own or to form a firm with one or more colleagues, one might expect similar processes to operate. It seems reasonable to expect that lawyers who worked on law reform would be different from those who worked on service cases in terms of the types of colleagues interested in going into practice with them, the potential clients known, and the potential clients likely to be attracted.

Only about 15% of the lawyers in Legal Services spent a majority of their time on law reform work, but half spent an average of at least 1 day a week. Analysis indicates that insofar as doing law reform work has an effect on subsequent careers, it affects lawyers who did 1 day a week or more rather than those who did less than one day a week. White male lawyers who were engaged in law reform work are less likely to be found in private practice than are other Legal Services lawyers. However, contrary to expectations, the particular type of job taken outside of private practice does not seem to have been affected by the law reform experience.

On the other hand, having done law reform work does seem to affect two of the three indicators of type of current work for lawyers in private practice. Lawyers who did law reform work are much more likely to be successful, by traditional criteria. Controlling for all the variables discussed in the previous section (including prior job), the mean status of practice for these lawyers is 3.8, as compared to 2.8 for lawyers who almost exclusively did service work. (This higher status of practice does not, however, reduce the percentage of minority clients, which is the same for both groups.) In addition, lawyers who did law reform work in Legal Services are more likely to do social-change oriented pro bono work in private practice; the adjusted percentage is 48% versus 39% for lawyers who had almost all service cases. This difference is not, however, statistically significant. It is important to note that for both these dependent variables the effect of variation in experience within the organization is additive to the effect of the participation in the organization itself. The high status of practice score for lawyers who worked on law reform and the low social reform pro bono score for lawyers who did not are still substantially different from those of the control group.

A program characteristic somewhat related to law reform work is the quality of local office in which the lawyer served. Some programs achieved high reputations in social reform circles for the quality of their work and their aggressiveness in pursuit of client interests. Usually these local programs engaged in a good deal of law reform work, but they did extensive service work as well. It is of interest, then, whether difference in milieu affected subsequent careers. The data indicate that lawyers in private practice who were in these elite programs (as defined by our panel) have a slightly lower status of practice than lawyers from the other local programs but that they are less likely to have minority clients. However, these differences are not statistically significant. (There is no difference in the percentage rendering reform-oriented pro bono work.)

Two other variations in experience for which indicators are available are length of service in the organization and service as a local program director. Lawyers who left the program after staying for relatively long periods of time might be more likely to choose to remain outside of private practice, and subsequent jobs may also depend on the type of work—service or law reform—done in Legal Services. But analysis shows that length of service has no direct or interactive effects on subsequent career. For the local program directors, one might expect that since they had been in administrative jobs they would acquire skills and contacts that would be likely to lead to similar employment. The data indicate, however, no clear tendency in this regard. In addition, former directors in private practice are not different from former staff lawyers in terms of status of practice, percentage of minority clients, or propensity to do social reform pro bono work.

CONCLUSIONS

Given the limits of the data, the conclusions here must be tentative;[12] but within these limitations, the data for white male Legal Services lawyers clearly indicate that participation in the program leads to a

[12] Limitations in study design as well as some of the methodological problems involved in assessing the impact of programs such as Legal Services on the careers of participants are discussed in Erlanger (1977).

redistribution of service among lawyers in private practice. Former Legal Services lawyers in private practice have less prestigious practices (as measured by the traditional indicators of types of clients, types of work setting, and professional income), and they do more pro bono work oriented to social reform than do other lawyers of comparable background and experience. Former Legal Services lawyers who do not go into private practice also seem to have careers quite different from those of their counterparts in the bar; most especially, they seem to shun corporate counsel and nonlaw jobs. Variations in experience within the program affect subsequent career, but they are not so important as the effect of participation itself.

IV

CONCLUSIONS

9

Structured Opportunity and Careers in Legal Rights Activities

SUMMARY OF FINDINGS

Three types of questions were raised in Chapter 1: One dealt with the apparent rise and decline of legal rights activities; another with the nature of the involvement of lawyers who engaged in legal rights activities; and the third with the implications of legal rights work for the poor. In this chapter, we summarize the findings on these questions and discuss their policy implications.

We defined legal rights activities to include legal representation of groups or individuals who for whatever reasons were unable to obtain their share of legal services. Within this broad spectrum, we described the history and activities of organizations and private practitioners engaged in legal rights activities. Contrary to popular accounts emphasizing fads and lack of permanence, we found a rich variety of legal rights activities. Lawyers were providing services to the unrepresented in a range of settings—in government programs, in the voluntary sector, as part of private practice, and through the organized bar. There was also great variety in the style and goals of the several kinds of legal rights activities. Within each of the settings, one could find traditional services, aggressive services, or mixtures. At least by the mid-1970s, there was no slackening in the growth and proliferation of legal rights activities; indeed, the situation was the reverse.

The growth of legal rights activities has not been uniform with respect to either amount or character. Rather, it reflected larger political and social conditions in society. Prior to the 1960s, there were two types of emphasis. One was traditional legal rights represented through legal aid, the assigned counsel and a rudimentary public defender system, and the pro bono activities of private practitioners. This tradition, although stretching back to the nineteenth century, was a miserly effort on the part of the bar. Yet in terms of professional time it far overshadowed the other emphasis, which was the aggressive work of the NAACP, the ACLU, and a few other organizations. In the activist period of the 1960s and early 1970s, the aggressive tradition expanded to include a great many organizations and involve substantial professional time. The older organizations, such as the NAACP, the NAACP Inc. Fund, and the ACLU grew; OEO Legal Services came into being as well as the Nader groups, public interest law firms, and law communes. These organizations attracted a great deal of attention. At the same time, traditional legal rights activities also expanded. Defender programs and legal aid societies received infusions of federal funding, and there was also a growth of bar association and private service organizations for the poor. In terms of size and resources, the pre-1960s disparity continued; traditional legal rights activities—as evidenced by pro bono activities of private practitioners, many bar association organizations, most defender programs, and parts of Legal Services— were much larger than aggressive legal rights activities. Looking at the profession as a whole, then, we note the overall growth of legal rights activities with the continued domination of traditional activities.

The effects of organizations, of course, cannot be measured simply by counting their existence. The kinds of professionals they attract affect the work of the organizations and their impact on society. Who, then, works in legal rights activities?

During the period of the study, OEO Legal Services rose in prominence and then fell on hard times politically. At the same time, there was a rise in alternative opportunities for legal rights careers. Despite these changes, however, we found that recruitment into Legal Services remained fairly strong and constant; sizable numbers of young lawyers continued to seek positions, and to be recruited from a broad base of the professional population representing a wide spectrum of law schools and academic performance.

Not only did recruitment remain strong, perhaps even more significant are the findings concerning the continued commitments of these lawyers. The hypothesis of this study is that there is a steady stream of lawyers whose involvement in legal rights activities is long-term; that is, at least within the time frame of this study, their legal rights activities have continued beyond the usual time in a particular legal rights job. Our standard for measuring this involvement is deviation from conventional professional career choices. Indicators of such commitment are (a) long-term continuation in Legal Services jobs; (b) nonprivate practice jobs, including teaching, government, or not-for-profit organizations but excluding jobs in commercial establishments such as banks and corporations; (c) jobs in public interest law firms that are either foundation supported, self-designated by the lawyers, or law communes, and (d) private practice which either has pro bono activities different from those of other private practitioners or is of a lower status on the traditional dimensions than is the practice of lawyers of similar age, social background, and education.

We have compared data on two types of lawyers—surveys of lawyers who are or have been in legal rights activities jobs and a random sample of those lawyers who have never been in legal rights activities jobs. For the moment, we are assuming that all lawyers are potentially mobile. For example, if we find a lawyer who has stayed in Legal Services 2 years beyond the normal duration for Legal Services lawyers, we assume that he or she had the choice of leaving Legal Services and getting a law job in private practice or in the business community.

We regard the inference that remaining in Legal Services is evidence of a continuing involvement in legal rights as a relatively noncontroversial judgment. Other nonconventional career choices may not be so obviously linked to continuing commitments. It may seem strange that we count as a continued involvement a former Legal Services lawyer who is now a law school professor enjoying the prestige, comforts, and tenure of academic life at a comfortable salary. Still, former Legal Services lawyers on faculties differ from the average law school teachers. Legal academics are, without doubt, paying a large price for their tastes; but for most, these tastes are not legal rights commitments. Most law professors are not former legal rights activities lawyers; they are simply paying for a different way of life. However, former legal rights lawyers are, for the most part, teaching courses related to their prior work, such as poverty, consumer, criminal, clinical, and related matters. Few are completely embedded in the conventional curriculum. Former Legal Services lawyers are, in fact, not appreciably more likely than other lawyers to be academics: The difference lies in the courses they teach. Similarly, former Legal Services lawyers disproportionately enter government work; moreover, they tend to select government work that favors the disadvantaged (e.g., the Civil Rights Division of the U.S. Department of Justice).

The third unconventional career choice is public interest or related kinds of jobs. As noted in Chapters 4 and 6, either these firms are entirely financed by charitable contributions, or, if they are in the private sector, they are self-proclaimed public interest law firms and law communes. These lawyers have consciously identified themselves with legal rights activities; compared to their peers, they perform a different kind of legal work and at a considerable economic sacrifice.

The fourth career choice involves the most controversial and interesting finding of the study. As pointed out in Chapter 1, those who noted the exit of lawyers from Legal Services and other legal rights activities jobs to private practice assumed that that career change represented the end of social reform involvement. Private practice was usually viewed as homogeneous, as law for the rich against the poor and unrepresented. But this assumption is unwarranted. There are many reasons why lawyers leave legal rights activities jobs, especially Legal Services, and move into private practice. The nature and types of practice these lawyers went into had to be examined before passing judgment as to whether private practice necessarily meant the end of legal rights involvement. We took as evidence of a continuing involvement the existence of either of two conditions in private practice: (a) The pro bono work performed by the lawyer was greater in quantity and more oriented toward social reform than the norm of the bar; or (b) the practice was of a lower status than the norm of the bar. By lower status, we refer to the traditional criteria of status (not necessarily those held by legal rights lawyers): a less wealthy clientele; more individual work than business work; less corporate, commercial, real estate work; smaller firms; more minority clients; and lower professional incomes. If the former legal rights lawyers are choosing a practice lower in status than their matched cohorts, then this amounts to a redistribution of private practice services and is evidence of a continuing commitment to social reform.

We have two sets of independent variables to relate to long-term career choices. One set deals with the standard battery of background variables—socioeconomic position of the family, political and religious influences, education, and so forth. Popular accounts hold that lawyers recruited into legal rights activities come from liberal, elitist backgrounds or, conversely, from lower-class backgrounds. We found that the background variables were not related to the career choice. Lawyers who took jobs in legal rights activities were little different from the rest of the bar in terms of background characteristics. What is the explanation for the lack of relationship?

When the lawyers entered the activities we are concerned with—first civil rights and poverty and later environment, consumer, and other public interest law work—these were not radical positions. These activities were supported by influential, legitimate parts of society—government (during the Kennedy and Johnson years), foundations, the national media, and other important segments of white, northern liberal support. Their appeal was not to the fringe elements of society but to broader elements, and certainly to the middle or upper middle class. The vast majority of lawyers come from these classes. There are differences in backgrounds of lawyers, but they are not great. Small proportions of the bar come from poor families, but it is not clear whether such backgrounds produce radicalism. It would be expected, then, that the dominant reform ideas of the time, while not affecting all lawyers, would at least be widely diffused. Most legal rights activities are not especially radical or deviant. Legal Services never had the poor professional reputation of legal aid. For a time, it was highly fashionable, and it certainly remains professionally respectable. Many of the newer legal rights jobs are glamorous. Working conditions for most of the jobs are not particularly onerous, and the lawyers can and do live respectable middle-class lives. In other words, with legal rights activities, we are talking about a mild type of professional reformism that would be expected to have a broadly based appeal. To the extent that specific legal rights jobs deviate from this model, then background variables would become more relevant. For example, working in a law commune requires a great deal more sacrifice and commitment, and here we expected and found more of the popular stereotype—white radicals of liberal background and elite education. The newer public interest law firms chiefly recruit lawyers with elite educational backgrounds. But without these two exceptions, one would expect a large-scale, mildly reformist, establishment-supported activity to have a diffuse, widespread appeal among younger lawyers; and this is what we found.

In contrast, the second set of independent variables is crucial. These are the actual job experiences in legal rights activities. The hypothesis of this study is that it is the *structured* experience (i.e., the legal rights activities job) that will have the most important predictive effect on continued participation in legal rights activities. The hypothesis was tested and confirmed for Legal Services lawyers, the largest group by far in the sample. We found that—controlling for age and other background factors—Legal Services lawyers who left their jobs went disproportionately into government, other jobs outside of private practice (but not commercial establishments), or public interest jobs; or, if they went into private practice, they did more and a different kind of pro bono work or had lower-status practices.

What explains this relationship? Since there has never been an experiment dealing with the career paths of lawyers, we can only draw inferences as to the causes of the observed relationships. This returns us to the question of choice and the effects of the experience in legal rights activities. Specifically, would these lawyers have chosen the alternative career paths anyway, without regard to the legal rights activities experience; or once they had chosen legal rights jobs, was the attraction or availability of careers in traditional private practice thereby decreased? On the basis of our research design and findings, these questions cannot be answered definitively. As previously stated, relationships between background and political socialization variables, on the one hand, and career choices, on the other, do not explain away our findings. Of course, this does not necessarily mean that our findings are correct; it could be that our variables were faulty in their ability to measure the relevant characteristics; for example, it may be that those who go into legal rights activities are already on a different career track but cannot be discriminated by the questions that we asked. Although we cannot be sure that this did not happen, we think that the weight of the evidence is the other way; there was a strong relationship between Legal Services work and subsequent career choices. What follows is our view of the causal relationships.

We think that the legal rights activities experience has an additive effect on widely diffused general reformist tendencies. Our interpretation focuses on lawyers who have been somewhat influenced by the ideology of the times—civil rights, the War on Poverty, Ralph Nader, the environmental and consumer movements, and so forth—and would like to participate in a concrete manner. However, they are from the middle class and have had little or no contact with minorities, the poor, or nontraditional work settings. Unless they have such experiences, their reformist tendencies are not fulfilled, and through fear of the unknown they enter into regular professional career paths. Perhaps they do pro bono work, but it is of a traditional nature—for example, for charities and individual service cases rather than for organizations challenging the status quo. On the other hand, if they have actual work experience in a legal rights organization, the fears of the unknown are removed, and they learn that they can work and function in a formerly strange social milieu. We think that this process is especially true with upper-middle-class lawyers working with the poor and minorities, people with whom they would not be likely to come into contact in law school or in traditional private practice positions.

If, as we suggest, one of the important determinants of career choice is the actual experience with different social classes, especially the poor and minorities, then there may be functional equivalents to Legal Services jobs. Thus, we would expect the same effects on lawyers who worked in civil rights (e.g., the NAACP, Inc. Fund) or worked directly with minorities and the poor in nonlegal jobs—for example, civil rights work during college. Unfortunately, not enough lawyers in our surveys participated in these types of experiences to test this hypothesis. In the main, we are restricted to former Legal Services lawyers.

Our theory of the importance of experience with unknown social classes explains the career paths of the Legal Services lawyers but does not explain the career paths of the smaller, but still not insignificant, number of lawyers who go into environmental, consumer, and other kinds of public interest law work. Because of the recent origin of most of the public interest law firms, not enough lawyers have left them to permit definitive answers about subsequent career paths to be found; but of those who have left, the evidence clearly indicates that lawyers formerly associated with public interest law firms generally do not go into traditional private practice. As with the former Legal Services lawyers, they disproportionately enter government or other kinds of public interest law work (see Weisbrod, Handler, and Komesar, forthcoming).

We again stress the importance of structured career opportunities as the important additive element affecting career choice. But how much of an additive element is less certain. Public interest lawyers, as distinguished from Legal Services lawyers, come from more elite backgrounds; therefore, without public interest law jobs, they would tend to go into large firms, government, or teaching. In these jobs, they would be able to pursue some legal rights activities, especially causes and interests that were more oriented toward the middle and upper-middle classes. Their legal rights activity would be less than that of former Legal Services lawyers but probably somewhat more and of a different kind than that of their age-matched cohorts in the bar with less elite backgrounds.

In what ways do structured opportunities determine subsequent career choices? The experience socializes and trains reform-minded lawyers into particular work and social settings. This serves to break down barriers, remove fears of the unknown, familiarize them with particular issues, and open up choices that they may have been only dimly aware of. Structured experiences produce two other effects that determine subsequent career paths. The lawyers become specialized in a particular kind of practice, and this serves to limit their opportunities in a number of different ways. Poverty lawyers, particularly those with heavy service caseloads, develop skills that are not readily marketable with traditional law firms, especially those with business clients. Public interest lawyers develop litigation skills that are sometimes marketable with high-status law firms, but these lawyers suffer other disabilities. High-status law firms are usually large, and such firms try to avoid lateral entry at levels above the youngest associates. The firms make exceptions, but usually only for a lawyer with particularly sought after experience—e.g., securities, antitrust—which usually does not apply to a former public interest lawyer. In addition, there is some impressionistic evidence that private practice lawyers may discriminate against lawyers who have been involved in legal rights activities.

The other effect of the legal rights experience is to restrict relevant market information. We know from job seeking in other occupations that people more often find jobs through informal networks (relatives, friends, coworkers, etc.) than through formal, traditional market sources such as ads, employment services, and so forth. We would expect the same behavior among lawyers. Legal Services lawyers operate in a particular milieu—lower courts and agencies, other Legal Services lawyers, lawyers in lower-status practice. This is where they will hear about other job opportunities. They will have little contact with lawyers in elite practice, and thus little opportunity to learn about or seek out jobs in higher-status practice. In other words, steps along the career ladder usually restrict job opportunities rather than expand them, and lawyers who hold nontraditional jobs are less likely to have high status jobs subsequently.

What this means is that structured opportunities in legal rights activities are important in two significant respects: They serve directly to increase the number of lawyers doing this type of work and they serve to direct lawyers to different types of clients and different types of issues. Although our findings do not necessarily rule out self-selection, they emphasize three effects of the structured opportunity—socialization and training, specialization, and restricting market information—which both affirm the choices made by self-selection and operate apart from them.

MEETING LEGAL NEEDS OF THE POOR

We have described both the proliferation of legal rights activities and organizations, and the steady stream of recruits into them, people whose commitments seem to survive their specific legal rights jobs. What implications do these findings have for the legal needs of the poor? How do the history and nature of legal rights activities relate to the legal needs of the poor and the capacity of the legal profession to respond to those needs?

Legal needs are social constructs composed of a perception first, that something is wrong and, second, that what is wrong ought to be corrected through the legal system. There are a great many social relationships which meet neither of these conditions. Many problems or wrongs remain hidden from view, and people are often unaware that wrongs are being committed against them. A common example is to be found in cases where officials do not disclose the existence of entitlements or remedies. Unless clients obtain information from other sources, they are not likely to be aware of any problem. At other times, wrongs are recognized but not considered amenable to correction by the legal system. People can feel aggrieved by government decisions or professional malpractice, for instance, but not think of the problem in terms of legal remedies. Besides the perception that a problem exists and that it is or ought to be correctable through the legal system, the final step is to persuade the sources of the law—courts, agencies, or legislatures—the need should officially be recognized as such.

Prior to the War on Poverty, few of the activities and transactions of the poor were considered legal needs. The problems of the poor were either hidden from view or otherwise unrecognized or, if recognized, not considered to be legal problems. It was known, of course, that the poor committed crimes and had their share of family problems— nonsupport, desertion, illegitimacy, and so forth—but there was little recognition of other private law problems that arise out of consumer transactions, housing, or employment. It was recognized that the poor had problems in their relations with government, in attempting to exercise the franchise, and in dealings with schools, welfare departments, and other public programs; but for many of these areas, it was thought that relations with government, although troublesome, were not capable of correction by the legal system. In technical terms, the benefits of many social programs were considered to be gratuities or privileges which the government could grant, grant conditionally, or withhold; and these relationships did not establish any legal rights or entitlements with the recipients. The theory held that since recipients were not forced to accept social welfare benefits they therefore could not complain about the conditions under which the benefits were offered (see Van Alstyne, 1968; Reich, 1964).

During the past two decades, a tremendous growth in the legal needs of the poor occurred; problems of the poor were exposed; it was argued that they were correctable through the legal system; and in a great many instances, these arguments were persuasive. Although there were many reasons for this growth, there is little doubt that a crucial role was played by aggressive legal rights organizations.

The foundation of this development was the emergence of new concepts of entitlements and of procedural due process to protect those entitlements. As discussed in Chapter 2, the pioneering work was undertaken primarily by the NAACP and later the NAACP Inc. Fund. These organizations sensitized the federal judiciary and, through the courts, the rest of the country to the existence and nature of racial discrimination and to the view that these social wrongs should be corrected through new interpretations of the equal protection and due process clauses of the Constitution. From this foundation, aggressive legal rights organizations uncovered other problems of the poor in welfare, housing, education, employment, and private transactions and cast these problems in terms of legal needs. Courts, agencies, and legislatures were persuaded that significant relations with government were legal entitlements rather than privileges or gratuities and that administrative discretion could be challenged through the exercise of due process rights.

Changes in sensitivities and perceptions and the development of new legal doctrine coincided with the rapid growth of social programs—the expansion of welfare, food stamps, health, education, employment, and antidiscrimination legislation. Statutory and administrative development was responsive to the law fashioned by aggressive legal rights, and the new programs specified legal entitlements and due process protection for the recipients. During this period, there was also the rediscovery of the traditional private law problems of the poor—family, consumer, housing, employment, crime, and delinquency. Aggressive legal rights organizations applied remedies for the poor that heretofore had only been used for the middle class; in addition, they also fashioned new remedies (such as withholding of rent) or created new structures (such as paraprofessionals and lay advocates) to handle high-volume routine tasks.

The influence of aggressive legal rights activities can be highlighted by contrasting them with the work of traditional legal aid before the advent of OEO Legal Services. Traditional legal aid, as noted, had been in existence since before the turn of the century. During that long period, the poor suffered from many problems, but for the most part these problems were either not recognized or considered incorrectable by the legal system. Legal aid restricted itself to conventional private law problems, such as contract, debt, and some family law, and even in these areas avoided cases that could offend conventional morality (there were restrictions on taking bankruptcy and divorce cases) and never undertook test-case or law reform litigation. The approach of traditional legal aid contrasted sharply to aggressive legal rights activities.

In sum, legal rights organizations, during the last two decades, have brought the energies of thousands of lawyers to bear on the problems of the poor and produced a proliferation of new concepts of public law entitlements and procedural protections and the application of remedies for traditional private law problems. The new types of organizations, by providing a structured cutting edge, have extended the recognition of legal rights of the poor and helped provide the professional talent that defined and enforced those rights. Legal Services lawyers have been the main actors in this process. Our findings indicate that the organizations, as they cycle lawyers into other professional placements, have a carryover effect in sensitizing graduates toward continuing legal rights questions.

Granted that legal rights activities have defined new rights for the poor and provided large amounts of legal services. Are the poor better off because of these efforts? Can we say that the poor have been extricated from poverty; or that earnings have increased; or that there is better schooling, housing, and health, or improved family and social relations as a result of Legal Services? As noted, OEO Legal Services was part of the War on Poverty's strategy to help the poor help themselves; as such, it was conceived as a means toward achieving antipoverty ends.

Legal Services can be viewed as an in-kind transfer. This raises the question of whether the poor would not be made better off by receiving cash and then deciding for themselves whether or not to purchase legal services. A free good will always result in high consumption; whereas under a cash system, consumer sovereignty would determine the value of the service to the poor. There are several reasons why cash grants would not be effective for legal services. The legal profession market does not seem closely to approximate a normal competitive market; we lack both theory and data as to how people select professionals, but we do know that there are problems of information and the delivery of services which we would expect to be especially severe with the poor. When OEO Legal Services was started, specific attention was paid to locating offices in neighborhoods and conducting outreach programs. A cash system would presumably rely on competitive forces to produce these results, which would be problematic in view of the slender resources available to the poor for lawyers. In addition, this is the type of commodity that has to be consumed before one knows its value; the poor (as is true with other social classes) would have to be educated as to the value of legal help before they could be expected to purchase it.

Requiring the services of lawyers, especially for the nonbusiness client, tends to be an infrequent, one-time, crisis affair. It is the type of thing the average person does not normally anticipate or prepare for, and it would be unreasonable to expect the poor to save their grants in the event legal assistance should be needed. Moreover, legal help is usually needed when the person is least able to afford it—through the loss of a job, or a welfare grant, or an apartment, or through the breakup of a family. These problems have been recognized for the middle class, and there has been a growth in prepaid legal insurance programs. There are many problems still to be ironed out in these plans, and in any event, they have not been applied to the poor; but until some such scheme is available, one would not expect that much legal assistance would be purchased under a cash grant system.

Finally, legal rights activities provide services to the poor that could not be financed under a cash grant system. We have already mentioned the location of offices in poverty neighborhoods. Another important function is law reform. Some class action suits could be financed on a contingency basis if there was an award of money damages, but these cases are relatively rare and inapplicable to many of the important problems of the poor. For example, litigation seeking to prevent changes in benefit levels or Medicaid regulations would not provide money damages out of which lawyers could be paid. These suits would simply not be brought if the only financing method required cash grants to individual clients. Legal Services offices also engage in community work and in client education and self-help programs; under a cash grant system, it would obviously not pay for lawyers to teach clients to handle their own cases. It is upon these kinds of benefits that Earl Johnson (1974, 224–234) focuses in his evaluation of the Legal Services program.

Johnson argues that the program was cost effective. In his analysis, costs were defined as federal budgetary outlays, and benefits were similarly defined in economic terms only; no allowance was made for other supposed benefits such as increased personal freedom, participation in decision making, and so forth. Johnson distinguished among three types of benefits—consumer resources (material goods and services having an immediate impact, such as food, housing, and clothing); opportunity resources to enhance capacities (training programs); and redistribution resources, which induce decision makers to alter distribution systems to provide more goods and services to the poor. The test for Legal Services was whether it produced more of these benefits to the poor than would have been provided if the total budget for the poor were merely distributed to them in cash. To answer this question, Johnson used only redistributive resources. He found that between 1965 and the end of 1972 federal outlays for Legal Services were

$290 million, whereas the total benefits to the poor resulting from about seven law reform cases amounted to over $2 billion, which exceeded the cost by a ratio of 7 to 1.

Johnson (1974) readily admits that his analysis is imprecise, but he argues that the differences between the costs and these benefits are so large that the judgment that Legal Services is cost effective is an informed appraisal. His test is severe, and counts as benefits neither consumer resources nor opportunity resources nor any of the noneconomic benefits. On the other hand, he may (as he also admits) be counting as benefits results from test cases which may not have materialized in fact or may have been wiped out by subsequent legislation or other changes in programs.[1] In any event, to the extent that Johnson is correct, the results of this study lend even more support to the conclusion that Legal Services is a cost effective antipoverty program. Johnson only counted benefits from the program itself, whereas because of the spillover effects on subsequent career paths, the former Legal Services lawyers continue to work for the poor in other professional settings. This work includes not only service (consumption resources) but also law reform.

PROSPECTS FOR LEGAL RIGHTS ACTIVITIES

In some respects, the creative role of aggressive legal services repeats a characteristic of the American legal profession. Because there is relatively open recruitment into the legal profession (Carlin, 1976), and because stratification systems within it are weak, there is still room for flexibility and the generalist problem solver. Historically, the profession has always attracted roving, restless entrepreneurs, exploring the corners and frontiers of society for new roles and new business. In the nineteenth century, frontier lawyers used their legal tools to facilitate economic and social development. In this century, lawyers pressed into other social and economic issues, and once again fashioned the legal tools—land use planning, estate and tax planning, and public administration (Handler, 1967, pp. 151–156). Aggressive legal rights lawyers are in this tradition; what is different is the subject matter. Instead of using their entrepreneurial talent for economic interests and middle- and upper-class problems, these lawyers have turned to the poor and disenfranchised in American society. They uncovered social problems and created new roles for themselves by casting these problems in terms of legal needs.

---

[1] There are, of course, differing judgments as to cost effectiveness (see, for example, Horowitz, 1977, p. 52; Hazard, 1969, p. 699).

Aggressive legal rights activities have played an important role in the perception and definition of the legal needs of the poor. What is the likelihood that this process will continue? The underlying social problems of the poor have not only not been significantly ameliorated but may even have increased since the War on Poverty. As the economic picture has darkened, there has been a retrenchment in the conception and protection of rights. Courts and administrative agencies are cutting back on the definition of substantive rights and procedural protections, producing uncertainty in the applicable law. There is increasing pressure to make social welfare programs more efficient and more regulatory. Eligibility definitions are being tightened, benefits are being excluded for certain classes of recipients, and there is more emphasis on fraud investigation, enforcement of nonsupport laws, and reduction of administrative error.

There is also an increase in administrative complexity. There is reorganization (e.g., Supplemental Security Income), which always raises problems—at least during the initial stages of a new program. There is also the growth of in-kind programs, in such areas as food, health, and employment, which raise problems of eligibility and conflicting benefits and incentives. There are trends toward decentralization and revenue sharing—for example, Title XX Social Services—which raise additional problems as new administrative structures are created or expanded at the state and local levels. There are always sorting-out periods when administrative programs are changed raising hosts of new questions and problems for the recipient populations (see Handler, forthcoming; Rabin, 1976b).

In addition, the private law needs of the poor have also probably increased. Rising or even continued high unemployment and inflationary pressures are bound to increase the consumer, housing, family, and criminal law problems of the poor. There has been increasing pressure to resist enforcement of antidiscrimination law. Hard times, in short, increase the public law regulatory and private legal problems of the poor.

It is obvious that meeting all the legal needs of the poor is beyond the capacity of the legal profession as presently organized. There are not enough lawyers, and it would no doubt be far too costly to attempt to meet all legal needs with the services of lawyers. Thus, there are calls for lay advocates, various kinds of plans that would deliver legal services in less costly ways, the dissemination of legal knowledge so that other helping professions and the poor themselves can avoid legal difficulties, more efficient methods of resolving conflicts that do arise, and reform of administrative programs and laws to reduce legal problems.

But whatever alternatives are adopted, success in meeting the legal needs of the poor will continue to depend largely on the response of the legal profession. Legal rights lawyers have also found the going harder as the private legal problems of the poor extended more into middle- and upper-middle-class interests. Housing problems of the poor have proved far more difficult when they involve private landlords rather than public landlords. Local bar associations became less supportive of neighborhood Legal Services when the consumer and credit problems of the poor reached the local banks as well as the loan sharks.

Whether the legal needs challenge will be met depends, in part, on whether reform-minded young lawyers will continue to be attracted to legal rights activities and whether legal rights organizations will continue to define and extend the legal needs of the poor. We have discussed our findings concerning recruitment, training, and exit from legal rights activities. We know that recruitment into legal rights activities has continued; the work of the Legal Services offices has remained steady in the aggressive tradition; and the lawyers, when they leave, continue their commitments—in government, teaching, and most notably in private practice, where their pro bono work and the nature of their regular practice is different from the norm in terms of clients, issues, and the kind of service rendered. If events continue along these lines, the legal rights area should continue to be active.

What are the prospects for legal rights activities organizations? Thus far, contrary to predictions, the organized bar has supported a fairly aggressive Legal Services program. The reason for this support does not lie in the professional ethics of the bar enjoining lawyers to support pro bono activities; this canon of professional ethics had been in existence for a half-century before the War on Poverty without much noticeable effect. Rather, the support stems from the fact that traditional legal ethics demand autonomy for lawyers in order to preserve the sanctity of the attorney–client relation. During the formative years of Legal Services, the American Bar Association insisted that the governing boards of neighborhood Legal Services programs be lawyer dominated; at the time, this was a conservative strategy designed to blunt the influence of citizen groups on the conduct of Legal Services business. Although the governing boards of neighborhood offices were often controlled by local lawyers, many of these offices were able to develop aggressive law reform units. Then, during the Nixon years, the administration sought to control the aggressive offices by subjecting Legal Services to political supervision. The American Bar Association rallied to the defense of the program on the grounds that political interference would violate the professional attorney–client relationship. There was a protracted struggle over the organization of Legal Services at the national level. The result was an independent corporation, run by prestigious professional elites and committed to the professional integrity of Legal Services.

One of the first acts of the new corporation was to find a way to preserve the law reform back-up centers, which had been a target of the enemies of Legal Services. There has also been an increase in the corporation's budget. The result is that at least for the immediate future Legal Services will retain its present characteristics. There will be reform not only at the back-up centers but also in many of the neighborhood offices. It will be recalled in Chapter 3 that the proportion of time devoted to law reform remained constant in the neighborhood offices although law reform strategies may have changed. There is no reason to think that time devoted to law reform will diminish. In addition to their law reform work, the neighborhood offices will continue to serve as the training ground for social-minded young lawyers in the aggressive tradition as long as social conditions in the larger society continue to stimulate young lawyers toward these aims. The organized bar, in part because of traditional legal ethics, will continue to be supportive of independence for Legal Services.

Legal rights activities are broader than Legal Services; they encompass a variety of types of social reform, including public interest law, aggressive pro bono activities, law communes, and so forth (Handler *et al.*, Chapter 4). There has also been bar support for many of these activities, again it is based on traditional legal ethics. The American Bar Association, as well as several influential local bar associations, support public interest law on the grounds that underrepresented interests are entitled to be heard before legally constituted decision-making bodies. Whatever the private feelings of leaders of the organized bar, the organizations do support the idea of full legal representation free of outside political interference. The effects of this position are to allow the young recruits into aggressive legal rights activities to perform the professional services that we have described.

The support of the profession for aggressive legal rights is, of course, limited. There is an independent Legal Services Corporation, but it is a reformist, not a radical, organization. There is also support of public interest law, but the public interest law supported by the bar associations is also reformist; and even then, the support has been more in rhetoric than in dollars. And, of course, there is little or no support from the organized bar for the more radical legal rights activities such as those of the National Lawyers Guild or the law communes. The bar's support stems from traditional values, which can only be stretched so far; but within these limits, it is spreading to other groups and institutions. In addition to the organized profession, there are various statutes and administrative rules now providing funds for the support of advocacy representation before particular agencies or for civil rights; and perhaps more significantly, there seems to be greater general acceptance of the idea of the need for advocacy for the unrepresented in a variety of contexts, such as hospitals, nursing homes, schools, and correctional institutions.

The importance of this support for the organizational structure of legal rights activities is crucial because it is the legal rights organizations that sensitize the country to the legal needs of the underrepresented and provide the structured opportunities that recruit, train, and "graduate" young lawyers working for the poor. The Legal Services program, the most important example, not only delivers legal services to the poor but also has important spillover effects for the rest of society. Lawyers are trained to deal with different types of clients for different kinds of issues. When they leave Legal Services, this training and socialization carry on; the lawyers either continue to serve the poor and unrepresented through their increased pro bono efforts or serve the middle and lower-middle classes through lower-status private practice. Legal Services, then, not only serves the poor directly but also is instrumental in producing a modest redistribution of private practice.

In addition, the continued recruitment, training, and exit of young lawyers in this work will mean the small but steady growth of a constituency within the legal profession—in private practice, government, and the law schools, as well as the legal rights organizations—which will continue to work for legal rights. Compared to the bar as a whole, this is a small group—but it is an active, interested constituency. Moreover, because of the nationwide spread of Legal Services programs, the growth of this constituency of "graduates" will be decentralized. It is to be hoped that in turn this could lead to more receptivity in many more localities to the idea of expanding the scope and variety of structures and organizations to meet the legal needs of the poor—lay advocacy, prepaid plans, etc. A number of these programs are already under way, but the continued growth of aggressive legal services should be influential in directing some of these efforts for the poor.

What this means is that turnover in Legal Services is not necessarily a deficit; in fact, it can be considered a benefit to society. Turnover provides more structured opportunities for reform-minded recruits and then feeds more graduates into nontraditional kinds of law work. Longer tenure in Legal Services would mean fewer lawyers experiencing the Legal Services process and would ultimately decrease the proportion of former Legal Services lawyers in other types of practice. Of course, turnover may have other negative effects on the Legal Services program—poor service to clients, higher cost of on-the-job training, and so forth—which have to be weighed along with its benefits. But we find that the investment and training for Legal Services lawyers are not lost when they leave; there is a payoff in their subsequent careers.

To increase the number of lawyers working on legal rights activities in both the short and long runs, then, the single most important policy recommendation is to increase the number of structured opportunities available for new recruits.

In terms of its size and of the numbers of lawyers recruited, trained, and graduated, the Legal Services program is far and away the most significant of all legal rights activities. Other legal rights activities are, at the present time, considerably smaller than Legal Services but nevertheless still important. Because of the newness of many of these activities, especially public interest law firms, we are less confident that our findings concerning Legal Services are generalizable to them. We expect that similar kinds of career paths will eventually be established. Public interest lawyers will not generally go to the other side of the street when they leave. To the extent that we are correct, turnover will also have positive spillover effects.

These data present a view of the legal profession not usually found in the literature. It looks primarily at nonelites and finds that there are young lawyers who carve out careers with strong public service components. We find that legal rights activities are a growing area of law. If all else remained equal, we would expect legal rights lawyers to have a steadily increasing influence on the profession and society at large as turnover increased their numbers. Assuming an even mildly supportive political environment, the legal profession should be at least as responsive as it has been so far to the legal needs of the poor, if not more responsive. Professions and professional organizations tend to generate their own momentum. Once engaged, with activities decentralized among state and local groups, the organized bar is unlikely to back away from poverty and public interest law as long as the political and financial costs are not too high. But the environment does not remain constant. There is now a massive increase in new members of the profession. If new structured opportunities are not made available to the proportionate increase in the bar, then we predict that even if legal rights activities grow in absolute terms, they will decline in relative importance to the rest of the bar. If this occurs, a major opportunity to increase the rights of groups underrepresented in the legal system will be lost.

Explanation of Methodology

SAMPLES

The samples on which this study is based were drawn as follows:

1967 Legal Services

All available names of lawyers in Legal Services in 1967 were collected and stratified by (a) North–South; (b) city size—under 100,000, between 100,000 and 600,000, over 600,000; and (c) quality of program—excellent, medium, or poor—as rated by several Legal Services regional directors. Over 900 names were available. All of the names in small cells created by the stratification technique were used (e.g., those in the southern cities), and samples were drawn from the cells in which names were numerous (e.g., programs of middle quality in middle-sized northern cities). In all, 284 interviews were completed, 83% of those attempted.

No complete roster of names of Legal Services lawyers exists for 1967. The names used for sampling were obtained from national and regional Legal Services offices, from early Legal Services conference lists and publications, and from interviews with program directors and lawyers. We estimate that our list was at least 80% complete. Reginald Heber Smith fellows and VISTA lawyers were excluded from the lists from which samples were drawn.

1972 Legal Services

The National Clearinghouse for Legal Services made available a complete list of 1972 Legal Services lawyers. Reggie and VISTA lawyers were removed, and a random sample was drawn. Interviews with 176 lawyers were completed, 83% of those attempted. In order to have the most accurate portrayal of Legal Services for both cohorts, duplicates were not eliminated from the sample; that is, a lawyer in Legal Services in both 1967 and 1972 was eligible for sampling for both years.

Reginald Heber Smith Fellows

Random samples of Reggies were drawn for 1967 and 1972. We completed interviews with 88% for 1967 (37 interviews) and 87% for 1972 (49 interviews).

National Sample of Bar

Two sources were used to construct the national sample of the bar: *Martindale–Hubbell Law Directory 1972*; and the best available lists of lawyers for 15 states selected randomly. A master sample of 4000 names was drawn randomly from *Martindale* and stratified into age groups. Disproportionate random sampling was then carried out, with younger age groups more heavily represented.

In order to offset any bias in *Martindale* listings, we drew 15 states at random (with the probability of being chosen conditional on the number of lawyers in the state) and obtained the best lists of lawyers available. Samples were drawn for each state thus selected; the resultant names were then cross-checked with *Martindale* and discarded if located. Approximately 20% of the names failed to appear in *Martindale*. These names were stratified by age. Younger lawyers were randomly sampled, and names of all older lawyers were used.

The number of interviews and the percentage completed for the various age and source groups are shown in Table A.1.

Completed interviews were weighted to reflect the age distribution of lawyers in the census in 1970 (corrected for law school graduating classes of 1970 and 1971) and the varying sampling ratios used.

Since the weights distort cell sizes, all tables that follow show unweighted Ns. However, all percentages are computed with the appropriate weights.

Lawyers in the contrast group who refused to participate were sent a two-page, self-administered schedule in June and July 1974. Three mailings were carried out, and 228 questionnaires were returned (48%). Preliminary analysis reveals only modest and substantively insignifi-

Table A.1

National Sample of Bar

Source and birth date	Number of completed interviews	Percentage completed
Martindale–Hubbell		
1944 and later	179	82
1939–1943	224	83
1929–1938	217	74
Before 1929	538	66
Fifteen states		
1944 and later	74	80
Before 1944	218	53
Total	1450	69

cant differences between those completing the long form and those completing the short.

Public Interest Lawyers

All civil rights, public interest, consumer, environmental, and related organizations (defined very broadly) were canvassed as to the aims and work of their organizations and the names of full-time paid lawyers associated with them since 1968. From the resulting list of 450 names, a random sample was drawn. We completed 110 interviews, 77% of those attempted. Lawyers in the following organizations are included in this study as public interest lawyers: American Civil Liberties Union, Appalachian Research and Defense Fund, Center for Constitutional Rights, Center for Law in the Public Interest, Center for Law and Social Policy, Center for Study of Responsive Law, Centro de la Raza, Citizens Advocate Center, Citizens Communication Center, Common Cause, Environmental Defense Fund, Environmental Law Institute, Fortune Society, Institute for Public Interest Representation, Lawyers' Committee for Civil Rights under Law, Mexican-American Legal Defense and Education Fund, Migrant Services, National Association for the Advancement of Colored People Legal Defense and Education Fund, Inc., National Committee against Discrimination in Housing, National Conference of Black Lawyers, National Lawyers' Guild, National Wildlife Federation, Natural Resources Defense Council, Public Advocates, Public Law Institute, Puerto Rican Legal Defense and Education Fund, Sierra Club Legal

Defense Fund, Southern Poverty Law Center, Stern Family Community Law Fund, Washington Research Project.

Lawyers in pro Bono Departments or Committees in Traditional Firms

Law firms which had listed themselves with the American Bar Association as having explicit pro bono arrangements were asked to identify lawyers who held past or present pro bono responsibilities. All names were used in the sample. Interviews with 113 lawyers were completed, 86% of those attempted.

Organizations of Lawyers: Bar and Other Voluntary

Lawyers in bar organizations (and counterbar organizations) in which lawyers functioned in social reform or public interests contexts and full-time paid lawyers in volunteer legal services organizations were randomly sampled. The names of the organizations were obtained from the American Bar Association's Project to Assist Interested Law Firms in Pro Bono Publico Programs. Both present and past job holders were included. Seventeen interviews were completed with lawyers from the Chicago Council of Lawyers, the Beverly Hills Bar Association Law Foundation, the Council of New York Law Associates, Community Law Office, Chicago Volunteer Legal Services Foundation, and similar organizations.

Mixed Public Interest Private Firms

These firms were identified through use of lists prepared by the American Bar Asssociations Project to Assist Interested Law Firms in Pro Bono Publico Programs and through information provided by public interest lawyers. All past and present lawyers in such firms were included, and 52 interviews were completed (86%).

Law Communes

All lawyers with past or present work in a law commune were sampled. A wide variety of sources were used to locate the names of participants: periodical articles, organizations active in such work, and knowledgeable individuals. In all, 53 interviews were completed (83%).

INTERVIEWS

Telephone interviews were conducted with all the above groups (except the contrast group from the 15 states) between August and December 1973. The remaining contrast group interviews were conducted in April and May 1974. The Survey Research Laboratory of the University of Wisconsin conducted all interviews by telephone. Respondents were sent a copy of the interview schedule in advance. (Interview and questionnaire schedules appear in Appendix B.)

LAW SCHOOL RATINGS

A panel of lawyers rated all United States law schools on a scale from 1 (excellent) to 6 (lowest quality). See Table A.2 for the distribution of law schools by quality.

National elite schools would be Quality 1, leading regional law schools Quality 2, etc. All unaccredited law schools were rated 6.

Table A.2

Distribution of Law Schools by Quality

Quality[a]	Number	Percentage
1	8	4.7
2	15	8.9
3	20	11.8
4	61	36.1
5	14	8.3
6	51	30.2
Total	169	100.0

[a] On a continuum from 1 = excellent to 6 = poorest or unaccredited.

AREA OF PRACTICE

On the questionnaire, lawyers in private practice were asked what were their major areas of practice; from which area they derived the largest portion of their earnings; and what was their legal specialty. In this study, the area from which a lawyer derived the largest portion of earnings was designated as the area of practice. If this information was missing, the legal specialty was used. If this item was also missing, the first area of practice listed was used. In this way, each lawyer had an area of practice (there was no missing information). The responses were grouped into eight areas of practice: corporate, wills, realty, criminal and juvenile, litigation, civil, marital, and other.

STATUS OF PRACTICE INDEX AND COMPONENTS

Business Client Wealth Score

The question asked of all lawyers in private practice (915 in the national sample, 111 in the 1967 Legal Services sample) was "what percentage of the firm's (or your own, for solo practitioners) time is spent on each of the following kinds of clients?"

1. Major national and international corporations
2. Large businesses—grossing over $10 million per year
3. Medium businesses
4. Small businesses—grossing $100,000 or less per year
5. Individuals

A score was derived by combining the types of business clients with the percentage of time spent on each. The business clients were ranked from 4 to 1, with major national and international corporations assigned 4. For each lawyer, the percentage of time indicated for major national and international corporations was multiplied by 4, the percentage of time for large businesses multiplied by 3, and so forth. These sums were added and divided by the total time spent with business clients to obtain a business client wealth score ranging from 4 (high) to 0 (low).

From these, 49 respondents in the national sample of the bar and 5 respondents in the 1967 Legal Services sample were excluded because of missing data.

Individual Client Wealth Score and Example

All lawyers who indicated that they or their firms spent 20% or more of their time on individuals were asked to indicate the percentage of that time spent on individuals with annual incomes less than $5000, between $5000 and $15,000, between $15,000 and $35,000, and over $35,000. These items were scaled from 1 to 4, respectively, and multiplied by the percentage of time spent with that client income group. The sum of these figures was divided by 100, to obtain an Individual Client Wealth Score, which ranged from 4 (high) to 1 (low).

For lawyers spending less than 20% of their time with individuals, individual client wealth scores were not computed (160 for the national sample and 7 for the Legal Services sample). Another 73 lawyers in the national sample and 8 in the Legal Services sample were also missing information here.

Total Client Wealth Score

The Business and Individual Client Wealth scores were integrated to give a total client wealth score for each lawyer. The following equivalents were set:

5 = Major national and international corporations
4 = Large businesses—grossing over $10 million per year; individuals with incomes over $35,000 per year
3 = Medium businesses; individuals with incomes between $15,000 and $35,000 per year
2 = Small businesses—grossing $100,000 or less per year; individuals with incomes between $5,000 and $15,000 per year
1 = Individuals with incomes lower than $5,000 per year

For each lawyer, the percentage of time indicated for each type of client was multiplied by the appropriate number (1–5); these figures were summed and divided by 100.

In order that a total client wealth score could be computed for as many lawyers as possible, lawyers lacking an individual client wealth score were assigned a score for that part, based on the relationship between percentage of time with individuals and client wealth. Generally, the less the time spent with individual clients, the greater the wealth of those clients.

The resulting total client wealth score ranged from 5 (high) to 1 (low). An example of the calculation of the three scores follows.

Lawyer A	Rank value
10% Major national and international corporations	4
20% Large businesses	3
30% Medium businesses	2
10% Small businesses	1
30% Individuals	

Computation of business client wealth score
10(4) + 20(3) + 30(2) + 10(1) = 170
170/70 (percentage of time spent on business clients) = 2.43 (business client wealth score)

Individual clients   Rank value
   0% under $5,000 income   1
  30% with incomes $5,000–15,000   2
  35% with incomes $15,000–35,000   3
  35% with incomes over $35,000   4

Computation of individual client wealth score
  0(1) + 30(2) + 35(3) + 35(4) = 305
  305/100 = 3.0 (individual client wealth score)

Computation of total client wealth score
[(Sum of Col. 2 × Col. 3 + Col. 3 × Col. 4)/100]

1	2	3	4	5	6
Type business client	Percent-age	Rank	Percent-age	Type individual client	
Major national, international	10	5			= 50
Large	20	4	10.5	$35,000 annual income	= 122
Medium	30	3	10.5	Income $15,000–35,000	= 121.5
Small	10	2	9.0	Incomes $5,000–15,000	= 38
		1	0	Incomes under $5,000	= 0
					331.5

331.5/100 = 3.3 (total client wealth score)

Status of Practice Index

The components of the Status of Practice Index are total earnings, firm size, and total client wealth score. Adjusted earnings were obtained by dividing earnings from major job by percentage of total earnings from that job and multiplying by 100. Earnings over $75,000 were treated as equal to $85,000. To correct for a skewed distribution, we used the log of actual firm size. Actual firm sizes ranged from 1 (solo practitioner) to an upper limit of 175. The computation of the total client wealth score has been shown.

To combine these three measures into an overall status index, first, missing data on the total client wealth score and on income were replaced with values predicted separately by regression equations for the national and Legal Services samples. There was almost no missing information on firm size. Then, for each lawyer in the national sample, the number of standard deviations from the mean was computed on each variable, and the standard deviations were added together to obtain the scale (Blalock, 1960, Chapter 7). For each lawyer in the Legal

Services sample, the scale was obtained the same way, using the means of the national sample. To enhance readability, a constant was added to make the scores positive; the scores ranged from 0 to 14.

In most instances, these computations were performed separately for communities of different sizes. In some tables, the status scale was also divided into three categories—low, medium, and high. Respondents were classified as high if their scores were more than one standard deviation above the mean; as low, if their scores were less than one standard deviation below the mean.

Appendix **B**

Questionnaire

_____Office Number   University of Wisconsin-Extension
Project 589   Wisconsin Survey Research Laboratory

A STUDY OF LAWYERS

1. First we have a few background questions...in what year were you born?   19 ____

2. What is the predominant nationality of your family on your father's side?

    _____

3. Was your father born in the United States?   /Yes/   /No/

4. What was your mother's religious preference?
    /Protestant/   /Catholic/   /Jewish/   Other: _____

5. What is your religious preference?
    /Protestant/   /Catholic/   /Jewish/   Other: _____
        | (TO Q 6)   (TO Q 6)   (TO Q 6)
        ↓
    5a. What denomination? _____

6. When you were growing up, were religious beliefs very important, somewhat
    important, or unimportant in your family? /   Very   / /Somewhat / /   Un-   /
                                               /important/ /important/ /important/

7. How important are your personal religious beliefs to you now--very important,
    somewhat important, or unimportant? /   Very   / /Somewhat / /   Un-   / /   No   /
                                         /important/ /important/ /important/ /beliefs/

8. In what state did you live most of the time until you were 18?
    _____(STATE)

9. Did you grow up in a big city, a suburb, a small city or town, or a rural area?
    /Big city/   /Suburb/   /Small city/town/   /Rural area/

10. Were you living with both your parents most of the time up to age 18?
                        /Yes/   /No/
                      (TO Q 11) |
                                             ↓
    10a. Who was the head of your family while you were growing up?

          _____

Interviewer's Name: _____   Sample No.: _____

Date: _____   Time Started: _____

11. Roughly speaking, what was your family's total annual income while you were in high school? $_____ /Don't know/

12. What is the highest grade of school or year of college your (FATHER OR PERSON WHO HEADED FAMILY) completed?

_____(GRADE OF SCHOOL), OR _____(YEAR OF COLLEGE)
(TO Q 13)

12a. What degrees did your (FATHER OR OTHER HEAD) earn?

/None/, or _____, _____, _____

13. What kind of work did your (FATHER OR PERSON WHO HEADED FAMILY) do most of the time you were in high school? _____

14. Was that a salaried job, or one in which (HE OR OTHER HEAD) was self-employed?

/Salaried/   /Self-employed/   /Both/

15. What was your (FATHER'S OR OTHER HEAD'S) political preference--Democrat, Republican, Independent, or something else?

/Democrat/   /Republican/   /Independent/   Else: _____   /None/   /DK/

16. At the time you were growing up, would you say (he;she) was liberal, middle-of-the-road, or conservative? /Liberal/   /Middle/   /Conservative/   /Don't know/

17. What is the highest grade of school or year of college your mother completed?

/No mother/   /Mother was head/   _____(GR. OF SCH.), OR _____(YR. OF COLL.)
(TO Q 21)   (TO Q 21)   (TO Q 18)

17a. What degrees did your mother earn? /None/, or _____, _____, _____

18. What kind of work did your mother do most of the time you were in high school?

/Never worked/, or _____
(TO Q 19)

18a. Was that a salaried job, or one in which she was self-employed?

/Salaried/   /Self-employed/   /Both/

19. What was your mother's political preference...Democrat, Republican, Independent, or something else?

/Democrat/   /Republican/   /Independent/   Else: _____   /None/   /DK/

20. At the time you were growing up, would you say she was liberal, middle-of-the-road, or conservative? /Liberal/   /Middle/   /Conservative/   /Don't know/

21. Was either parent active in politics? (Which one?)

/Neither/   /Father/   /Mother/   /Both/

22. How important was politics in your household when you were growing up--very important, somewhat important, or not important at all?

/Very/   /Somewhat/   /Not/

23. To what extent were your parents active in social reform or service organizations when you were growing up--a great deal, some, little, or none?

/Great deal/   /Some/   /Little/   /None/

24. What colleges or universities did you graduate from, including law school? What degrees did you obtain, and in what years?

INSTITUTION	DEGREE	YEAR
_____	_____	19 ___
_____	_____	19 ___
_____	_____	19 ___
_____	_____	19 ___
_____	_____	19 ___
_____	_____	19 ___

25. When you were in college or law school, or during those summers, did you participate in political activities such as civil rights work, voter registration, or student protest?   /Yes/   /No/
                                                                                                        (TO Q 26)

    25a. What did you do? _____

_____

26. Are you now married, divorced, separated, widowed, or never married?

/Married/   /Divorced/   /Separated/   /Widowed/   /Never married/
                                                                    (TO Q 27)

    26a. Is this your first marriage?

    /Yes/   /No/

        26b. What are the ages of your children--if any?

        /No children/, or _____, _____, _____, _____, _____

27. Have you ever been in military service?   /Yes/   /No/
                                                                (TO Q 28)

    27a. What years were you on active duty? 19 ___ to 19 ___; 19 ___ to 19 ___

    27b. What was your usual military job? _____

28. What is your race and sex?   RACE: _____   SEX: /Male/   /Female/

29. Are you currently active in politics?   /Yes/   /No/
                                                               (TO Q 30)

   29a. Is your political activity primarily in national, state, or
        local politics?   /National/   /State/   /Local/

   29b. What do you do...for example, hold office, manage campaigns, or what?

   _____

   _____

30. Have you ever been active in politics in the past?   /Yes/   /No/
                                                                       (TO Q 31)

   30a. Was this in national, state, or local politics?
        /National/   /State/   /Local/

   30b. What kinds of political activity have you done in the past?

   _____

   _____

31. Are you now a Democrat, a Republican, an Independent, or what?
    /Democrat/   /Republican/   /Independent/   Other: _____

32. Do you think of yourself as conservative, moderate conservative, middle-of-
    the-road, liberal, or left-liberal?
    /Conservative/   /Moderate conservative/   /Middle/   /Liberal/   /Left-liberal/

33. Why did you decide to go to law school? (Any other reason?) _____

   _____

   _____

34. Was there any particular person or event while you were growing up that
    strongly influenced you to be a lawyer? (What, or who was it?)
    /Nothing/, or _____

   _____

   _____

35. In what quarter of your law school class did you graduate--first, second,
    third, or fourth?   /First/   /Second/   /Third/   /Fourth/   /Don't know/

36. What was your Law School Aptitude Test (LSAT) percentile score?
    _____   /Never took it/   /Don't know/

37. Did your law school offer courses on consumer protection?

/Yes/   /No/   /Don't know/
           (TO Q 38)   (TO Q 38)

37a. Did you take any?   /Yes/   /No/

38. Did they offer courses on poverty and welfare?

/Yes/   /No/   /Don't know/
           (TO Q 39)   (TO Q 39)

38a. Did you take any?   /Yes/   /No/

39. Did they offer any advanced courses in criminal law?

/Yes/   /No/   /Don't know/
           (TO Q 40)   (TO Q 40)

39a. Did you take any?   /Yes/   /No/

40. Did you have the opportunity to be on law review?   /Yes/   /No/
                                                                     (TO Q 41)

40a. Were you on it...or did you decline to join, decline to compete, or
     quit the review?   /On it/   /Declined/join/   /Decline/complete/   /Quit/

41. Was your law school associated with a Legal Aid program, or did it have some
    other clinical program?   /Yes/   /No/

41a. What program was there? _____   41c. Were you in Legal Aid during
     _____   law school?   /Yes/   /No/
     _____   (TO Q 42)

41b. Were you in it?   /Yes/   /No/
                                  (TO Q 42)

41d. How many years did you work in the office?   _____(# YRS)

41e. How many hours a week did you spend on the average?   _____(HRS)

41f. While you were working there, did you think the office was of
     high, average, or low quality?   /High/   /Average/   /Low/

41g. In what way, if any, did the experience affect your subsequent
     career decisions? _____
     _____

42. Did you belong to the American Bar Association Law Student Division
during law school?   /Yes/   /No/

43. Did you belong to the National Lawyers Guild then?   /Yes/   /No/

44. How did you finance your law school training? _____

_____

45. Were you a law clerk for a judge?   /Yes/   /No/
                                           | (TO Q 46)
                                           |
                                           ▼
    45a. For what court were you a clerk? _____

    45b. In what years?   19 ___ to 19 ___;   19 ___ to 19 ___

46. While you were in law school, did you seriously consider taking a job in
Legal Services or in an organization like a Legal Aid office, a public
interest firm, or a defender program?   /Yes/   /No/

GO ON TO NEXT PAGE

PRESENT EMPLOYMENT STATUS

1. Now we have some questions about your present work. Are you now employed? /Yes/ /No/
   (TO Q 2)

   1a. Are you retired, looking for a job, or what?
       /Retired/ /Looking/ Other: _____
       (GO TO PAST EMPLOYMENT
       STATUS: PAGE 50)

   1b. How do you happen to be unemployed now? _____
       _____
       _____

   1c. Have you ever been employed since graduating from law school?
       /Yes/ /No/
       (GO TO PAST EMPLOYMENT   (GO TO GENERAL ATTITUDE
       STATUS; PAGE 50)   SCHEDULE; PAGE 83)

2. Are you employed full or part time? /Full/ /Part/
   (TO Q 3)

   2a. On the average, how many hours a week do you work? _____(# HOURS)

3. Do you hold more than one job now? Please consider part-time Public Defender
   or Judicare work as separate from your other legal work. /Yes/ /No/
   (TO Q 4)

   3a. What jobs do you have now, about what percent of your working time do you
       spend on each, and about what percent of your earnings come from each?

JOB	% TIME	% EARNINGS
_____	_____	_____
_____	_____	_____

4. How many of your present jobs are non-law jobs?
   /None/, or _____(#)
   (GO TO PRESENT LEGAL   (GO TO PRESENT NON-LAW
   ACTIVITY FORM, PAGE 9)   JOB FORM, PAGE 8)

Questionnaire   213

Sample # _____   PRESENT NON-LAW JOBS   Interviewer's Name: _____

1. What kind of non-law work do you do? _____

2. What year did you start this job?   19 ____

3. Why did you choose this job rather than a full-time law job? _____
   _____

4. At the time you took this job, what other options did you have? _____
   _____

5. Do you plan to move to a law job in the next few years?
                        /Yes/   /No/
                          | (TO Q 6)
                          ↓
   5a. What kind of law work do you plan to go into? _____
   ____ _____

6. Comparing your present earnings to what you thought during law school that you
   would earn at this time, do you earn more, about the same, or less than you
   expected?   /More/   /Same/   /Less/

7. When do you think you will reach your maximum earnings...
   in how many years?   ____(# YRS)

8. What do you think your maximum annual earnings will be? $_____   /DK/

9. Are your annual earnings from the job under $10,000, between 10 and $15,000,
   between 15 and $20,000, between 20 and $30,000, between 30 and $50,000, or
   over $50,000?
   / Under /   /$10,000-/   /$15,000-/   /$20,000-/   /$30,000-/   /$50,000/
   /$10,000/   / $14,999/   / $19,999/   / $29,999/   / $49,999/   /or over/

10. Do you now have another non-law job?   /Yes/   /No/
                                      (FILL OUT ANOTHER
                                      PRESENT NON-LAW JOB FORM)

    10a. Are you now also in a job related to the law?
            /Yes/   /No/
    (TO PRESENT LEGAL ACTIVITY   (TO PAST EMPLOYMENT
       FORM; PAGE 9)   STATUS; PAGE 50)

PRESENT LEGAL ACTIVITY FORM

1. I would like to ask some more questions about your current law work. First, I'll read a list of law jobs. Please tell me which one or more of these kinds of work you are doing. If you have more than one job, you will want to indicate more than one choice. It may be that none of the choices fits your job?

A. Private Law Firm. /Yes/ (TO SCHEDULE A; PAGE 10) /No/

B. Solo Practice. /Yes/ (TO SCHEDULE B; PAGE 14) /No/

C. OEO Legal Services, working in...

   1. Judicare, a national or regional office, a back-up-center, or a clearinghouse? /Yes/ (TO SCHEDULE C-1; PAGE 17) /No/

   2. Neighborhood project? /Yes/ (TO SCHEDULE C-2; PAGE 19) /No/

D. Law work in an office for the poor not funded by the Office of Economic Opportunity, such as a local Legal Aid facility, a bar-funded office, a firm-sponsored office, etc. /Yes/ (TO SCHEDULE D; PAGE 23) /No/

E. Public defender program. /Yes/ (TO SCHEDULE E; PAGE 25) /No/

F. A Reginald Heber Smith fellow or a VISTA lawyer.
   /Yes/ (TO SCHEDULE F; PAGE 27) /No/

G. Law work in a public interest law firm supported by foundation or general memberships. /Yes/ (TO SCHEDULE G; PAGE 28) /No/

H. Law work in a public interest firm, combining both private practice and public interest work. /Yes/ (TO SCHEDULE H; PAGE 31) /No/

I. Law work on the legal staff of a foundation or a not-for-profit corporation. /Yes/ (TO SCHEDULE I; PAGE 35) /No/

J. Law work in a law commune. /Yes/ (TO SCHEDULE J; PAGE 37) /No/

K. NONE OF THE ABOVE (E.G., GOVERNMENT, TEACHER, JUDGE, CORPORATE OR BUSINESS). /Yes/ (TO SCHEDULE K; PAGE 41) /No/ (ADMINISTER SCHEDULES CHECKED "YES")

TOTAL # _____

SCHEDULE A: PRIVATE LAW FIRM

1. In what city and state is your firm located? _____, _____

2. How many lawyers are employed in the firm full time, and how many part time?

_____(# FULL)   _____(# PART)

3. Does the firm specialize in any particular line of work, or work
    only for particular kinds of clients?   /Yes/   /No/
                                                                (TO Q 4)

    3a. Could you explain? _____

    _____

4. What percent of the firm's time is spent on each of the following kinds
    of clients?   (READ EACH TYPE AND RECORD %)

        %   TYPE OF CLIENT
    _____   A. Major national and international corporations

    _____   B. Large businesses--grossing over $10 million per year

    _____   C. Medium businesses

    _____   D. Small businesses--grossing $10,000 or less per year

    _____   E. Individuals (IF 20% OR MORE; ASK QUESTION 4a)

    4a. Roughly, what percent of the individuals represented by the firm have
         incomes in each of these ranges?   (READ EACH CATEGORY AND RECORD %)

            %   INCOME RANGE   /Don't know/
        _____   Under $5,000

        _____ $5,000 - $15,000

        _____ $15,000 - $35,000

        _____   Over $35,000

5. What is your position in the firm? _____

6. Looking back over the past twelve months, what have been your major areas of
    practice? _____

    _____

7. From which area just mentioned did you derive the largest portion of your earnings?

    _____

8. What, if any, is your legal specialty? _____

9. Have you spent a substantial amount of time in court during the past
    twelve months?   /Yes/   /No/
                                           (TO Q 10)

    9a.   What kinds of courts do you spend most of your time in? _____

_____

10. During the past twelve months have you spent a substantial amount of time
    dealing with government agencies in a professional capacity?
                          /Yes/   /No/
                                           (TO Q 11)

    10a. With what agencies do you spend most of your time? _____

_____

11. I'll read a list of seven things which may affect choices about cases. Would
    you tell me which three are most important in your choice? A. Novel questions
    of law or legal precedent; B. Expected duration of litigation; C. Altruistic
    motives; D. Subject matter; E. Jurisdiction of case; F. Ability of client to
    pay; and G. Chance of success. Which three of these are most important in
    your choice of cases?
                          _____, _____, _____ (LETTER)

12. What proportion of the clients the firm works for are members of
    minority groups?   /None/, or _____%
                      (TO Q 13)

    12a. Which minority groups are represented? _____

13. Does the firm do any pro bono work?
        /Yes/   /No/

                          13a.   Does the firm have an explicit policy against doing
                                 pro bono work?   /Yes/   /No/
                                                                  (TO Q 14)

                          13b.   What is this policy? _____

                          _____

    13c. Does the firm have an explicit policy or regular way of handling
          pro bono work?   /Yes/   /No/
                                              (TO Q 13e)

          13d. What is the policy? _____

          _____

13e. Have questions of conflict of interest ever arisen over the firm's pro bono work? /Yes/   /No/
                                                                 (TO Q 14)

 13f. How were they handled? _____

 _____

 13g. How many such questions have arisen in the past year?   _____ (#)

14. Have actual or possible conflicts of interest inhibited the firm's willingness, or your willingness, to take certain kinds of pro bono work?
                    /Yes/   /No/
                                    (TO Q 15)

 14a. Without naming names, could you elaborate? _____

 _____

15. Do you spend any of your billable hours doing pro bono work?
                    /Yes/   /No/
                                    (TO Q 16)

 15a. Roughly, what percent of your billable hours in the past twelve months did you spend doing pro bono work?   _____ %

 15b. Without naming names, would you give me some examples of the kinds of groups or individuals you do pro bono work for, the kinds of problems you are working with, and what you have done?

WORKED FOR	PROBLEMS	WHAT R HAS DONE
1) _____	1) _____	1) _____
2) _____	2) _____	2) _____
3) _____	3) _____	3) _____

 15c. I'll read a list of six things which may affect choices about pro bono cases. Would you tell me which three are most important in your choice? A. Novel questions of law or legal precedent; B. Expected duration of litigation; C. Altruistic motives; D. Subject matter; E. Jurisdiction of case; F. Chance of success. Which three of these are most important in your choice of pro bono cases?   _____, _____, _____ (LETTERS)

16. IS R READING FROM HIS COPY OF SCHEDULE?

/Yes/   /No/

16a. Which letter under Question 16a   19b. Are your annual earnings from
      best represents your annual   this job under $10,000, between
      earnings from this job?   10 and $12,000, between 12 and
                                                   $14,000, between 14 and $16,000,
      _____ a. Under $10,000   between 16 and $18,000, between
                                                   18 and $20,000, between 20 and
      _____ b. $10,000-$11,499 $30,000, between 30 and $50,000,
                                                   between 50 and $75,000, or over
      _____ c. $11,500-$12,999 $75,000?

      _____ d. $13,000-$14,499   _____ Under $10,000

      _____ e. $14,500-$15,999   _____ $10,000-$11,999

      _____ f. $16,000-$17,499   _____ $12,000-$13,999

      _____ g. $17,500-$18,999   _____ $14,000-$15,999

      _____ h. $19,000-$20,499   _____ $16,000-$17,999

      _____ i. $20,500-$24,999   _____ $18,000-$19,999

      _____ j. $25,000-$29,999   _____ $20,000-$29,999

      _____ k. $30,000-$49,999   _____ $30,000-$49,999

      _____ l. $50,000-$74,999   _____ $50,000-$74,999

      _____ m. $75,000 or over   _____ $75,000 or over

                        THIS IS SCHEDULE A
          FILL OUT SCHEDULE L (GREEN) FOR THIS JOB, PAGES 43-44

Questionnaire

SCHEDULE B: SOLO PRACTICE

1. In what city and state do you practice? _____, _____

2. Looking back over the past twelve months, what have been your major areas of practice? _____

3. From which area just mentioned did you derive the largest portion of your earnings? _____

4. What--if any--is your legal specialty? _____

5. Have you spent a substantial amount of time in court during the past twelve months? /Yes/   /No/
                                                        (TO Q 6)

   5a. What kinds of courts do you spend most of your time in? _____
   _____

6. During the past twelve months have you spent a substantial amount of time dealing with government agencies in a professional capacity? /Yes/   /No/
                                                                    (TO Q 7)

   6a. With what agencies do you spend most of your time? _____
   _____

7. What percentage of your time do you spend on each of the following kinds of clients? (READ EACH TYPE AND RECORD %)

%	TYPE OF CLIENT
_____	A. Major national and international corporations
_____	B. Large businesses--grossing over $10 million a year
_____	C. Medium businesses
_____	D. Small businesses--grossing $100,000 or less a year
_____	E. Individuals (IF 20% OR MORE, ASK Q 7a)

7a. Roughly, what percent of the individuals you represent have incomes in each of these ranges? (READ EACH CATEGORY AND RECORD %)

%	INCOME RANGES	/Don't know/
_____	Under $5,000	
_____	$5,000 - $15,000	
_____	$15,000 - $35,000	
_____	Over $35,000	

8. I'll read a list of seven things which may affect choices about cases. Would you tell me which <u>three</u> are most important in your choice? A. Novel questions of law or legal precedent; B. Expected duration of litigation; C. Altruistic motives; D. Subject matter; E. Jurisdiction of case; F. Ability of client to pay; and G. Chance of success. Which three of these are most important in your choice of <u>cases</u>?
                    _____, _____, _____(LETTERS)

9. What percent of the clients you work for are members of minority groups?

   /None/, or _____%
   (TO Q 10)

   9a. Which minority groups are represented? _____

10. Roughly, what percent of your billable hours in the past twelve months did you spend doing <u>pro bono</u> work?
                    /None/, or _____%
                    (TO Q 12)

   10a. Without naming names, would you give me some examples of the kinds of groups or individuals you do pro bono work for, the kinds of problems you are working with, and what you have done?

GROUPS OR INDIVIDUALS WORKED FOR	PROBLEMS	WHAT R HAS DONE
_____	_____	_____
_____	_____	_____
_____	_____	_____
_____	_____	_____
_____	_____	_____

11. I'll read a list of six things which may affect choices about <u>pro bono</u> cases. Would you tell me which <u>three</u> are most important in your choice? A. Novel questions of law or legal precedent; B. Expected duration of litigation; C. Altruistic motives; D. Subject matter; E. Jurisdiction of case; F. Chance of success. Which three of these are most important in your choice of <u>pro bono</u> cases?
                    _____, _____, _____(LETTERS)

12. IS R READING FROM HIS COPY OF SCHEDULE?

/Yes/   /No/

12a. Which letter under Question 12a   12b. Are your annual earnings from
best represents your annual   this job under $10,000, between
earnings from this job?   10 and $12,000, between 12 and
                                              $14,000, between 14 and $16,000,
_____ a. Under $10,000   between 16 and $18,000, between
_____ b. $10,000-$11,499   18 and $20,000, between 20 and
                                              $30,000, between 30 and $50,000,
_____ c. $11,500-$12,999   between $50 and $75,000, or over
_____ d. $13,000-$14,499 $75,000?

_____ e. $14,500-$15,999   _____ Under $10,000

_____ f. $16,000-$17,499   _____ $10,000-$11,999

_____ g. $17,500-$18,999   _____ $12,000-$13,999

_____ h. $19,000-$20,499   _____ $14,000-$15,999

_____ i. $20,500-$24,999   _____ $16,000-$17,999

_____ j. $25,000-$29,999   _____ $18,000-$19,999

_____ k. $30,000-$49,999   _____ $20,000-$29,999

_____ l. $50,000-$74,999   _____ $30,000-$49,999

_____ m. $75,000 or over   _____ $50,000-$74,999

                                              _____ $75,000 or over

THIS IS SCHEDULE B

FILL OUT SCHEDULE L (GREEN) FOR THIS JOB, PAGES 43-44

SCHEDULE C-1:

OEO JUDICARE, NATIONAL OR REGIONAL OFFICE, BACK-UP CENTER, OR CLEARINGHOUSE

1.   Is your job in Judicare, a national office, a regional office, or in a back-up center or clearinghouse?

/Judicare/   /National/ /Regional/ /Back-up or clearinghouse/

1a.   What is the name, city, and state of the program?

1e.   What is the name, city, and state of the organization where you work?

_____ ,

_____ , _____

_____ ,

_____ , _____

1b.   What percent of your working time is devoted to Judicare work? _____ %

1f.   What is your job title?

_____

1c.   What is your job title?

1g.   What are your main activities?

_____

1d.   What are your main activities?

1h.   Would you tell me what your annual salary for this job is? $ _____

FILL OUT SCHEDULE L (GREEN) FOR THIS JOB, PAGES 43-44

2.   How many staff lawyers are in the program, and how many private lawyers?

_____ (# STAFF)   _____ (# PRIVATE)

3.   Approximately, how many Judicare cases did you personally handle in 1972?

/None/, or   _____ (#)
(TO Q 4)

3a.   What kinds of Judicare cases do you handle most of the time? _____

_____

4.   Overall, what is your impression of the Judicare program in which you participate-- is it excellent, good, fair, or poor? /Excellent/ /Good/ /Fair/ /Poor/
(GO TO Q 5)

4a.   What makes it less than good? _____

_____

5. Is law reform work being done in the Judicare program?

/Yes/   /No/
           (TO Q 6)

5a. Could you give some examples of the law reform work being done? _____

_____

_____

6. All Judicare programs have restrictions on how much you can earn, and what the fees are. Do you agree or disagree with these restrictions?

/Agree/   /Disagree/
(TO Q 7)

6a. Why do you disagree? _____

_____

7. Approximately what were your earnings from Judicare in 1972?

$ _____

THIS IS SCHEDULE C-1
FILL OUT SCHEDULE L (GREEN) FOR THIS JOB, PAGES 43-44

SCHEDULE C-2:   OEO NEIGHBORHOOD PROJECT

1. What is the name, city and state of the program?

    _____, _____, _____

2. Does the program have more than one office?   /Yes/   /No/
                                                                     (TO Q 3)

    2a. Are you assigned to the main office or a branch office?
         /Main/   /Branch/

3. What is your position? _____

4. What percent of the office's time is for service cases, as opposed to law
    reform or legislative work?   _____% SERVICE CASES (IF 80% OR LESS ASK Q 4a)

    4a. What are the major areas in which the office does law reform work?
         1. _____ 2. _____ 3. _____

5. How do you personally divide your time between service cases and law reform
    or legislative work?   _____% SERVICE CASES (IF 80% OR LESS, ASK Q 5a)

    5a. What are the major areas in which you do law reform work?
         1. _____ 2. _____ 3. _____

6. What are the major areas in which you handle service cases? _____
    _____

7. What specialization, if any, is there in the office?
    /None/, or _____

8. What, if any, is your specialty?
    /None/, or _____
    (TO Q 9)
    8a. What percent of your time do you devote to your specialty? _____%

9. Approximately how many open files do you have as of now? _____(# FILES)

10. Have you spent a substantial amount of time in court during the past
    twelve months?   /Yes/   /No/
                                              (TO Q 11)

    10a. What kinds of courts do you spend most of your time in? _____
    _____

11. During the past twelve months have you spent a substantial amount of time
    dealing with government agencies in a professional capacity?

             /Yes/   /No/
               | (TO Q 12)
               |
    11a. With what agencies do you spend most of your time? _____

    _____

12. In community work, how many hours a month--if any--do you personally spend

    A. Speaking to neighborhood client groups?   _____(# HRS)

    B. Helping organize client or neighborhood groups?   _____(# HRS)

    C. Counseling, for example, about welfare or consumer problems?   _____(# HRS)

13. What percent of your clients are in each of these categories? (READ EACH
    AND RECORD %)
                         %
              _____   A. Black

              _____   B. Chicano

              _____   C. Puerto Rican

              _____   D. Native American

              _____   E. White

              _____   F. Other (SPECIFY): _____

14. I'll read a list of six things which may affect choices of cases. Would you
    tell me which three are most important in your choice? A. Novel questions of
    law or legal precedent; B. Expected duration of litigation; C. Altruistic
    motives; D. Subject matter; E. Jurisdiction of case; F. Chance of success.
    Which three of these are most important in your choice of cases?

                    _____, _____, _____(LETTERS)

15. How did you originally hear about this job? _____

    _____

16. If you left this project, what would you do? (Please be as specific as possible.
    For example, if you would practice law, what type of law and where would you
    practice?) _____

    _____

17. What is the average number of months attorneys are employed in the office?

                                                _____(# MOS)

    17a. Has this changed in recent years? /Yes/   /No/
                                              | (TO Q 18)
                                              |
         17b. How has it changed? _____

         _____

18. Overall, would you say this office is excellent, very good, good, fair, or poor? /Excellent/ /Very good/ /Good/ /Fair/ /Poor/

19. Why do you say that? _____

_____

20. Is the project administered by a Legal Aid Society or an organization which was in existence prior to OEO funding? /Legal Aid Society/ /Org. in existence/ /DK/

21. Has the local bar association generally been helpful to Neighborhood Legal Services, indifferent, or has the bar hindered it?
    /Helpful/ /Indifferent/ /Hindered/

22. If there are branch offices in your program, what problems if any arise between the branch office and the main office? /No branch office/ /No problem/, or

_____

_____

23. Is there pressure from outside sources for the project to do _more_ law reform work? /Yes/ /No/
    (TO Q 24)

    23a. From what sources does this pressure come? _____

    _____

24. Is there pressure from outside sources for the project to do _less_ law reform work? /Yes/ /No/
    (TO Q 25)

    24a. From what sources does this pressure come? _____

    _____

25. Is there internal pressure for the project to do more law reform work? /Yes/ /No/

26. Is there internal pressure for the project to do less law reform work? /Yes/ /No/

27. Have there been any objections, either from within your program or from outside it, to the types of cases you handle, or to any matter you handled or considered handling? /Yes/ /No/
    (TO Q 28)

    27a. Without naming names, could you describe the situation? _____

    _____

28. Aside from the restrictions contained in the OEO guidelines, are there kinds of cases which your office is unwilling or unable to handle?

/Yes/   /No/
             (TO Q 29)

    28a. What are they? _____

_____

29. Has the office ever been criticized on issues of legal ethics?

/Yes/   /No/
             (TO Q 30)

    29a. Without naming names, could you describe the situation? _____

_____

30. Would you tell me what the annual salary for this position is?

$ _____

THIS IS SCHEDULE C-2[1]

FILL OUT SCHEDULE L (GREEN) FOR THIS JOB, PAGES 43-44

[1] Responses to Schedules D and E were not analyzed for this study.

<u>SCHEDULE F: REGINALD HEBER SMITH FELLOW OR A VISTA LAWYER</u>

1. Are you presently a Reginald Heber Smith Fellow or a VISTA lawyer?

   /Smith fellow/   /VISTA lawyer/

2. Do you have any assignments as a (Smith fellow; VISTA lawyer) that are
   <u>not</u> to Legal Services projects or offices?   /Yes/   /No/
                                                       (TO Q 3)

   2a. Are you assigned to: 1) Judicare, a national or regional office, a
       back-up center, a clearinghouse, or to 2) a neighborhood project?

       /Judicare, national or regional   /   /A neighborhood project/
       /office, back-up center, clearinghouse/   (GO TO SCHEDULE C-2, PAGE 19)
       (GO TO SCHEDULE C-1, PAGE 17)

3. What assignments do you have of this type...that is, what are you
   doing and for how many months?

   _____ JOB _____   # MONTHS
   _____   _____
   _____   _____
   _____   _____
   _____   _____

4. Do you also have an assignment to a Legal Services office?

   /Yes/   /No/
                           (TO Q 5)

   4a. Are you assigned to: 1) Judicare, a national or regional office, a
       back-up center, a clearinghouse, or to 2) a neighborhood project?

       /Judicare, national or regional   /   /A neighborhood project/
       /office, back-up center, clearinghouse/   (GO TO SCHEDULE C-2, PAGE 19)
       (GO TO SCHEDULE C-1, PAGE 17)

5. Would you tell me your annual salary for this position? $ _____

THIS IS SCHEDULE F

FILL OUT SCHEDULE L (GREEN) FOR THIS JOB, PAGES 43-44

Questionnaire

SCHEDULE G: FIRMS SUPPORTED BY FOUNDATIONS OR GENERAL MEMBERSHIPS

1. What is the name, city and state of the firm?
   _____, _____, _____

2. What is your position in the firm? _____

3. In what year did the firm start? 19_____

4. How many lawyers are employed full time, and how many part time?
   _____(# FULL)   _____(# PART)

5. What are the main sources of financial support for the firm--foundation
   grants, public membership, government grants, or other sources? (CHECK ALL
   THAT APPLY)
                        /Foundation grants/ /Public membership/

   /Government grants/ Other: (SPECIFY) _____

6. Does the source of your funding cause any problems for your firm--like
   financial insecurity, or concern over kinds of cases?

              /Yes/   /No/
                │   │
   6a. What do you have in mind?   6b. Do you expect it to cause
                                              problems in the future?
   _____
   _____   /Yes/   /No/
   _____   │   (TO Q 7)
   _____
   _____   6c. What do you have in mind?
   _____
                                          _____
                                          _____

7. What are the major areas in which the firm specializes? _____
   _____

8. What, if any, is your specialty?
   _____
   /None/, or
   (TO Q 9)
                                          │
   8a. What percent of your working time do you spend in your specialty? _____%

9. Have you spent a substantial amount of time in court during the past twelve months?

/Yes/   /No/
            (TO Q 10)

9a. What kinds of courts do you spend most of your time in? _____

_____

10. During the past twelve months, have you spent a substantial amount of time dealing with government agencies in a professional capacity?

/Yes/   /No/
            (TO Q 11)

10a. With what agencies do you spend most of your time? _____

_____

11. I'll read a list of seven things which may affect choices about cases. Would you tell me which three are most important in your choice? A. Novel questions of law or legal precedent; B. Expected duration of litigation; C. Altruistic motives; D. Subject matter; E. Jurisdiction of case; F. Ability of client to pay; and G. Chance of success. Which three are most important in your choice of cases?

_____, _____, _____ (LETTERS)

12. Have you had conflict of interest problems in your own work in the firm?

/Yes/   /No/
            (TO Q 13)

12a. How did you handle the problem? _____

_____

13. Does the firm have a general policy about conflict of interest?

/Yes/   /No/
            (TO Q 14)

13a. What would that be? _____

_____

14. What do you think the future of the firm will be? _____

_____

15. IS R READING FROM HIS COPY OF SCHEDULE?

/YES/   /NO/

15a. Which letter under Question 15a   15b. Are your annual earnings from this
      best represents your annual   job under $10,000, between 10 and
      earnings from this job? $12,000, between 12 and $14,000,
                                                       between 14 and $16,000, between 16
      ____ a. Under $10,000   and $18,000, between 18 and $20,000,
                                                       between 20 and $30,000, between 30
      ____ b. $10,000 - $11,499   and $50,000, between 50 and $75,000,
                                                       or over $75,000?
      ____ c. $11,500 - $12,999

      ____ d. $13,000 - $14,499   ____ Under $10,000

      ____ e. $14,500 - $15,999   ____ $10,000 - $11,999

      ____ f. $16,000 - $17,499   ____ $12,000 - $13,999

      ____ g. $17,500 - $18,999   ____ $14,000 - $15,999

      ____ h. $19,000 - $20,499   ____ $16,000 - $17,999

      ____ i. $20,500 - $24,999   ____ $18,000 - $19,999

      ____ j. $25,000 - $29,999   ____ $20,000 - $29,999

      ____ k. $30,000 - $49,999   ____ $30,000 - $49,999

      ____ l. $50,000 - $74,999   ____ $50,000 - $74,999

      ____ m. $75,000 and over   ____ $75,000 and over

THIS IS SCHEDULE G.
FILL OUT SCHEDULE L (GREEN) FOR THIS JOB, PAGES 43-44

SCHEDULE H:
PUBLIC INTEREST FIRM, COMBINING PUBLIC INTEREST AND PRIVATE PRACTICE

1. What is the name, city and state of the firm?

   _____ , _____ , _____

2. In what year was the firm founded?   19 ____

3. What is your position in the firm? _____

4. How many full-time and part-time lawyers are in the firm? ____(# FULL) ____(# PART)

5. What percent of the _firm's_ time is spent on _public interest_ cases as compared to "regular" cases? _____% PUBLIC INTEREST

6. What are the major areas in which the FIRM does _public interest_ work?
   1. _____
   2. _____
   3. _____

7. What percent of _your own time_ with the firm is in the area of _public interest_ as compared to "regular" cases? _____% PUBLIC INTEREST

8. What are the major areas in which _you_ do _public interest_ work?
   1. _____
   2. _____
   3. _____

9. What are the major areas in which the FIRM does "regular" legal work?
   1. _____
   2. _____
   3. _____

10. What are the major areas in which _you_ do "regular" legal work?
    1. _____
    2. _____
    3. _____

11. What percent of its income does the _firm_ derive from "regular" cases? ____%

12. What percent of its income does the _firm_ derive from _public interest_ case fees? ____%

13. What are the other major sources of income for the firm--grants, gifts, etc.?

_____

_____

14. Have the firm's regular clients or sponsors tried to influence the types
    of public interest cases the firm takes?   /Yes/   /No/
                                                                 (TO Q 15)

    14a. Without naming names, could you describe the situation? _____

    _____

15. Regarding your public interest cases, have you spent a substantial amount
    of time in court during the past twelve months?   /Yes/   /No/
                                                                  (TO Q 16)

    15a. What kinds of courts do you spend your time in? _____

    _____

16. Regarding your regular cases, have you spent a substantial amount of time
    in court during the past twelve months?   /Yes/   /No/
                                                                (TO Q 17)

    16a. What kinds of courts do you spend your time in? _____

    _____

17. Regarding your public interest cases, have you spent a substantial amount of
    time dealing with government agencies in a professional capacity during the
    past twelve months?   /Yes/   /No/
                                           (TO Q 18)

    17a. With what agencies do you spend most of your time? _____

    _____

18. Regarding your regular cases, have you spent a substantial amount of time
    dealing with government agencies in a professional capacity during the
    past twelve months?   /Yes/   /No/
                                           (TO Q 19)

    18a. With what agencies do you spend most of your time? _____

    _____

19. What percentage of the firm's time on "regular" clients would you say is spent among each of the following types of clients? (READ EACH TYPE AND RECORD %)

%	TYPE OF CLIENT
_____	A. Major national and international corporations
_____	B. Large businesses--grossing over $10 million a year
_____	C. Medium businesses
_____	D. Small businesses--grossing $100,000 or less a year
_____	E. Individuals (IF 35% OR MORE, ASK Q 19a)

19a. Roughly, what percent of the individuals represented by the firm have incomes in each of these ranges? (READ EACH CATEGORY AND RECORD %)

%	INCOME RANGE	/Don't know/
_____	Under $5,000	
_____	$5,000 - $15,000	
_____	$15,000 - $35,000	
_____	Over $35,000	

20. I'll read a list of seven things which may affect choices about public interest cases. Would you tell me which three are most important in your choice? A. Novel questions of law and legal precedent; B. Expected duration of litigation; C. Altruistic motives; D. Subject matter; E. Jurisdiction of case; F. Ability of client to pay; and G. Chance of success. Which three are most important in your choice of public interest cases?
_____, _____, _____ (LETTERS)

21. What kinds of conflict of interest problems, if any, have arisen between your public interest clients and your regular clients?
/None/, or _____

_____

22. Does the firm have a policy for handling such possible conflicts of interest when they arise? /Yes/   /No/
                                                              (TO Q 23)

22a. What is the policy? _____

_____

23. What do you think the future of the firm will be? _____

_____

24. IS R READING FROM HIS COPY OF SCHEDULE?

/Yes/   /No/

24a. Which letter under Question 24a   24b. Are your annual earnings from this
     best represents your annual   job under $10,000, between 10 and
     earnings from this job? $12,000, between 12 and $14,000,
                                                    between 14 and $16,000, between 16
   _____ a. Under $10,000   and $18,000, between 18 and $20,000,
                                                    between 20 and $30,000, between 30
   _____ b. $10,000-$11,499   and $50,000, between 50 and $75,000,
   _____ c. $11,500-$12,999   or over $75,000?

   _____ d. $13,000-$14,499   _____ Under $10,000
   _____ e. $14,500-$15,999   _____ $10,000-$11,999
   _____ f. $16,000-$17,499   _____ $12,000-$13,999
   _____ g. $17,500-$18,999   _____ $14,000-$15,999
   _____ h. $19,000-$20,499   _____ $16,000-$17,999
   _____ i. $20,500-$24,999   _____ $18,000-$19,999
   _____ j. $25,000-$29,999   _____ $20,000-$29,999
   _____ k. $30,000-$49,999   _____ $30,000-$49,999
   _____ l. $50,000-$74,999   _____ $50,000-$74,999
   _____ m. $75,000 and over   _____ $75,000 and over

THIS IS SCHEDULE H[2]

FILL OUT SCHEDULE L (GREEN) FOR THIS JOB, PAGES 43-44

[2]Responses to Schedule I were not analyzed for this study.

SCHEDULE J: LAW COMMUNE

1. What is the name, city and state of the commune?

   _____, _____, _____

2. In what year did the commune come into existence?   19 _____

3. How many full-time lawyers, part-time lawyers, and legal workers are in the commune?   _____(# FULL)   _____(# PART)   _____(# LEGAL WORKERS)

4. Overall, what percentage of the commune's time is spent on "straight" cases as compared to cases for the poor, students, draft, consumer, environmentalists, minorities, political protest groups, etc.?   _____% STRAIGHT

5. Do you divide your time about the same way?   /Yes/   /No/
                                                  (TO Q 6)

   5a. What percent of your time do you spend on "straight" cases?   _____% STRAIGHT

6. Looking at the cases that you wouldn't call "straight" what are the major kinds of cases the commune has taken in the last year?
   1. _____
   2. _____
   3. _____
   4. _____

7. In which of these areas have you spent the most time and the next most time?
   _____(# MOST, Q-6)   _____(# SECOND, Q-6)

8. Among "straight" cases, what three kinds of cases have taken up most of the time of the commune?
   1. _____
   2. _____
   3. _____

9. Concerning the time you personally spend on "straight" cases, what three kinds of cases have taken up most of your time?
   1. _____
   2. _____
   3. _____

10. Overall, what percent of the commune's income is derived from "straight"
    cases as compared to all other sources?   ____% STRAIGHT (IF LESS THAN 80%,
                                                                ASK Q-10a)

    10a. Please indicate the other major sources of income.

         1. _____

         2. _____

         3. _____

11. What restrictions, if any, are there on the kinds of "straight" cases you take?

    /None/, or _____

    _____

12. Do the sources of income result in pressure about types of cases, etc.?

              /Yes/   /No/
                                     (TO Q 13)

    12a. What do you have in mind? _____

    _____

13. On what basis are financial resources allocated in the commune?_____

    _____

14. I'll read a list of seven things which may affect choices of "straight" cases.
    Would you tell me which three are most important in your choice? A. Novel
    questions of law and legal precedent; B. Expected duration of litigation;
    C. Altruistic motives; D. Subject matter; E. Jurisdiction of case; F. Ability
    of client to pay; and G. Chance of success. Which three are most important
    in your choice of "straight" cases?   ____, ____, ____(LETTERS)

15. Which three are most important in your choice of other cases?
                                    ____, ____, ____(LETTERS)

16. Have you spent a substantial amount of time in court during the
    past twelve months?   /Yes/   /No/
                                                 (TO Q 17)

    16a. What kinds of courts do you spend your time in? _____

    _____

17. During the past twelve months have you spent a substantial amount of time
    dealing with government agencies in a professional capacity?

              /Yes/   /No/
                                     (TO Q 18)

    17a. With what agencies do you spend most of your time? _____

    _____

18. What percent of the commune's time on "straight" cases is spent with business clients?

                          _____(% BUSINESS CLIENTS)

19. What kind of businesses are they? _____

20. What percent of the "straight" individuals your commune represents have annual incomes in each of these ranges? (READ EACH CATEGORY AND RECORD %)

%	INCOME RANGES	/Don't know/
_____	Under $5,000	
_____	$5,000 - $15,000	
_____	$15,000 - $35,000	
_____	Over $35,000	

21. If you have had any conflict of interest problems, what kind have they been? /None/, or _____

22. What do you think the future of the commune will be? _____

23. What factors are most important in shaping the commune's future? _____

24. IS R READING FROM HIS COPY OF SCHEDULE?

/Yes/   /No/

24a. Which letter under Question 24a best represents your annual earnings from this job?

_____ a. Under $5,000

_____ b. $5,000-$9,999

_____ c. $10,000-$11,499

_____ d. $11,500-$12,999

_____ e. $13,000-$14,499

_____ f. $14,500-$15,999

_____ g. $16,000-$17,499

_____ h. $17,500-$18,999

_____ i. $19,000-$20,499

_____ j. $20,500-$21,499

_____ k. $21,500 or over

24b. Are your annual earnings from this job under $5,000, between 5 and $10,000, between 10 and $12,000, between 12 and $14,000, between 14 and $16,000, between 16 and $18,000, between 18 and $20,000, or over $20,000?

_____ Under $5,000

_____ $5,000-$9,999

_____ $10,000-$11,999

_____ $12,000-$13,999

_____ $14,000-$15,999

_____ $16,000-$17,999

_____ $18,000-$19,999

_____ $20,000 or over

THIS IS SCHEDULE J

FILL OUT SCHEDULE L (GREEN) FOR THIS JOB, PAGES 43-44

Sample # _____   Interviewer's Name: _____

SCHEDULE K:
LAWYERS FOR WHOM OTHER SCHEDULES DO NOT APPLY
(E.G., GOVERNMENT, TEACHING, JUDGE, CORPORATION OR BUSINESS)

1. What is the name, city and state of your employer?

   _____ , _____ , _____

2. What is your job title? _____

3. Please tell me in some detail what types of law-related work you do?

   _____

   _____

4. IS RESPONDENT A TEACHER (Q's 2-3)?

   /Yes/   /No/
                           (TO Q 5)

   4a. What courses do you teach? _____

   _____

   4b. In what areas do you do research? _____

   _____

5. Do you engage in litigation?   /Yes/   /No/
                                                     (TO Q 6)

   5a. About what percent of your time?   _____ %

   5b. What are the major kinds of cases you handle? _____

   _____

   5c. Have you spent a substantial amount of time in court during the past
       twelve months?   /Yes/   /No/
                                               (TO Q 6)

       5d. What kinds of courts do you spend your time in? _____

       _____

6. During the past twelve months have you spent a substantial amount of
   time dealing with government agencies in a professional capacity?

   /Yes/   /No/
                           (TO Q 7)

   6a. With what agencies do you spend most of your time? _____

   _____

7. Later, I am going to ask you about pro bono work you do outside working hours, but in your work, what percent--if any--of your time do you spend on pro bono work?
   /None/, or ____ %
   (TO Q 8)

7a. Without naming names, would you give me some examples of the kinds of groups or individuals you do pro bono work for, the kinds of problems you are working with, and what you have done?

WORKED FOR	PROBLEMS	WHAT R HAS DONE

8. IS R READING FROM HIS COPY OF SCHEDULE?

/Yes/   /No/

8a. Which letter under Question 8a best represents your annual earnings from this job?

   ____ a. Under $10,000
   ____ b. $10,000-$11,499
   ____ c. $11,500-$12,999
   ____ d. $13,000-$14,499
   ____ e. $14,500-$15,999
   ____ f. $16,000-$17,499
   ____ g. $17,500-$18,999
   ____ h. $19,000-$20,499
   ____ i. $20,500-$24,999
   ____ j. $25,000-$29,999
   ____ k. $30,000-$49,999
   ____ l. $50,000-$74,999
   ____ m. $75,000 and over

8b. Are your annual earnings from this job under $10,000, between 10 and $12,000, between 12 and $14,000, between 14 and $16,000, between 16 and $18,000, between 18 and $20,000, between 20 and $30,000, between 30 and $50,000, between 50 and $75,000, or over $75,000?

   ____ Under $10,000
   ____ $10,000-$11,999
   ____ $12,000-$13,999
   ____ $14,000-$15,999
   ____ $16,000-$17,999
   ____ $18,000-$19,999
   ____ $20,000-$29,999
   ____ $30,000-$49,999
   ____ $50,000-$74,999
   ____ $75,000 and over

THIS IS SCHEDULE K

FILL OUT SCHEDULE L (GREEN) FOR THIS JOB, PAGES 43-44

Sample # _____   Interviewer's Name: _____

SCHEDULE L:
GENERAL QUESTIONS ON EACH TYPE OF LEGAL POSITION

| FILL OUT FOR EACH SCHEDULE A THROUGH K WHICH WAS COMPLETED |

1. THIS SCHEDULE L ACCOMPANIES SCHEDULE: _____(LETTER OF SCHEDULE)

2. In what year did you first get this job?   19 ____

3. What were the main reasons you chose this job? _____
    _____
    _____

4. At the time you took this job, what other options did you have? _____
    _____

5. IS RESPONDENT IN OEO LEGAL SERVICES (SCHEDULES C-1 OR C-2)?

                        /Yes/   /No/

5a. Aside from the current instability   5d. How satisfied are you with
     of OEO Legal Services, are you   your job...very satisfied,
     very satisfied, satisfied, dis-   satisfied, dissatisfied, or
     satisfied, or very dissatisfied   very dissatisfied?
     with your job?
                                                  /Very/ /Sat/ /Dissat/ / Very /
     /Very/ /Sat/ /Dissat/ / Very /   / sat/   /dissat/
     / sat/   /dissat/

                                              5e. What are the things you
5b. What are the things you particu-   particularly like about
     larly like about your job?   your job?
                                                   _____
     _____
     _____   _____
     _____
                                                   _____

5c. Aside from the current instability
     of OEO Legal Services, what are the   5f. What are the things you particu-
     things you particularly do not like   larly do not like about your
     about your job? (Anything else?)   job? (Anything else?)

     _____   _____
     _____   _____
     _____   _____

6. When you took this job, did you plan to stay in this kind of work?

/Yes/   /No/   /Don't know/
(TO Q 7)   (TO Q 7)

6a. Why not? _____

_____

6b. About how many months or years did you plan to stay
in this kind of work? _____(MOS), OR _____(YRS)

6c. What kind of work did you hope to move to? _____

_____

7. When you chose this job, how important were financial considerations in your
choice...very important, important, or not important?

/Very important/   /Important/   /Not important/

8. When you chose this job, how important were family considerations in your
choice...very important, important, or not important?

/Very important/   /Important/   /Not important/

REFER TO PRESENT LEGAL ACTIVITY FORM, PAGE 9, AND GO TO NEXT SCHEDULE
INDICATED. IF NONE INDICATED, GO TO NEXT PAGE.

GENERAL QUESTIONS ON PRESENT LEGAL OCCUPATIONS

[TO BE COMPLETED BY ALL R'S WITH AN OCCUPATION RELATED TO THE LAW]

1. Comparing your present earnings to what you thought during law school you
   would earn at this time, do you earn more, about the same, or less than
   you expected? /More/   /About same/   /Less/

2. When do you think you will reach your maximum earnings--in how many
   years from now? _____(# YRS)

3. What do you think your maximum annual earnings will be? $ _____

4. In 1972, roughly what percent of your total gross family income was
   derived from your work as a lawyer? _____%

5. What do you see yourself doing five years from now? _____
   _____
   _____

6. DOES R NOW HOLD MORE THAN ONE JOB?   (Q-3; PRESENT EMPLOYMENT STATUS, PAGE 7)

   /Yes/   /No/
                            (TO Q 7)

   6a. What conflicts of interest problems, if any, have you experienced
       because you have more than one job?
       /None/, or _____
       (TO Q 7)   _____

   6b. How serious have such problems been...very serious, somewhat serious,
       or not serious? /Very/   /Somewhat/   /Not/

7. Lawyers have a set of special skills. Do you feel your current job calls for
   a very high, medium high, medium, or low use of those special skills? (IF
   LAWYER HOLDS MORE THAN ONE JOB, RECORD THE JOB HE IS USING AS THE BASIS OF
   HIS COMPARISON; JOB _____   )

        /Very high/   /Medium high/   /Medium/   /Low/
                         (TO Q 7b)   (TO Q 7b)   (TO Q 7b)

   7a. Could you name two other legal specialties which also call for very high
       use of a lawyer's special skills? Be as specific as possible. For example,
       if "litigation", do you have a particular kind of litigation in mind ?

       1) _____
          _____

       2) _____

                          (GO TO Q 10)

7b. Could you name two jobs that call for greater use of a lawyer's special
     skills? Be as specific as possible. For example, if "litigation", do
     you have a particular kind of litigation in mind?

     1) _____

     2) _____

8. Do you ever feel you should move into a job that makes more or better
    use of your special skills as a lawyer?   /Yes/   /No/
                                                                 (TO Q 9)

8a. Is this feeling very strong, strong, or not very strong?

     /Very strong/   /Strong/   /Not very strong/

9. Does anyone pressure you to move into a job making more use of the
    special skills of a lawyer?   /Yes/   /No/
                                                     (TO Q 10)

9a. Who does this? _____

9b. Do you feel quite a lot of pressure, some, or very little?

     /Quite a lot/   /Some/   /Very little/

10. I'll read some examples of work that lawyers do. For each, would you tell
     me whether you personally feel the work itself requires...(1) very high,
     (2) high, (3) medium, or (4) low use of the special skills of a lawyer?

              #   WORK LAWYERS DO
         _____   A. Negotiating complicated business deals.

         _____   B. Nader-type investigations of government agencies to determine
                        their fulfillment of legal obligations.

         _____   C. Planning for large estates.

         _____   D. Criminal defense, such as done by Edward Bennett Williams.

         _____   E. Chief litigating lawyer in a very large firm.

         _____   F. Handling major desegregation or environmental impact
                        suits for plaintiff.

         _____   G. Handling major class actions seeking benefits for the poor.

11. If you were to change jobs now, do you think your chances for obtaining a
     desirable job would be excellent, good, fair, or poor?

     /Excellent/   /Good/   /Fair/   /Poor/

12. Will you be seeking a job change in the next year?

/Yes/   /Depends/   /No/
                         (TO Q 13)

12a. Why? _____

_____

12b. What kind of position will you seek? _____

13. Do you feel that you should do more pro bono or social reform work, you're doing the right amount now, or that you should do less pro bono or social reform work?

/More/   /Right amount/   /Less/
              (TO Q 14)

13a. What, specifically, do you feel you should do (instead)? _____

_____

_____

13b. Who, if anyone, pressures you to do (more;less) pro bono work?

/No one/, or _____

13c. How strong is this feeling that you should do (more; less) pro bono work...very strong, strong, moderate, or weak?

/Very strong/   /Strong/   /Moderate/   /Weak/

14. Most lawyers from time to time express disappointment in their clients. How often have you felt this way...some, rarely, or not at all?

/Some/   /Rarely/   /Not at all/
                           (TO Q 15)

14a. What have you found disappointing? _____

_____

15. Of these three types of law firms--the private firm, OEO Legal Services, and public interest law firm--which one do you think is most likely to avoid unconventional or controversial clients or issues?

/Private firm/ /OEO Legal Services/ /Public interest firm/ /All same/ /DK/

16. Which one is least likely to avoid unconventional or controversial clients or issues?

/Private firm/ /OEO Legal Services/ /Public interest firm/ /All same/ /DK/

17. Of the private firms, OEO Legal Services, and public interest firms, which one do you think is most likely to seek novel questions of law or to establish legal precedent?

/Private firm/   /OEO Legal Services/   /Public interest firm/   /All same/   /DK/

18. Which one is least likely to do this?

/Private firm/   /OEO Legal Services/   /Public interest firm/   /All same/   /DK/ 3
   (GO TO NEXT PAGE)   (GO TO NEXT PAGE)   (GO TO NEXT PAGE)

³Page 49 is omitted.

PAST EMPLOYMENT STATUS AND LEGAL ACTIVITY FORM

Now I would like to ask you about all the income producing jobs you have had since graduating from law school. Beginning with the first job after law school, ex-cluding clerking, please tell me about each one in order up to but not including your present one. If you have done part-time Public Defender or Judicare work, please list such work as a separate job. We'd like to know the type of law practice it was, the year you started and ended it, and your employer's name then.

> NUMBER JOBS IN CHRONOLOGICAL ORDER AND FILL IN INFORMATION ON EACH BELOW AND ON NEXT PAGE. THEN, STARTING WITH FIRST JOB, GO TO APPROPRIATE SCHEDULE. REPEAT UNTIL A SEPARATE SCHEDULE FOR EACH JOB HAS BEEN COMPLETED. NOTE: IF R NOW RETIRED, ASK ONLY ABOUT LAST JOB.

/No past job; present job /
/is first since law school/   JOB   YEAR
(TO GENERAL ATTITUDE FORM, PAGE 83)   #   START   END   NAME OF FIRM OR EMPLOYER

A. Private Law Firm (SCHEDULE AA) . ___ 19 ___   19 ___   _____
    (GO TO PAGE 52)
                                      ___ 19 ___   19 ___   _____

                                      ___ 19 ___   19 ___   _____

                                      ___ 19 ___   19 ___   _____

B. Solo Practice (SCHEDULE BB). . . ___ 19 ___   19 ___   _____
    (GO TO PAGE 54)
                                      ___ 19 ___   19 ___   _____

                                      ___ 19 ___   19 ___   _____

C. OEO Legal Services, working in...

    1. Judicare, a national or
        regional office, a back-up
        center, or a clearinghouse
        (SCHEDULE CC-1). . . . . . . ___ 19 ___   19 ___   _____
        (GO TO PAGE 56)
                                      ___ 19 ___   19 ___   _____

    2. Neighborhood project
        (SCHEDULE CC-2). . . . . . . ___ 19 ___   19 ___   _____
        (GO TO PAGE 58)
                                      ___ 19 ___   19 ___   _____

D. Law work in an office for the
    poor not funded by OEO; e.g.,
    a local legal aid facility, a
    bar funded office, a firm
    sponsored office, etc.
    (SCHEDULE DD). . . . .   ___ 19 ___   19 ___   _____
    (GO TO PAGE 62)
                                      ___ 19 ___   19 ___   _____

E. Public defender program
    (SCHEDULE EE). . . . .   ___ 19 ___   19 ___   _____
    (GO TO PAGE 64)
                                      ___ 19 ___   19 ___   _____

(CONTINUED ON NEXT PAGE)

PAST EMPLOYMENT STATUS AND LEGAL ACTIVITY FORM: (CONTINUED)

	JOB #	YEAR START	YEAR END	NAME OF FIRM OR EMPLOYER
F. A Reginald Heber Smith Fellow or a VISTA lawyer (SCHEDULE FF) (GO TO PAGE 66)	___ ___	19 ___ 19 ___	19 ___ 19 ___	_____ _____
G. Law work in a public interest firm supported by foundation or general memberships (SCHEDULE GG). . . . . (GO TO PAGE 68)	___ ___	19 ___ 19 ___	19 ___ 19 ___	_____ _____
H. Law work in a public interest firm, combining both private and public interest work (SCHEDULE HH). . . . . (GO TO PAGE 71)	___ ___	19 ___ 19 ___	19 ___ 19 ___	_____ _____
I. Law work on the legal staff of a foundation or a not-for-profit corporation (SCHEDULE II) (GO TO PAGE 75)	___ ___	19 ___ 19 ___	19 ___ 19 ___	_____ _____
J. Work in a law commune (SCHEDULE JJ). . . . . (GO TO PAGE 76)	___	19 ___	19 ___	_____
K. LAW-RELATED WORK IN NONE OF THE ABOVE, E.G., GOVERNMENT, TEACHER, JUDGE, CORPORATE OR BUSINESS (SCHEDULE KK). . . . . (GO TO PAGE 79)	___ ___ ___	19 ___ 19 ___ 19 ___	19 ___ 19 ___ 19 ___	_____ _____ _____
X. JOB NOT RELATED TO LAW (SCHEDULE XX). . . . . (GO TO PAGE 82)	___ ___ ___ ___	19 ___ 19 ___ 19 ___ 19 ___	19 ___ 19 ___ 19 ___ 19 ___	_____ _____ _____ _____

(ALL PAST LEGAL JOBS SCHEDULES HAVE SCHEDULE LL ATTACHED. FILL IT OUT EACH TIME)

SCHEDULE AA: PAST PRIVATE LAW FIRM

Sample #: _____   Job #: _____   Interviewer's Name: _____

Now let's talk about your job at _____.
                                                    (NAME OF FIRM)

1. In what city and state was the firm located?

    _____, _____

2. How many lawyers were employed in the firm full time, and how many
    part time?   _____(# FULL TIME)   _____(# PART TIME)

3. Did the firm specialize in any particular kind of work or clients?
                      /Yes/   /No/
                                             (TO Q 4)

    3a. Could you explain? _____

    _____

4. What was your position in the firm? _____

5. What were the main kinds of legal work you did? _____

    _____

6. Roughly, what percent of your billable hours in that job did you spend
    doing pro bono work?   /None./, or _____ %
                              (TO Q 7)

    6a. Without naming names, would you give me some examples of the kinds of
         groups or individuals you did pro bono work for, the kinds of problems
         you worked with, and what you did?

WORKED FOR	PROBLEMS	WHAT R DID
1) _____	1) _____	1) _____
2) _____	2) _____	2) _____
3) _____	3) _____	3) _____

7. IS R READING FROM HIS COPY OF SCHEDULE?

                    /Yes/   /No/

7a. Which letter under Question 7a   7b. Were your highest annual earnings
    best represents your highest   from this job under $10,000,
    annual earnings from this job?   between 10 and $12,000, between
                                                12 and $14,00, between 14 and
    _____ a. Under $10,000 $16,000, between 16 and $18,000,
                                                between 18 and $20,000, between
    _____ b. $10,000-$11,499   20 and $30,000, between 30 and
                                                $50,000, between 50 and $75,000,
    _____ c. $11,500-$12,999   or over $75,000?

    _____ d. $13,000-$14,499   _____ Under $10,000

    _____ e. $14,500-$15,999   _____ $10,000-$11,999

    _____ f. $16,000-$17,499   _____ $12,000-$13,999

    _____ g. $17,500-$18,999   _____ $14,000-$15,999

    _____ h. $19,000-$20,499   _____ $16,000-$17,999

    _____ i. $20,500-$24,999   _____ $18,000-$19,999

    _____ j. $25,000-$29,999   _____ $20,000-$29,999

    _____ k. $30,000-$49,999   _____ $30,000-$49,999

    _____ l. $50,000-$74,999   _____ $50,000-$74,999

    _____ m. $75,000 and over   _____ $75,000 and over

             FILL OUT ATTACHED SCHEDULE LL FOR THIS JOB, NEXT PAGE

SCHEDULE BB: PAST SOLO PRACTICE

Sample #: _____   Job #: _____   Interviewer's Name: _____

Now let's talk about your solo practice from 19 _____ to 19 _____.

1. In what city and state was that practice?

_____, _____

2. What were the main kinds of legal work you did? _____

_____

_____

3. Roughly, what percent of your billable hours in that
    job did you spend doing <u>pro bono</u> work?

         /None/, or _____%
         (TO Q 4)

3a. Without naming names, would you give me some examples of the kinds
     of groups or individuals you did <u>pro bono</u> work for, the kinds of
     problems you worked with, and what you did?

GROUPS OR INDIVIDUALS WORKED FOR _____ PROBLEMS _____ WHAT R DID

1)_____   1)_____   1)_____

_____   _____   _____

2)_____   2)_____   2)_____

_____   _____   _____

3)_____   3)_____   3)_____

_____   _____   _____

4. IS R READING FROM HIS COPY OF SCHEDULE?

                    /Yes/   /No/

4a. Which letter under Question 4a   4b. Were your highest annual earnings
    best represents your highest   from this job under $10,000,
    annual earnings from this job?   between 10 and $12,000, between
                                                12 and $14,000, between 14 and
    _____ a. Under $10,000 $16,000, between 16 and $18,000,
                                                between 18 and $20,000, between
    _____ b. $10,000-$11,499   20 and $30,000, between 30 and
    _____ c. $11,500-$12,999 $50,000, between 50 and $75,000,
                                                or over $75,000?
    _____ d. $13,000-$14,499
                                                _____ Under $10,000
    _____ e. $14,500-$15,999
                                                _____ $10,000-$11,999
    _____ f. $16,000-$17,499
                                                _____ $12,000-$13,999
    _____ g. $17,500-$18,999
                                                _____ $14,000-$15,999
    _____ h. $19,000-$20,499
                                                _____ $16,000-$17,999
    _____ i. $20,500-$24,999
                                                _____ $18,000-$19,999
    _____ j. $25,000-$29,999
                                                _____ $20,000-$29,999
    _____ k. $30,000-$49,999
                                                _____ $30,000-$49,999
    _____ l. $50,000-$74,999
                                                _____ $50,000-$74,999
    _____ m. $75,000 and over
                                                _____ $75,000 and over

            FILL OUT ATTACHED SCHEDULE LL FOR THIS JOB, NEXT PAGE

254

Appendix B

SCHEDULE CC-1:

PAST OEO JUDICARE, NATIONAL OR REGIONAL OFFICE, BACK-UP OR CLEARINGHOUSE

Sample #: _____   Job #: _____   Interviewer's Name: _____

Let's talk about your OEO job from 19 ____ to 19 ____.

1. Was this OEO job in Judicare, a national office, a regional office, or in a
   back-up center or clearinghouse?

   /Judicare/   /National/ /Regional/ /Back-up or clearinghou

1a. What was the name, city, and   1h. What was the name, city, and state
    state of the program?   the organization where you worked?

    _____,   _____

    _____, _____   _____, _____

1b. What percent of your working   1i. What was your job title?
    time was devoted to Judicare
    work? ____%   _____

1c. What was your job title?   1j. What were your main activities?

    _____   _____

1d. What were your main activities?   _____

    _____   (TO Q 2, BELOW)

    _____

1e. How many staff lawyers were in the program, and how many private
    lawyers? _____(# STAFF)   _____(# PRIVATE)

1f. Approximately how many Judicare cases did you personally handle the
    last year you held the job?   /None/, or _____(#)
                                   (TO Q 2)

    1g. What kinds of Judicare cases did you handle most of the time? _____

    _____

2. What were the things you particularly liked about the job? (Anything else?)

3. What were the things you particularly didn't like about the job?
    (Anything else?) _____

    _____

    _____

4. When you took the job, did you plan to stay in that kind of work?

              /Yes/   /Didn't know/   /No/
             (TO Q 5)   (TO Q 5)

    4a. Why not? _____

    _____

5. IS THIS JOB IN JUDICARE (Q-1)?   /Yes/   /No/
                                         (TO Q 6)

    5a. Would you tell me what your highest annual salary was for
         that job? $_____(FILL OUT ATTACHED SCHEDULE LL
                                     FOR THIS JOB, NEXT PAGE)

6. Overall, what were your impressions of the Judicare program--was it
    excellent, good, fair, or poor? /Excellent/   /Good/   /Fair/   /Poor/
                                       (GO TO Q 7)

    6a. What did you have in mind? _____

    _____

7. Was law reform work being done in the Judicare program?

              /Yes/   /No/
                               (TO Q 8)

    7a. Could you give me some examples of the work? _____

    _____

8. Approximately, what were your earnings from Judicare in the last year
    of your job? $_____

                 FILL OUT ATTACHED SCHEDULE LL FOR THIS JOB, NEXT PAGE

SCHEDULE CC-2: PAST OEO NEIGHBORHOOD PROJECT

Sample #: _____   Job #: _____   Interviewer's Name: _____

Let's talk about your OEO neighborhood project job from 19 _____ to 19 _____.

1. What was the name, city, and state of this office?

   _____, _____, _____

2. Did the program have more than one office?   /Yes/   /No/
                                                             (TO Q 3)

   2a. Were you assigned to the main office or to a branch office?
       /Main/   /Branch/

3. What was your position? _____

4. What percent of the office's time was for service cases, as opposed to
   law reform or legislative work? _____% SERVICE CASES (IF 80% OR LESS, ASK Q 4a)

   4a. What are the major areas in which the office did law reform work?
       1._____ 2. _____ 3. _____

5. How did you personally divide your time between service cases and law
   reform or legislative work? _____% SERVICE CASES (IF 80% OR LESS, ASK Q 5a)

   5a. What are the major areas in which you did law reform work?
       1. _____ 2. _____ 3. _____

6. What were the major areas in which you handled service cases? _____

   _____

7. What specialization, if any, was there in the project?
   /None/, or _____

   _____

8. What, if any, was your speciality? /None/, or _____
                                        (TO Q 9)

   8a. What percent of your time did you devote to your specialty? _____%

9. Approximately, how many open files did you have going at any
   any one time? _____ (# FILES)

10. What percent of your time did you spend in court? /None/, or _____ %
                                                       (TO Q 11)

    10a. What kinds of courts did you spend most of your time in? _____
    _____

11. What percent of your time did you spend dealing with government
    agencies? /None/, or _____ %
              (TO Q 12)

    11a. What agencies were usually involved? _____
    _____

12. In community work, how many hours a month--if any--did you personally spend...
    A. speaking to neighborhood-client groups? _____ (# HRS)

    B. helping organize clients or neighborhood groups? _____ (# HRS)

    C. counseling, for example, about welfare or draft problems? _____ (# HRS)

13. What percent of your clients were in each of these categories?
    (READ EACH AND RECORD %)
                              _____ % A. Black
                              _____ % B. Chicano
                              _____ % C. Puerto Rican
                              _____ % D. Native American
                              _____ % E. White
                              _____ % F. Other (SPECIFY): _____

14. How did you originally hear of the job in Legal Services? _____
    _____

15. What were the things you particularly liked about the job? (Anything else?)
    _____
    _____

16. What were the things you particularly didn't like about the job? (Anything else?)
    _____
    _____

17. When you took the job, did you expect to stay in that kind of work?

 /Yes/   /Didn't know/   /No/
 (TO Q 18)   (TO Q 18)

17a. Why not? _____

_____

18. What was the average number of months attorneys stayed in the project? _____ (# MOS)

19. Overall, would you say the quality of the office, at the time you were there, was excellent, very good, good, fair, or poor?

 /Excellent/ /Very good/ /Good/ /Fair/ /Poor/

20. Was the project administered by a Legal Aid Society or an organization which was in existence prior to OEO funding?

 /Legal Aid Society/ /Organization in existence/ /DK/

21. Was the local bar association generally helpful to neighborhood Legal Services, indifferent, or did the bar hinder it? /Helpful/ /Indifferent/ /Hindered/

22. If there were branch offices in the program, what problems--if any--arose between the branch office and the main office?

 /No branch office/ /No problems/, or _____

_____

23. Was there pressure from outside sources for the project to do more law reform work?

 /Yes/   /No/
                (TO Q 24)

23a. From what sources did this pressure come? _____

_____

24. Was there pressure from outside sources for the project to do less law reform work? /Yes/   /No/
                                                           (TO Q 25)

24a. From what sources did this pressure come? _____

_____

25. Was there internal pressure for the project to do more law reform? /Yes/ /No/

26. Was there internal pressure for the project to do less law reform? /Yes/ /No/

27. Were there any objections, either from within your program or from outside it, to the types of cases you handled, or to any matter you handled or considered handling?   /Yes/   /No/
                                                                        (TO Q 28)

   27a. What happened? _____
   _____

28. Was the office ever criticized on issues of legal ethics?
       /Yes/   /No/   /Don't know/
                    (TO Q 29)   (TO Q 29)

   28a. What happened? _____
   _____

29. Would you tell me your highest annual salary for this position? $ _____

FILL OUT ATTACHED SCHEDULE LL FOR THIS JOB, NEXT PAGE[4]

[4] Past job schedules roughly parallel to present job schedules were included for Schedules DD, EE, FF, GG, HH, II, JJ, and KK. For purposes of brevity these schedules are not shown.

SCHEDULE LL:
GENERAL QUESTIONS ON EACH TYPE OF PAST LEGAL POSITION

1. What were the main reasons you chose this job? _____

    _____   _____

2. When you chose this job, how important were financial considerations in
    your choice...very important, important, or not important?

    /Very important/   /Important/   /Not important/

3. When you chose this job, how important were family considerations
    in your choice...very important, important, or not important?

    /Very important/   /Important/   /Not important/

4. At the time, what other job options did you have? _____

    _____

5. How satisfied were you with the job...very satisfied, satisfied, dissatisfied,
    or very dissatisfied?   /Very sat/   /Sat/   /Dissat/   /Very dissat/

6. How difficult was it for you to find another job you wanted when you
    left this one...very difficult, difficult, somewhat easy, or very easy?

    /Very difficult/   /Difficult/   /Somewhat easy/   /Very easy/

7. Why did you leave this job? _____

    _____

8. Did you feel your job called for a very high, medium high, medium, or
    low use of lawyerly skills?   /Very high/   /Medium high/   /Medium/   /Low/
                                   (SEE DIRECTIONS BELOW)

    8a.   How important a factor was this in your decision to leave the
           job...very important, important, or not important?

           /Very important/   /Important/   /Not important/

REFER TO PAST EMPLOYMENT STATUS AND LEGAL ACTIVITY FORM AND ADMINISTER
SCHEDULE FOR NEXT JOB NUMBER.

IF THIS JOB IS THE LAST ONE BEFORE PRESENT JOB, GO TO GENERAL ATTITUDES FORM,
PAGE 83[5]

[5]For purposes of brevity Schedule XX (page 82) is omitted.

GENERAL ATTITUDES

1. Recently it has been proposed that the organized bar take special steps to dedicate itself to delivering legal services to those groups with relatively little access to the legal system. In terms of the bar's activity, do you think there is too much, the right amount, or too little going on?

/Too much/   /Right amount/   /Too little/   /Don't know/
                       (TO Q 2)   (TO Q 2)

1a. What do you have in mind?   1b. What more would you like to see?

_____

_____

_____

_____

2. Could you tell me if you have followed the OEO Legal Services program very closely, somewhat closely, not very closely? /Have been/   / Very / /Somewhat/ / Not / / in it / /closely/ /closely / /closely/

3. What criticisms do you have of the OEO Legal Services program?

/Don't know it/   /No criticisms/, or _____

_____

_____

4. Do you think there should be any restrictions on OEO Legal Services taking suits against the government?   /Yes/   /No/   /Don't know/
                                             (TO Q 5)   (TO Q 5)

4a. Under what circumstances? _____

_____

5. Do you think OEO Legal Services are taking business away from other lawyers?

/Yes/   /No/   /Don't know/

6. Do you think that OEO Legal Services' lawyers have sought out clients to generate cases?   /Yes/   /No/   /Don't know/

7. What is your attitude toward OEO Legal Services' lawyers seeking out clients to generate cases? _____

_____

8. Would you say you have followed the Judicare programs very closely, somewhat closely, or not very closely? /Have been/ / Very / /Somewhat/ / Not /
   / in it / /closely/ /closely / /closely/

9. From what you know of Judicare programs, would you say they have been largely successful, partly successful, or not successful?
   /Largely/ /Partly/ /Not/ /Don't know/

10. Concerning litigation activity by environmental groups, do you think they have been given too much access, about the right amount of access, or too little access to the legal system?

    /Too much/   /About right/   /Too little/   /DK/
                      (TO Q 11)   (TO Q 11)

    10a. What restrictions would you   10b. What would you suggest to increase
         suggest? _____   access? _____

    _____   _____

    _____   _____

11. Concerning litigation activity by consumer protection groups, do you think they have been given too much access, about the right amount of access, or too little access to the legal system?

    /Too much/   /About right/   /Too little/   /DK/
                      (TO Q 12)   (TO Q 12)

    11a. What restrictions would you   11b. What would you suggest to increase
         suggest? _____   access? _____

    _____   _____

    _____   _____

12. There is great diversity of opinion as to the financing of public interest lawyers. For example, a U. S. district court has held in a case involving highway and housing relocation that the defendant must pay the lawyer's fee for the plaintiff since the plaintiff acted as a "private attorney general." Under what circumstances, if any, do you favor such awards?
    /None/ /Don't know/, or _____

    _____

13. Do you think federal and state agencies should supply legal assistance for people who want to appear before them or to challenge them?

    /Yes/   /No/   /Don't know/
                       (TO Q 14)   (TO Q 14)

    13a. What do you have in mind? _____

    _____

14. To what extent do you think lawyers are generating cases or seeking out clients in the areas of consumer and environmental protection--a lot, some, or not very much?

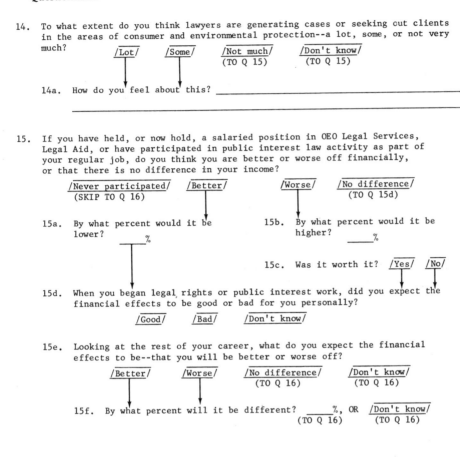

/Lot/   /Some/   /Not much/   /Don't know/
                   (TO Q 15)   (TO Q 15)

14a. How do you feel about this? _____

_____

15. If you have held, or now hold, a salaried position in OEO Legal Services, Legal Aid, or have participated in public interest law activity as part of your regular job, do you think you are better or worse off financially, or that there is no difference in your income?

/Never participated/   /Better/   /Worse/   /No difference/
(SKIP TO Q 16)   (TO Q 15d)

15a. By what percent would it be   15b. By what percent would it be
     lower?   %   higher?   %

                                        15c. Was it worth it? /Yes/ /No/

15d. When you began legal rights or public interest work, did you expect the financial effects to be good or bad for you personally?

           /Good/   /Bad/   /Don't know/

15e. Looking at the rest of your career, what do you expect the financial effects to be--that you will be better or worse off?

     /Better/   /Worse/   /No difference/   /Don't know/
                            (TO Q 16)   (TO Q 16)

     15f. By what percent will it be different? ____%, OR /Don't know/
                                                (TO Q 16)   (TO Q 16)

16. Outside of working hours, during the past two years, have there been any groups or individuals for which you have done free, or reduced-fee, legal work--like the Scouts, a charitable agency, a neighborhood association, a hospital, volunteer work in a ghetto law office, advising a legal aid office, etc.?

/Yes/   /No/
                       (TO Q 17)

16a. What groups or individuals--or what type of groups or individuals-- have you done law work for?

GROUP NAME OR TYPE	Q 16b. WHAT GROUP DOES	Q 16c. LAW WORK OF R'S	Q 16d. # HRS.	Q 16e. OFFICES HELD
1)				
2)				
3)				
4)				
5)				

(ASK Q's 16b - 16e FOR EACH GROUP LISTED)

16b. What does _____ do? (RECORD ABOVE)

16c. What kind of law work or law problems did you work on for _____?
(RECORD ABOVE)

16d. About how many hours of your time altogether was involved for _____?
(RECORD ABOVE)

16e. What offices--if any--did you hold in _____? (RECORD ABOVE)

17. In the past five years, have you belonged to any action, monitoring, or lobbying
     groups of lawyers? For example, lawyers who attempt to observe riots, or take
     positions on foreign policy, or study particular issues.

                        /Yes/   /No/

17a. What are the names of these   17b. Have you belonged to such groups
      groups, what does each group   in the past?   /Yes/   /No/
      do, and are you active or not   (TO Q 18)
      active in each?
      (RECORD BELOW)   17c. What are the names of each group
                                                you belonged to, what did the
                                                group do, were you active or not
                                                very active in each, and why did
                                                you leave each group? (RECORD
                                                BELOW)

NAME OF GROUP	WHAT GROUP DOES OR DID	ACTIVE?	Q-17c. REASON FOR LEAVING

18. What are the names of the bar organizations you belong to? /None/, or LIST BELOW
                                                                  (END)

NAME OF BAR ORGANIZATION	Q18a. ACTIVE? YES	NO	Q18b. WHAT R DOES
ABA			
State:			
County:			
City:			

(ASK Q 18a FOR EACH ORGANIZATION LISTED)

18a. Are you quite active in _____? (CHECK YES OR NO ABOVE)

18b. (IF "YES" TO Q 18a) What do you do in _____? (RECORD ABOVE)

TIME INTERVIEW ENDED: _____

References

Agnew, S. T. 1972. What's wrong with the Legal Services program? *American Bar Association Journal, 58,* 930–932.

American Bar Association. 1908. *Canons of professional ethics.* Chicago.

American Bar Association. 1970. What price professionalism? *American Bar Association Journal, 56,* 172–173.

American Bar Association. 1971. A cloudy Legal Services picture. *American Bar Association Journal, 57,* 243–244. (a)

American Bar Association. 1971. Toward better Legal Services. *American Bar Association Journal, 57,* 901–902. (b)

American Bar Association. 1971. *Pro bono report.* Chicago. (c)

American Bar Association. 1973. *Pro bono report.* Chicago.

Appleby, M. 1969. Overview of Legal Services. In H. H. Weissman (Ed.), *Justice and the poor,* pp. 25–38. New York: Association Press.

Ashman, A., and Woodard, R. 1970. Private law firms serve the poor. *American Bar Association Journal, 56,* 565–567.

Auerbach Corporation. 1971. *Office of Legal Services individual project evaluations, final report.* Washington, D.C.: Office of Educational Opportunity, Office of Legal Services.

Auerbach, J. S. 1976. *Unequal justice: Lawyers and social change in modern America.* New York: Oxford University Press.

Bamberger, E. C., Jr. 1965–1966. The Legal Services Program of the Office of Economic Opportunity. *Notre Dame Lawyer, 41,* 847–852.

Berman, J. L., and Cahn, E. S. 1970. Bargaining for justice: The law students' challenge to law firms. *Harvard Civil Rights–Civil Liberties Law Review, 5,* 16–31.

Biderman, P. 1971. The birth of communal law firms. In J. Black (Ed.), *Radical lawyers,* pp. 280–288. New York: Avon. (a)

Biderman, P. 1971. Insurgency in the courts. In J. Black (Ed.), *Radical lawyers,* pp. 289–297. New York: Avon. (b)

Blalock, H. M. 1960. *Social statistics.* New York: McGraw-Hill.

Boasberg, E. 1970. Urban law and the private bar. *Urban Lawyer, 2,* 105–110.

Borosage, R. 1970. The new public interest lawyers. *Yale Law Journal, 79,* 1069–1152.

Bowler, C. A. 1973. National legal services—The answer or the problem for the legal profession. *Illinois Institute of Technology/Chicago–Kent Law Review, 50,* 415–434.

Braudy, S. 1971. The new people. *Glamour,* April: 174–175, 254–256.

Braungart, R. 1971. Family status, socialization and student politics. *American Journal of Sociology, 77,* 108–129.

Brill, H. 1973. The uses and abuses of legal assistance. *Public Interest, 31,* 38–55.

Brownell, E. 1951. *Legal aid in the United States.* Rochester, N.Y.: Lawyers Cooperative.

Cahn, E. S., and Cahn, J. C. 1964. The War on Poverty: A civilian perspective. *Yale Law Journal, 73,* 1317–1352.

Cahn, E. S., and Cahn, J. C. 1970. Power to the people or the profession? The public interest in public law. *Yale Law Journal, 79,* 1005–1048.

Carlin, J. E. 1962. *Lawyers on their own.* New Brunswick, N. J.: Rutgers University Press.

Carlin, J. E. 1966. *Lawyers' ethics.* New York: Russel Sage Foundation.

Carlin, J. E. 1970. Store front lawyers in San Francisco. *Trans-Action, 6,* 64–74.

Carlin, J. E., and Brill, H. 1973. Communications in *Public Interest, 33,* 128–131.

Carlin, J. E., and Howard, J. 1965. Legal representation and class justice. *UCLA Law Review, 12,* 381–437.

Carlin, J. E.; Howard, J.; and Messinger, S. 1969. Civil justice and the poor. *Law and Society Review, 1,* 9–89.

Carter, B. 1963. A lawyer leaves Mississippi. *Reporter, 28,* 33–35.

Casper, J. D. 1972. Lawyers before the Warren Court: 1957–1966. Urbana: University of Illinois Press.

Champagne, A. 1974. The internal operation of OEO Legal Services projects. *Journal of Urban Law, 51,* 649–663.

Cohen, J. 1968. Multiple regression as a general data-analytic system. *Psychological Bulletin, 70,* 426–443.

Council of New York Law Associates. 1974. *Annual report.* New York.

Countryman, V., and Finman, T. 1966. *The lawyer in modern society.* Boston: Little, Brown.

Cramton, R. C. 1975. The task ahead in Legal Services. *American Bar Association Journal, 61,* 1339–1343.

Erlanger, H. S. 1977. Social reform organizations and the subsequent careers of participants: A follow-up study of early participants in the OEO Legal Services Program. *American Sociological Review, 42,* 233–248.

Fellers, J. D. 1975. State of the legal profession. *American Bar Association Journal, 61,* 1053–1059.

Feuillan, J. 1973. Making peace with poverty: Legal Services under fire. *Legal Services Reporter, 3,* 1–60.

Finman, T. 1971. OEO Legal Service programs and the pursuit of social change. *University of Wisconsin Law Review, 4,* 1001–1084.

Ford Foundation. 1973. *The public interest law firm: New voices for new constituencies.* New York.

Gerlach, L. P. 1971. Movements of revolutionary change. *American Behavioral Scientist, 14,* 812–835.

Goodman, L. H., and Walker, M. H. 1975. *The Legal Services Program: Resource distribution and the low income population.* Washington, D.C.: Bureau of Social Science Research.

Goulden, J. C. 1973. *The superlawyers.* New York: Dell.

Green, M. J. 1975. *The other government: The unseen power of Washington lawyers.* New York: Grossman.

Griffin, B. W. 1967. Comments. In *Proceedings of the Harvard Conference on Law and Poverty*, pp. 27–43. 17–19 March 1967, Cambridge, Massachusetts.

Gross, R., and Osterman, P., eds. 1972. *The new professionals*. New York: Simon & Schuster.

Grosser, C. 1964. The need for a neighborhood legal service and the New York experience. *Proceedings of the Conference on the Extension of Legal Services to the Poor*, November 12–14, 1964, pp. 73–80. Washington, D.C.: U.S. Government Printing Office.

Halpern, C. R., and Cunningham, J. M. 1971. Reflections on the new public interest law: Theory and practice at the Center for Law and Social Policy. *The Georgetown Law Journal, 59*, 1095–1126.

Handler, J. F. 1966. Controlling official behavior in welfare administration. *California Law Review, 54*, 479–510.

Handler, J. F. 1967. *The lawyer and his community: The practicing bar in a middle-sized city*. Madison: University of Wisconsin Press.

Handler, J. F. 1976. Public interest law: Problems and prospects. In *Law and the American future*, M. L. Schwartz (Ed.), pp. 99–115. Englewood Cliffs, New Jersey: Prentice Hall, for the American Assembly, Columbia University.

Handler, J. F. Forthcoming. *Protecting the social service client: Legal and structural controls on official discretion*.

Handler, J. F.; Hollingsworth, E. J.; Erlanger, H. S.; and Ladinsky, J. 1975. The public interest activities of private practice lawyers. *American Bar Association Journal, 61*, 1388–1394.

Hannon, P. J. 1969. The leadership problem in the Legal Services Program. *Law and Society Review, 4*, 235–253.

Harrison, G., and Jaffe, S. M. 1972. Public interest law firms: New voices for new constituencies. *American Bar Association Journal, 58*, 459–467.

Hazard, G. C. 1969. Social justice through civil justice. *University of Chicago Law Review, 36*, 699–712.

Hegland, K. 1971. Beyond enthusiasm and commitment. *Arizona Law Review, 13*, 805–817.

Heifetz, H. 1969. Introduction. In H. H. Weissman (Ed.), *Justice and the law*, pp. 15–23. New York: Association Press.

Hiestand, F. J. 1970. The politics of poverty law. In B. Wasserstein and M. J. Green (Eds.), *With justice for some*, pp. 160–189. Boston: Beacon Press.

Honnold, J. 1966. The bourgeois bar and the Mississippi Movement. *American Bar Association Journal, 52*, 226–232.

Horowitz, D. L. 1977. *The courts and social policy*. Washington, D.C.: Brookings Institution.

Hornstein, B. G. 1973. Effective indigent criminal defense services in Nebraska state courts. *Creighton Law Review, 7*, 1–26.

Hunter, A. 1968. *An empirical study of student political activism*. Unpublished doctoral dissertation, University of Wisconsin, Madison.

James, M. E. 1973. *The people's lawyers*. New York: Holt, Rinehart & Winston.

Johnson, D. O. 1963. *The challenge to American freedoms: World War I and the rise of the American Civil Liberties Union*. Lexington: University of Kentucky Press.

Johnson, E., Jr. 1967. *Proceedings of the Harvard Conference on Law and Poverty*, pp. 1–6. 17–19 March 1967, Cambridge, Massachusetts.

Johnson, E., Jr. 1968. A conservative rationale for the Legal Services Program. *West Virginia Law Review, 70*, 350–362.

Johnson, E., Jr. 1974. *Justice and reform: The formative years of OEO Legal Services Program*. New York: Russell Sage Foundation.

Karabian, W. 1972. Legal services for the poor: Some political observations. *University of San Francisco Law Review, 6,* 253–265.

Katz, J. 1976. *Routine and reform: A study of personal and collective careers in legal aid.* Unpublished doctoral dissertation, Northwestern University, Evanston, Illinois.

Kellogg, C. F. 1967. *NAACP: A history of the National Association for the Advancement of Colored People. Vol. 1:1909–1920.* Baltimore: Johns Hopkins Press.

Keniston, K. 1968. *Young radicals.* New York: Harcourt, Brace and World.

Kettelle Corporation, J. D. 1971. *Evaluation of Office of Economic Opportunity Legal Services Program–Final report.* Washington, D.C.: Office of Economic Opportunity Evaluation Division.

Klaus, W. R. 1976. Civil legal services for the poor. In M. L. Schwartz (Ed.), *Law and the American future,* pp. 131–142. Englewood Cliffs, New Jersey: Prentice-Hall, for the American Assembly, Columbia University.

Krislov, S. 1973. The OEO lawyers fail to constitutionalize a right to welfare: A study in the uses and limits of the judicial process. *Minnesota Law Review, 58,* 211–245.

Ladinsky, J. 1963. Careers of lawyers, law practice, and legal institutions. *American Sociological Review, 28,* 47–54.

Ladinsky, J. 1964. The social profile of a metropolitan bar. *Michigan State Bar Journal, 43,* 12–24.

Ladinsky, J. 1967. Higher education and work achievement among lawyers. *Sociological Quarterly, 8,* 222–232.

Law Students Civil Rights Research Council. 1972. *In the American tradition.* New York.

Lefcourt, R. 1971. The first law commune. In R. Lefcourt (Ed.), *Law against the people,* pp. 310–326. New York: Random House.

Legal Aid Briefcase. 1968. 26 (2), 94–144.

Leone, R. C. 1972. Public interest advocacy and the regulatory process. *Annals of the American Academy of Political Science, 400,* 46–58.

Levitan, S. A. 1969. *The Great Society's poor law.* Baltimore: Johns Hopkins Press.

Lipset, S. M. 1968. The activists: A profile. *Public Interest, 13,* 39–51.

Lochner, P. R., Jr. 1975. The no fee and low fee legal practice of private attorneys. *Law and Society, 9,* 431–474.

Lortie, D. C. 1959. Laymen to lawmen: Law school, careers, and professional socialization. *Harvard Educational Review, 29,* 352–369.

Marks, F. R.; Leswing, K.; and Fortinsky, B. A. 1972. *The lawyer, the public, and professional responsibility.* Chicago: American Bar Association.

Marshall, T. 1975. Financing public interest law practice: The role of the organized bar. *American Bar Association Journal, 61,* 1487–1491.

Mayer, M. 1967. The idea of justice and the poor. *Public Interest, 8,* 96–115.

Meier, A., and Rudwick, E. (Eds.) 1970. *Black protest in the sixties.* Chicago: Quadrangle Books.

Meier, A., and Rudwick, E. 1973. *CORE: A study in the civil rights movement, 1942–1968.* New York: Oxford University Press.

Miller, P. 1973. *Rights, rules, and remedies in law: A study of the OEO Legal Services Program.* Unpublished doctoral dissertation, University of California, Berkeley.

Moonan, W., and Goldstein, T. 1972. The new lawyer. In R. Gross and P. Osterman (Eds.), *The new professionals,* pp. 117–131. New York: Simon & Schuster.

Moore, B. C., Jr. 1970. The lawyer's response: The public interest law firm. In B. Wasserstein and M. J. Green (Eds.), *With justice for some,* pp. 299–333. Boston: Beacon Press.

Moynihan, D. P. 1969. *Maximum feasible misunderstanding.* New York: Free Press.

Murphy, R. D. 1971. *Political entrepreneurs and urban poverty.* Lexington, Massachusetts: D.C. Heath.

NAACP Legal Defense and Education Fund, Inc. 1969. *The quiet revolution.* New York.

Nagel, S. S. 1973. Effects of alternative types of counsel on criminal procedure treatment. *Indiana Law Journal, 48,* 404–426.

Naitove, M., and Nichols, M. 1972. Special section on law communes: The simple life isn't that simple. *Juris Doctor, 2,* 38–42.

National Legal Aid and Defender Association. 1964. *Annual report of the President.* Chicago.

National Legal Aid and Defender Association. 1973. *The other face of justice: A report of the National Defender Survey.* Chicago.

Newsweek. 19 January 1970, pp. 55–56. Ghetto law: Neighborhood Legal Services.

New York Times. 5 September 1971, pp. 1, 32. Law communes seeking social change.

Patterson, R. P., Jr. 1970. The importance of the legal aid society to the legal profession. *Catholic Lawyer, 16,* 264–273.

Pious, R. 1972. Congress, the organized bar, and the Legal Services Program. *Wisconsin Law Review, 27,* 418–446.

Pipkin, R. M. 1919. Legal aid and elitism in the American legal profession. In R. H. Smith (Ed.), *Justice and the poor,* pp. xi–xxvi. Reprint, 1972. Montclair, New Jersey, N. J.: Patterson Smith.

Platt, A., and Pollick, R. 1974. Channelling lawyers: The careers of public defenders. *Issues in Criminology, 9,* 1–31.

Pollitt, D. H. 1964. Timid lawyers and neglected clients. *Harper's, 229,* 81–86.

Pye, A. K. 1966. The role of Legal Services in the antipoverty program. *Law and Contemporary Problems, 31,* 211–249.

Pye, A. K., and Garraty, R. F., Jr. 1965–1966. The involvement of the bar in the war against poverty. *Notre Dame Lawyer, 41,* 847–852.

Rabin, R. L. 1976. Lawyers for social change: Perspectives on public interest law. *Stanford Law Review, 28,* 207–261. (a)

Rabin, R. L. 1976. Job security and due process: Monitoring administrative discretion through a reasons requirement. *University of Chicago Law Review, 44,* 60–93. (b)

Redlich, A. 1971. Art of welfare advocacy: Available procedures and forums. *Albany Law Review, 36,* 57–94.

Reich, C. 1964. The new property. *Yale Law Journal, 73,* 733–787.

Rosenthal, D. E.; Kagan, R. A.; and Quatrone, D. 1971. *Volunteer attorneys and legal services for the poor: New York's CLO Program.* New York: Russell Sage Foundation.

Rothstein, L. E. 1974. The myth of Sisyphus: Legal Services on behalf of the poor. *University of Michigan Journal of Law Reform, 7,* 493–515.

Salsich, P. W., Jr. 1969. Reform through legislative action: The poor and the law. *Saint Louis University Law Journal, 13,* 733–787.

Scheindlin, S. A. 1974. Legal Services—Past and present. *Cornell Law Review, 59,* 960–988.

Silver, C. R. 1968. The imminent failure of legal services for the poor: Why and how to limit caseload. *Journal of Urban Law, 46,* 217–248.

Silverstein, L. 1965. *Defense of the poor in criminal cases in American state courts.* Chicago: American Bar Foundation.

Simon, R. J.; Koziol, F.; and Joslyn, N. 1973. Have there been significant changes in the career aspirations and occupational choices of law school graduates in the 1960's? *Law and Society Review, 8,* 95–108.

Smigel, E. O. 1964. *The Wall Street lawyer.* New York: The Free Press of Glencoe.

Smith, R. H. 1919. *Justice and the poor.* Reprint, 1972. Montclair, New Jersey: Patterson Smith.

Stumpf, H. P. 1968. Law and poverty: A political perspective. *Wisconsin Law Review, 3,* 694–733.

Stumpf, H. P. 1973. *The failure of Legal Services, or let them clean out cellars*. Paper presented at Conference on the Delivery and Distribution of Legal Services, 11–12 October 1968, at Buffalo Law School, State University of New York.

Stumpf, H. P.; Culver, J. H.; and Turpen, B. 1975. The impact of OEO Legal Services. In D. B. James (Ed.), *Analyzing poverty policy*, Lexington, Massachusetts: D.C. Heath.

Sullivan, L. A. 1971. Law reform and the Legal Services crisis. *California Law Review, 59*, 1–28.

Theil, H. 1971. *Principles of econometrics*. New York: Wiley.

U.S. Bureau of the Census. 1974. *Statistical abstract of the United States: 1974*. Washington, D.C.: U.S. Government Printing Office.

Van Alstyne, W. W. 1968. The demise of the right–privilege distinction in constitutional law. *Harvard Law Review, 81*, 1439–1464.

Village Voice. 1 May 1969. Lawyers of the left: A crisis of identity. Voorhees, T. 1970. Legal aid: Past, present and future. *American Bar Association Journal, 56*, 765–768.

Wall Street Journal. 26 September 1968, pp. 1, 29. Shunning Wall Street.

Wall Street Journal. 20 May 1970, pp. 1, 15. Activist attorneys.

Wall Street Journal. 20 November 1973, p. 1. Labor letter.

Warkov, S., and Zelan, J. 1965. *Lawyers in the making*. Chicago: Aldine.

Washington, M. 1971. Constance Baker Motley: Black woman, black judge. *Black Law Journal, 1*, 173–179.

Washington Post. 8 February 1970, p. A3. Militants find new legal breed in collectives.

Watts, W.; Lynch, S.; and Whittaker, D. 1969. Alienation and activism in today's college age youth. *Journal of Counseling Psychology, 16*, 1–7.

Weisbrod, B.; Handler, J.; and Komesar, N. 1978. *Public interest law: An economic and institutional analysis*. Berkeley: University of California Press.

Wexler, S. 1971. The poverty lawyer as radical. In J. Black (Ed.), *Radical lawyers*, pp. 209–231. New York: Avon.

Wilensky, H. 1956. *Intellectuals in labor unions*. Glencoe, Illinois: Free Press.

Wright, E. 1967. Competition in Legal Services under the War on Poverty. *Stanford Law Review, 19*, 579–592.

Zald, M., and McCarthey, J. D. 1975. Organizational intellectuals and the criticism of society. *Social Science Review, 49*, 344–362.

A 8
B 9
C 0
D 1
E 2
F 3
G 4
H 5
I 6
J 7